BACH PERSPECTIVES

VOLUME 12

Bach and the Counterpoint
of Religion

BACH PERSPECTIVES

VOLUME 12

Bach and the Counterpoint of Religion

Edited by
Robin A. Leaver

**UNIVERSITY OF
ILLINOIS PRESS**
Urbana, Chicago, and Springfield

Library of Congress Cataloging-in-Publication Data
Names: Leaver, Robin A.
Title: Bach and the counterpoint of religion / edited by Robin A. Leaver.
Description: Urbana : University of Illinois Press, [2018] | Series: Bach
perspectives ; Volume 12 | Includes bibliographical references and index.
Identifiers: LCCN 2018013189 | ISBN 9780252041983 (cloth : alk. paper)
Subjects: LCSH: Bach, Johann Sebastian, 1685–1750—Criticism and
interpretation. | Sacred music—18th century—History and criticism.
| Church music—Austria—Vienna—18th century.
Classification: LCC ML410.B13 B13 2018 | DDC 782.2/2092—dc23
LC record available at https://lccn.loc.gov/2018013189

CONTENTS

PREFACE

From the earliest beginnings Bach studies have been closely connected with religion. It could not be otherwise, since much of Bach's music, especially the vocal music, was composed to be heard within Lutheran liturgical worship. However, whenever religion is overstressed—as it certainly was for much of the nineteenth and twentieth centuries—it leads to a distorted view of the composer, who is depicted almost exclusively as a church musician: the supreme Lutheran Cantor. On the other hand, if it is understressed—as it certainly was in the mid-twentieth century, as epitomized in the former East Germany—an equally distorted view of the composer is created, one that depicts him as a nonreligious musical genius: the secular-minded *Kapellmeister*. Even when careful and more balanced views of religious influences are pursued, problems arise because our knowledge and experience of religion are significantly different from what was current in eighteenth-century Germany. The situation is further complicated by the fact that in recent decades church historians have argued that studies of general interconfessional conflicts—such as the religious counterpoint of the Catholic *dux* and the answering Lutheran *comes*—as well as specific intraconfessional discord—such as the division between orthodoxy and Pietism within Lutheranism—have to be much more nuanced than has often been the case in the past.

The biennial conference of the American Bach Society in April 2016, held at the prestigious Catholic University of Notre Dame, sought to address some of these issues under the general title "J. S. Bach and the Confessional Landscape of His Time." Revisions and expansions of three of the Notre Dame papers form the nucleus of this volume: Mark Noll, the keynote speaker, examines the general background of European pietism and the piety expressed in Bach's cantatas; Joyce Irwin reviews the question of musical style that made use of dance forms, a contentious issue that was by no means confined to Lutherans; and Derek Stauff reveals the hidden confessional themes embedded within cantatas that are likely to pass unnoticed by modern audiences and performers. To these have been added four further studies. Three explore various aspects of the bridges and barriers between Catholics and Lutherans: Markus Rathey examines the mysticism of the Catholic medieval theologian Bernard of Clairvaux, which influenced many Lutheran authors, especially in the seventeenth century, as well as the author of the libretto of Bach's *Christmas Oratorio*; Janice Stockigt reexamines the 1733 Leipzig ceremony of paying homage to the new elector, a Catholic with Lutheran responsibilities, at which Bach's 1733 Missa may have been performed; and my own study discusses the hymnal prepared for the royal Catholic Chapel in Leipzig, which contained hymns and chants familiar to both Catholics and Lutherans alike.

In the final contribution, a study of the context of Bach's reception in Berlin by Sara Levy and her circle in the late eighteenth and nineteenth centuries, Rebecca Cypess outlines the influence of the Jewish Enlightenment within a society conditioned by Protestant Rationalism.

Two movements need further clarification. First, pietism was a European development of spirituality that affected most Protestant denominations, especially Moravians and Methodists (see Mark Noll's essay). But Lutheran Pietism had its own distinctive features, not least an ecclesiological agenda alongside its spirituality. Thus in this volume the general European movement is designated as "pietism" and its Lutheran manifestation as "Pietism."

Second, the term "Counter-Reformation" for the movement of Catholic reform has been avoided, since the term was coined by Protestant historians and has polemical overtones. In keeping with Catholic writers, the term used here is "Catholic Reformation."

I thank the members of the editorial board of the American Bach Society who read early drafts of the chapters and especially the president, Markus Rathey, and the society's general editor, Daniel R. Melamed, for their support and advice.

Robin A. Leaver, editor

ABBREVIATIONS

ARSI   Roman Jesuit Archives (Archivum Romanum Societatis Iesu Fondo Vecchia Compagnia), Bohemia.

BACH   *Bach: Journal of the Riemenschneider Bach Institute.*

BC-W/K   *The Book of Concord: The Confessions of the Evangelical Lutheran Church.* Edited by Robert Kolb and Timothy J. Wengert. Minneapolis: Fortress, 2000.

BDOK   *Bach Dokumente.* Edited by Andreas Glöckner, Anselm Hartinger, Karen Lehmann, Michael Maul, Werner Neumann, Hans-Joachim Schulze, and Christoph Wolff. 7 vols. Kassel: Bärenreiter; Leipzig: Deutscher Verlag für Musik, 1953–2008.

BJ   *Bach-Jahrbuch.*

BWV   [Bach-Werke-Verzeichnis] *Thematisch-systematisches Verzeichnis der musikalischen Werke von Johann Sebastian Bach.* Revised edition. Edited by Wolfgang Schmieder. Wiesbaden: Breitkopf & Härtel, 1990.

DADM   Diözesanarchiv Dresden-Meißen.

D-B   Staatsbibliothek, Berlin.

D-BAUd   Zentralabteilung, Archiv-Bibliothek Kunst, Bischöfliches Ordinariat Bautzen.

D-Dl   Sächsische Landesbibliothek—Staats- und Universitätsbibliothek, Dresden.

D-Dla   Sächsisches Staatsarchiv, Hauptstaatarchiv, Dresden.

Fk   Martin Falck. *Wilhelm Friedemann Bach: Sein Leben und seine Werke.* Leipzig: Kahnt, 1913.

GB-Lcm   Royal College of Music, London.

HStCal   *Königl. Polnischer und Churfürstl. Sächsischer Hof- und Staats-Calender.* Leipzig: Weidmann, 1728–29, 1731–33, 1735–57, cited by year.

KB   Kritischer Bericht (critical report) of the NBA.

KJV   King James Version of the Bible.

LW   *Luther's Works: American Edition.* Vols. 1–55. St. Louis and Philadelphia: Concordia and Fortress, 1955–86; vols. 56–, St. Louis: Concordia, 2009–.

NBA   [Neue Bach-Ausgabe] *Johann Sebastian Bach: Neue Ausgabe sämtlicher Werke.* Edited by Johann-Sebastian-Bach-Institut, Göttingen, and the Bach-Archiv, Leipzig. Kassel: Bärenreiter; Leipzig: Deutscher Verlag für Musik, 1954–2010.

NBR *The New Bach Reader: A Life of Johann Sebastian Bach in Letters and Documents.* Edited by Hans T. David and Arthur Mendel. Revised and enlarged by Christoph Wolff. New York: Norton, 1998.

RISM Répertoire International des Sources Musicales.

StA Bautzen Archivverbund Stadtarchiv und Staatsfilialarchiv Bautzen.

TWV *Thematisch Verzeichnis der Vokalwerke von Georg Philipp Telemann.* 2nd revised edition, edited by Werner Menke. Frankfurt: Klostermann, 1988–95.

WA *Luthers Werke: Kritische Gesamtausgabe.* 65 vols. Weimar: Böhlau, 1883–1993.

Wolff BLM Christoph Wolff. *Johann Sebastian Bach: The Learned Musician.* Updated edition. New York: Norton, 2013.

ZWV Wolfgang Reich. *Jan Dismas Zelenka: Thematisch-systematisches Verzeichnis der musikalischen Werke (ZWV).* Dresden: Sächsische Landesbibliothek, 1985.

Historical Proximity

John Wesley Visits Leipzig in 1738

Mark Noll

It is Thursday, July 27, 1738, and one of the most intriguing might-have-beens in the history of Western music and religion is just about *not* to take place. An Englishman who has been meandering west to east across Europe for the previous six weeks arrives at one of the gates of Leipzig in Saxony at five o'clock in the afternoon. The traveler has tarried from July 4 to July 19 at Marienborn, a village famous during the Cold War as a border crossing between East and West Germany but in the eighteenth century only a sleepy Saxon-Anhalt *Kleinstadt* less than one hundred miles northwest of Leipzig.

The attraction for the Englishman in Marienborn is its small community of about ninety Moravians, with whom he participates eagerly in worship, teaching, and fellowship. The Moravians, a quasi-Lutheran, semisectarian renewal movement, are led by Nikolaus Ludwig, count von Zinzendorf, a winsome, gregarious, charming—but also sometimes zany—German aristocrat. In Marienborn the English visitor converses with the count, he takes careful notes of a sermon Zinzendorf preaches on Sunday, July 9, and he carefully records the Moravian leader's words about the relationship between justification by faith and Christian assurance of salvation.[1] In both of these subjects—justification and the believer's assurance of justification—the Englishman sustains a passionate interest. After departing from Marienborn, he passes through towns and countryside where generations of Bachs have made music and practiced their Lutheran faith: Eisenach (where J. S. Bach was born), then Gotha (the ducal residence of a strong outpost of orthodox Lutheranism), then Weimar and Halle. He finally arrives in Leipzig on Thursday, July 27.

I would like to thank Paul Walker for the invitation that led to this essay, an anonymous reviewer for sparing readers mistakes and infelicities, and Robin A. Leaver for helpful additions.

1. Thursday, 6 July, through Wednesday, 12 July 1738, in *The Works of John Wesley*, ed. Richard P. Heitzenrater and John Baker, vols. 18–24, *Journals and Diaries* I–VII (Nashville: Abingdon, 1988–2003), 1:260–61.

The visitor passing through Bach country was thirty-five-year-old John Wesley, a Protestant pilgrim on his way to Herrnhut, Zinzendorf's country estate, another one hundred or so miles east of Leipzig. At Herrnhut only a few years before, the scraggly remnants of a Protestant-type movement dating from the fifteenth-century reforms of Jan Hus had found a refuge. In their native Moravia, the Czechs were identified as members of the Unitas Fratrum (Unity of the Brethren), but once they arrived in German-speaking lands they took the name of their ancestral Czech location. After the Moravians were settled at Herrnhut, they had absorbed through Zinzendorf several features of the pietist movement that was then renewing, but also embroiling, German Lutheranism. At Herrnhut decisive moments of spiritual renewal had also taken place. Out of that renewal had come a burst of new hymnody along with a comprehensive organization of choral singing for the entire community; that same experience had also led to the commissioning of missionaries to far-flung parts of the globe.

The chain of events that put John Wesley at the Leipzig city gates was complicated.[2] In January of that year, 1738, he had returned to England after spending more than two years in the American colonies as a defeated and discouraged preacher. Not only had his work as a Church of England priest been rebuffed both by settlers in the new colony of Georgia and by the Native Americans with whom the settlers intermingled, but Wesley's own search for peace with God had turned up empty. In his discouragement he wrote on January 24, "I went to America to convert the Indians; but oh! who shall covert me? . . . I have [merely] a fair summer religion."[3]

The only light that shone in Wesley's darkness came from a new set of friends he had met during his otherwise calamitous American sojourn. On board ship to the colonies and then in Georgia, he encountered a band of Moravians who, having been dispatched from Herrnhut, were on their way to Georgia in order to support German-speaking refugees who shortly before had been expelled from Roman Catholic Salzburg. With the Moravians Wesley studied German, with them he spoke earnestly and at length about his spiritual condition, and with them he eagerly sang the traditional Lutheran chorales and the newer musical compositions that constituted an integral part of Moravian worship.

After the dejected Wesley returned to England he continued in constant fellowship with other Moravians who had established several *ecclesiolae in ecclesiae* (small-group or cell-group fellowships) in and around London. During the early weeks of 1738, while Wesley was attending London Moravian gatherings, Johann Sebastian Bach

---

2. The definitive biography remains Henry Rack, *Reasonable Enthusiast: John Wesley and the Rise of Methodism*, 3rd ed. (London: Epworth, 2002).

3. Tuesday, 24 January 1738, in Wesley, *Journals and Diaries*, 1:211.

in far-away Leipzig was composing a secular cantata in honor of Frederick Augustus II, king of Poland, grand duke of Lithuania, and the elector of Saxony. This cantata, *Willkommen! Ihr herrschenden Götter der Erden*, was performed on April 28, after which Bach received payment of fifty thalers for himself and eight thalers for the town pipers who performed the work.[4]

It has been claimed that Bach distrusted the pietist movements of his day—presumably including the Moravians—because of complaints from leading pietists about the concerted church music prevailing among the orthodox Lutherans, music of which Bach (of course) had become the master.[5] Yet at a deeper emotional level, considerable resonance continued to exist among all the varieties of German Lutheranism that drew inspiration from the earlier books of Johann Arndt, the hymns of Paul Gerhardt, and Lutheran devotional writers like Heinrich Müller and Philip Nicolai. Motifs like the Bride-Bridegroom metaphor applied to the believer and Jesus figured prominently among the Moravians, as they did as well in Bach's church music.[6] At his death the inventory of Bach's estate contained books by several of these writers, including Johann Arndt's *True Christianity*, which the Moravians also honored.[7] In addition, for his chorale settings Bach enlisted hymns by Gerhardt and others that were also being sung by pietistic groups like the Moravians.

Back in London, Wesley experienced the spiritual breakthrough for which he had been ardently longing at a Moravian gathering on the evening of May 24, 1738. About this experience he wrote the following often-quoted words in his published journal: "In the evening I went very unwillingly to a society in Aldersgate Street, where one was reading Luther's Preface to the Epistle to the Romans. About a quarter before nine, while he was describing the change which God works in the heart through faith in Christ, I felt my heart strangely warmed. I felt I did trust in Christ, Christ alone for salvation, and an assurance was given me that he had taken away *my* sins, even *mine*, and saved *me* from the law of sin and death."[8]

The mood in Leipzig for J. S. Bach on that very same May 24 was equally pious, but in a completely different psychological register. On that day Bach wrote one of the few

4. BDOK 2:326–28, nos. 424–25a; NBR, 197–99, no. 200.

5. For helpful context, see chapters 9 and 10 of Christian Bunners, "Zinzendorf und die Brüdergemeine" and "Johann Sebastian Bach," in *Geschichte des Pietismus*, vol. 4, *Glaubenswelt und Lebenswelten*, ed. Hartmut Lehmann (Göttingen: Vandenhock and Ruprecht, 2004), 442–43 and 443–45, respectively.

6. See Markus Rathey's contribution to this volume.

7. BDOK 2:495–96, no. 627; NBR, 253–54, no. 279; see also Robin A. Leaver, *Bachs theologische Bibliothek / Bach's Theological Library* (Stuttgart: Hänssler, 1983), esp. 184–87, no. 51.

8. 24 May 1738, in Wesley, *Journals and Diaries*, 1:249–50.

extant personal letters that revealed, according to Martin Petzoldt's *Bach Almanach*, the sentiments of his own heart.[9] The occasion for the letter was the delinquency of Johann Gottfried Bernhard, the third son of Bach's first marriage. This young man had been employed as an organist in Sangerhausen but had piled up unpaid debts and then left town with no forwarding address. Bach was writing to a Sangerhausen town councilor with an appeal for understanding, along with an explanation for why he could not pay his son's debts until he found out where his son had fled. Memorably, he expressed his concerns with pious phrasing not unlike what John Wesley often used in his correspondence: "I must bear my cross in patience and leave my unruly son to God's Mercy alone, doubting not that He will hear my sorrowful pleading and in the end will so work upon him, according to His Holy Will, that he will learn to acknowledge that the lesson is owing wholly and alone to Divine Goodness."[10] Back in London, Wesley's spiritual breakthrough of May 24, for which Moravians had prepared the way in America and then midwifed in London, sparked his determination to visit the headquarters of the Moravian movement at Herrnhut in person.

John Wesley was much more than an ardent preacher and would-be spiritual adept. With his brother Charles, Wesley was also playing a crucial role in the transformation of English church music. Due to the extreme antipapalism of England's Protestant Reformation and then the strong biblicist influence of its Puritan movements, English hymnody had long been tethered to the metrical psalms. Only short years before Wesley set out for Herrnhut, a valetudinarian Dissenting pastor, Isaac Watts, had broken the stranglehold of metrical psalmody by composing hymns that pushed paraphrase into uncharted territory (*Our God, Our Help, in Ages Past*) or that abandoned psalmody entirely in order to write specifically Christian hymns for Christian worship (*When I Survey the Wondrous Cross*).

During his time in Georgia, John Wesley had published the first of what would be many hymn collections that expanded upon the freer compositions that Watts pioneered. His coeditor in this effort was his brother Charles, whose time in Georgia had otherwise been as inauspicious as John's. Their American effort from 1737, entitled *Collection of Psalms and Hymns*, included many selections from Isaac Watts, along with several by George Herbert and other English authors. Yet as a tribute to the hymn-singing Moravians, this book also included five of John Wesley's own translations of hymns he had learned from his Moravian companions.[11] Although in August 1737 John

---

9. Martin Petzoldt, *Bach Almanach* (Leipzig: Evangelischer Verlagsanstalt, 2000), 205.

10. BDOK 1:107–9, no. 42, here 107; NBR, 200–201, no. 203, here 200.

11. For an account of these translations, see J. R. Watson, *The English Hymn: A Critical and Historical Study* (Oxford: Clarendon, 1997), 206.

Wesley was charged in Charleston with "introducing into the church, and service at the altar, compositions of psalms and hymns not inspected or authorized by any proper judicature,"[12] back in England the brothers did not use hymns from their *Collection* in formal Anglican services, where the metrical psalms still prevailed. However, they did believe that such hymns could be of spiritual benefit for earnest seekers who gathered in Moravian-style small groups or classes.

Now that Charles was back in England, his own gifts in poetic composition, barely noticed before, burst into full flower when he too underwent a converting experience of God's grace in May 1738, only days before his brother's conversion. This experience, which began Charles Wesley's hyperenergetic career as a hymn writer, also featured a significant Lutheran element. Just as John's conversion had been prompted by a reading from Martin Luther's *Preface to Romans*, so Charles's experience of newfound faith took place as in his sickbed he read Luther's commentary on the book of Galatians and then heard a voice urging him to arise in the name of Jesus of Nazareth and be healed.[13] The hymn that Charles Wesley composed immediately upon his conversion was one of the earliest of the nearly ten thousand he would write before his death a half-century later:

> Where shall my wondering soul begin?
> How shall I All to Heaven aspire?
> A slave redeem'd from death and sin,
> A brand pluck'd from eternal fire,
> How shall I equal triumphs raise,
> And sing my great Deliverer's praise?[14]

And so to Leipzig on July 27. John Wesley—the brother, editor, and publisher of England's greatest Protestant hymn writer—had come to the city of the greatest musician in the entire history of Protestantism. The Englishman who had been converted to a liberating experience of God's grace through a word from Martin Luther had arrived in Leipzig, home of the composer whom Jaroslav Pelikan described as the most profound interpreter of Luther in the history of Protestantism before Søren Kierkegaard.[15] Wesley, who had proclaimed his devotion to Scripture by calling himself a *homo unius libri* (man of one book), was in position to speak with the *Kapellmeister* who

---

12. Cited in Luke Tyerman, *The Life and Times of the Rev. John Wesley*, 3rd ed. (London: Hodder and Stoughton, 1876), 1:155.

13. 17 and 21 May 1738, in *Charles Wesley: A Reader*, ed. John R. Tyson (New York: Oxford University Press, 1989), 96–99.

14. Frank Baker, *Representative Verse of Charles Wesley* (New York: Abingdon, 1962), 3.

15. Jaroslav Pelikan, *Bach among the Theologians* (Philadelphia: Fortress, 1986).

for the previous five years had been studying and annotating his own copy of Abraham Calov's commentary on Martin Luther's German translation of the Scriptures.[16] He had also on most Sundays of the year directed a cantata keyed to the biblical texts assigned for that day. Wesley, who throughout his life had to cope with many disappointments in his immediate family, was in the presence of Bach, whose domestic connections brought a measure of joy unknown by Wesley, but also a full measure of family heartache. Most significantly, the great English promoter of a hymnody focused on the saving mercy of Christ extended to conscience-smitten sinners found himself in the city where week after week works by the great German composer proclaimed in song the saving mercy of Christ extended to conscience-smitten sinners.

There exists, sadly, no record that Wesley met Bach or even that either was aware of the other's existence.[17] The relevant entries in Wesley's published journal read simply:

> Thur. 27 [July 1738]. We returned to Merseburg, and at five in the evening came to the gates of Leipzig. After we had sent in our pass, and waited an hour and a half, we were suffered to go to a bad inn in the town.

> Fri. 28. We found out Mr. Marschall and the other gentlemen of the university to whom we were directed. They were not wanting in any good office while we stayed, and in the afternoon went with us an hour forward in our journey.[18]

That was it. In the absence of evidence, however, it is impossible not to speculate on why Wesley did not meet Bach. Perhaps the composer was out of town, testing a newly built organ or visiting the Dresden opera. Perhaps Bach's testy relationship with the Leipzig city council—frayed most recently by controversy over appointment of prefects to lead the city churches' junior choirs—consumed all of Bach's time and attention.[19] Perhaps he was busy making music with friends at the university with whom he maintained warm relations. Or maybe the otherwise unknown "Mr. Marschall" lacked connections or had no interest in showing Wesley around.[20] We just do not know.

---

16. See Leaver, *Bachs theologische Bibliothek*, 46–51, no. 1; Robin A. Leaver, *J. S. Bach and Scripture: Glosses from the Calov Bible Commentary* (St. Louis: Concordia, 1985); Howard H. Cox, ed., *The Calov Bible of J. S. Bach* (Ann Arbor: UMI Research Press, 1985).

17. It is of interest that none of the indexes provided for the standard editions of John or Charles Wesley's letters, journals, or works contain a reference to J. S. Bach.

18. 27–28 July 1738, in *Journals and Diaries*, 1:264–65.

19. On Bach's relationship with the city council, see BDOK 1:99–106, nos. 40–41; NBR, 189–96, nos. 192–96.

20. There were two brothers at the university as students at that time, Johann Ludwig von Marschall (1720–1800) and Friedrich Wilhelm von Marschall (1721–1802). Both are known to have visited Herrnhut in 1738; see Wesley, *Journals and Diaries*, 1:264–65n62.

Yet if we suppose that Wesley on that Thursday evening or Friday morning had drifted by the St. Thomas Church or perhaps the St. Thomas School and had been in position to attend a rehearsal for the cantata to be sung on Sunday July 30,[21] we can reliably guess how he would have reacted and what he might have said to the cantata's composer.

July 30, 1738, was the Ninth Sunday after Trinity. The scriptural texts for the day were 1 Corinthians 10:6–13 ("Take heed lest ye fall") and the parable of the unjust steward from Luke 6. For these texts, Bach had probably composed five different cantatas, of which three are extant. Now let us suppose that in preparing for Sunday he had retrieved one of those cantatas to rehearse. And let us also suppose that Wesley had access to the libretto booklet that was customarily produced for successive Sundays and was thus able to review the text of the cantata before he heard it rehearsed. We can imagine that the Englishman would have been thrilled as he encountered so many of the themes, sentiments, and even specific expressions that were now also pouring forth in the hymns written by his brother.

One of Bach's cantatas for the Ninth Sunday after Trinity was BWV 94, *Was frag ich nach der Welt und allen ihren Schätzen* (What is the world and all its treasures to me). Wesley would have recognized the cantata's comparison of worldly riches, which pass away, and eternal security in Jesus as describing exactly his own estimation of what meant most in life. He could also have made a specific connection between phrases in Bach's composition and a new hymn that his brother Charles had just written. Cantata 94 ends with a chorale from a seventeenth-century hymn by Balthasar Kindermann:

Was frag ich nach der Welt!	What do I ask from the world!
Mein Jesus ist mein Leben,	My Jesus is my life,
Mein Schatz, mein Eigentum,	My treasure, my property,
Dem ich mich ganz ergeben.	To whom I have quite surrendered myself.[22]

The same contrast between meaningless earthly treasure and true riches in Christ began Charles Wesley's versification of the Beatitudes from Matthew 5:

---

21. Bach's rehearsal practice in Leipzig is very unclear. There were no music classes in the St. Thomas school on Thursdays and Saturdays, which might mean that rehearsals were held on these days, though there is evidence (e.g., the alto part of Cantata 174) that suggests that sometimes the rehearsal was very close to the first performance. On the weekly teaching of music in the St. Thomas School, see Markus Rathey, "Schools," in *The Routledge Research Companion to Johann Sebastian Bach*, ed. Robin A. Leaver (London: Routledge, 2017), 135.

22. Alfred Dürr, *The Cantatas of J. S. Bach with Their Librettos in German-English Parallel Text*, rev. and trans. Richard D. P. Jones (Oxford: Oxford University Press, 2005), 470.

> Jesu, if still the same Thou art,
>   If all Thy Promises are sure,
> Set up Thy Kingdom in my Heart,
>   And make me rich, for I am poor:
> To me be all Thy Treasures given,
>   The Kingdom of an Inward Heaven.[23]

John Wesley would have been even more drawn to the words of BWV 168, *Tue Rechnung! Donnerwort* (Settle my account! Word of thunder). With a libretto from Salomo Franck and Bartholmäus Ringwaldt, this cantata describes the unpayable debt that sinners owe to God, a debt that "mein Blut erkaltet" (freezes my blood; movt. 1). But then it goes on to praise "den Bürgen" (the surety) who "alle Schulden abgetan" (cancels all debts; movt. 4). The cantata then uses "blood and wounds" imagery to explicate the canceling of the debt: "Des Lammes Blut, o grosses Lieben! / Hat deine Schuld durchstrichen / und dich mit Gott verglichen" (The Lamb's blood, O great love! / Has cancelled out your debt / And settled you with God; movt. 4). And finally the prayer: "Heil mich mit deinen Wunden, / Wasch mich mit deinem Todesschweiß / in meiner letzten Stunden" (Heal me with your wounds, / Wash me in your death-sweat / In my last hours; movt. 6).[24]

As early as the summer of 1738, Charles Wesley had already written several hymns that echoed the themes and used the same imagery of Cantata 168. In the hymn he composed very shortly after his conversion, Charles borrowed the Moravian fixation on the side-wound of Christ on the cross but with phrases remarkably parallel to the Bach cantata:

> Come O my guilty Brethren come,
>   Groaning beneath your Load of Sin!
> His bleeding Heart shall make you room,
>   His open Side shall take you in.
> He calls you Now, invites you home—
>   Come, O my guilty Brethren, come!
>
> For you the purple Current flow'd
>   In Pardons from his wounded Side:
> Languish'd for you th'Eternal God,
>   For you the Prince of Glory dy'd.

---

23. Baker, *Representative Verse*, 21.

24. See Dürr, *Cantatas of J. S. Bach*, 474–75.

> *Believe*: and all your Guilt's forgiven,
> *Only Believe*—and yours is Heaven.[25]

As much as these two cantatas might have appealed to John Wesley, the third extant cantata for this Sunday in the church year, BWV 105, would have left him completely enthralled. Bach's text began with the outcry of Psalm 143: "Herr, gehe nicht ins Gericht mit deinem Knecht. Denn vor dir wird kein Lebendiger gerecht" (Lord, do not enter into judgment with your servant! For before you no man living shall be justified; movt. 1). This same sentiment had long been the cri de coeur of John Wesley before his contact with the Moravians introduced him to the grace of God found in Christ. The cantata ends with a seventeenth-century hymn text from Johann Rist, "Nun, ich weiß, du wirst mir stillen / mein Gewissen, das mich plagt" (Now I know that you will still / my conscience, which torments me; movt. 6). The same stanza announces that "keiner soll verloren werden" (no one will be lost) if only that one "ist Glauben voll" (is full of faith).[26]

Probably even before John Wesley left England on his German excursion, Charles had written the hymn that begins, "And can it be, that I should gain / An Int'rest in the Saviour's Blood." That hymn contains the same announcement of the free gift of the gospel to all who believe and climaxes with the same account of a guilty conscience stilled by Christ that brought Cantata 105 to a close:

> He left his Father's Throne above,
> (So free, so infinite his Grace!)
> Empty'd Himself of All but Love,
> And bled for *Adam's* helpless race. . . .
> No condemnation now I dread,
> Jesus, and all in Him, is Mine:
> Alive in Him, my living Head,
> And cloath'd in Righteousness Divine,
> Bold I approach th'Eternal Throne,
> And claim the Crown, thro' CHRIST, my own.[27]

If John Wesley could have perused the texts that Bach set to music for the Ninth Sunday after Trinity, he would have read an account remarkably similar to his own spiritual journey. To be sure, the emphasis in his brother's early hymns on the *reception* of new life in Christ differed slightly from the accent in the Bach cantatas on the

25. Baker, *Representative Verse*, 4.

26. See Dürr, *Cantatas of J. S. Bach*, 464–65.

27. Baker, *Representative Verse*, 10.

prevailing resources found in Christ for the believer. Yet the focus on the blood of the Lamb, the gratitude for divinely initiated redemption, the relief of a quiet conscience, and the emotion of joyful gratitude that infused the cantatas would have convinced Wesley that he had discovered a spiritual fellow traveler. In addition, since Wesley had gained reasonable facility in German, he would have been able to easily comprehend the relatively straightforward prosody of the cantatas.

But then let us suppose that Wesley not only read the cantata words but had actually been present when one of them was rehearsed—maybe even the first stanza of BWV 105, the cantata whose text so clearly described his own pilgrimage of faith. In the first movement alone, he would have heard a lengthy instrumental introduction followed by six minutes of meditative counterpoint, including a fugue, with soloists and the chorus intoning only two lines from Psalm 143.

At such music, John Wesley would have been appalled. Whatever fellow feeling, appreciation, or even joyful exultation he experienced from the cantata texts would have vanished in a twinkling once he heard the music. We can be quite certain about Wesley's reaction to the music, because a few years later he published a pithy tract entitled *Thoughts on the Power of Music*.[28] It amounted to an all-out, full-scale, unqualified denunciation of the musical conventions that Bach had perfected in his cantata series.

As Wesley explained why modern music had lost the power "to inspire love or hate, joy or sorrow, hope or fear, courage, fury, or despair, which ancient music had possessed," he outlined a blistering six-point indictment of, in effect, the church music of Lutheran Germany. First came a denunciation of harmony. According to Wesley, "The ancient composers studied melody alone; the due arrangement of single notes; and it was by melody alone, that they wrought such wonderful effects. . . . But the modern composers study *harmony*, which . . . is quite another thing; namely, a contrast of various notes, opposite to, and yet blended with, each other."

Second was his repudiation of "counterpoint," which in Wesley's indictment had "altered the grand design of music, so it has well-nigh destroyed its effects." To insure that no one had missed his meaning, he repeated, "It is counterpoint . . . which destroys the power of music."

Next he charged that modern music had lost its capacity for emotional effect. "Our composers," he wrote, "do not aim at moving the passions, but at quite another thing; at varying and contrasting the notes a thousand different ways. What has counterpoint

28. Wesley, *Thoughts on the Power of Music*, 9 June 1779, Inverness, in *The Works of John Wesley*, vol. 7, *A Collection of Hymns for the People Called Methodists*, ed. Franz Hildebrandt, Oliver Beckerlegge, and James Dale (Nashville: Abingdon, 1989), 766–69. All quotations in the following paragraphs are from this pamphlet.

to do with the passions? It is applied to a quite different faculty of the mind; not to our joy, or hope, or fear; but merely to the ear, to the imagination, or internal sense. . . . It no more affects the passions than the judgment."

Music unaccompanied by words then followed in Wesley's catalog of modern musical maladies. He fumed about "those modern overtures, voluntaries, or concertos, which consist altogether of artificial sounds, without any words at all." To Wesley's ear, music should reflect "judgment, reason, common sense," but these were exactly the results that "are utterly excluded, by delicate, unmeaning sound!"[29]

Then, as if harmony, counterpoint, emotional sterility, and unaccompanied "sound" were not enough, Wesley let fly on a feature that, over the course of his career, he complained about several times. In modern music he found it "glaringly, undeniably, contrary to common sense" for composers "allowing, yea, appointing, different words to be sung by different persons at the same time! What can be more shocking to a man of understanding than this?" About this modern error, Wesley mixed self-pity with apoplexy: "Pray, which of those sentences am I to attend to? I can attend to only one sentence at once; and I hear three or four at one and the same instant!"[30]

Last, but by no means least, Wesley was mortally offended—"to complete the matter," as he wrote—that "this astonishing jargon has found a place even in the worship of God! It runs through (O pity! O shame!) the greatest part even of our Church music! It is found even in the finest of our anthems, and in the most solemn parts of our public worship! Let any impartial, any unprejudiced person say, whether there can be a more direct mockery of God."[31]

In his otherwise thoroughly negative screed, Wesley did concede that the modern age had developed musical instruments, like the organ, that surpassed what the ancient world had known. He also allowed that some modern compositions could be very ef-

29. For later Moravian nervousness about musical accompaniment without words as interludes within hymns, see Lou Carol Fix, "The Organ in Moravian Church Music," in *The Music of the Moravian Church in America*, ed. Nola Reed Knouse (Rochester, NY: University of Rochester Press, 2008), 139.

30. Compare, for example, the comment in Wesley's journal dated 24 March 1765, made after he heard an oratorio in the Lock Hospital chapel, London: "There are two things in all modern pieces of music, which I could never reconcile to common sense. One is, singing the same words ten times over; the other, singing different words by different persons, at one and the same time" (Wesley, *Journals and Diaries*, 4:444).

31. In 1738 Wesley was perhaps more open to the church music of the time. Indeed, successively on the three days surrounding his Aldersgate experience that year he heard three anthems—almost certainly by Henry Purcell, Maurice Greene, and William Croft—at evensong in St. Paul's Cathedral, London, that made a deep impression on him; see Robin A. Leaver, "The Anthem as Homily," in *Liturgy and Music: Lifetime Learning*, ed. Robin A. Leaver and Joyce Ann Zimmerman (Collegeville, MN: Liturgical Press, 1998), 343–49.

fective—even capable of bringing individuals or even entire groups to tears. But such positive results occurred only, he declared, "when a fine solo was sung. . . . Then, and only then, the natural power of music to move the passions has appeared."

Otherwise, however, concerted church music of the sort he would have heard on the Ninth Sunday after Trinity at Leipzig's St. Thomas or St. Nicolai Church in 1738 was to the visiting Englishman entirely anathema. Whichever of the Bach cantatas was performed on that Sunday, it would have been guilty on all six counts.

We can only imagine the contentious conversation that might have ensued if Wesley and Bach had been able to talk after Wesley sat through the performance of one of these cantatas. Would Wesley have conceded the merit of the text but then asked in bewilderment how Bach could have destroyed the power of such truthful exposition with so much musical folderol? Would Bach have shown any appreciation for Wesley's approval of the cantata text before blasting away at the visitor's barbaric opinions—or perhaps before opening Calov's commentary on Luther's German Bible and thrusting his finger at one of the passages he had annotated from Exodus or 1 and 2 Chronicles as providing precedents for the music he attempted in Leipzig's churches?

We simply do not know. Yet what does become clear from this meeting that did not occur was how deep the divisions had become between the various Protestant confessions by the middle years of the eighteenth century. When Wesley and Bach passed, as it were, in the night, they represented diverse Protestant traditions that had gone their separate ways, including separate ways musically.

Protestantism had developed in multiple directions almost from its origins. Already by the mid-sixteenth century, Lutherans, Reformed of several stripes (Calvinists and Presbyterians), Anglicans, and a plethora of radical groups remained united in their opposition to the pope, but they already differed among themselves on many other matters. Now in the middle of the eighteenth century, contemporary cultural currents exacerbated that original Protestant fragmentation. Even as Wesley passed through Leipzig, the Protestant world was experiencing a series of aggravating tensions. Within the different confessions, advocates of renewal (like Pietists and Moravians in Germany and the Wesleys, along with George Whitefield and Jonathan Edwards, in the English-speaking world) harshly criticized defenders of inherited traditions and were in turn harshly criticized by these defenders. Adaptations to local circumstances further split up Protestants, with the Moravians' successful removal from Bohemia to Saxony one of the rare examples of transportable Protestantism. Additionally, all of these groups were confronting robust intellectual challenges. Some influential Lutherans, Calvinists, and Anglicans who found the eurekas of the Enlightenment compelling subjected traditional Christianity to the modifications of capital *R* Reason. Other influential Lutherans, Calvinists, and Anglicans turned in another direction, toward the freedom, ecstasy, and individualism of romanticism, which led to further ecclesiastical fractures.

Viewed from this angle, Wesley's denunciation of what he called "modern" church music offered only one more instance of Protestantism menaced by ever-increasing strain. Whatever theological agreement could arise from Wesley's resonance with Bach's cantata texts, his rejection of the musical settings for these texts illustrated confessional division magnified by taste, inclination, emotion, and standards of artistic propriety. Both Bach and Wesley embraced versions of the Christian faith that involved deep commitments to reason and emotion. But their differences in how they exercised reason and how they expected passion to support true faith differed so dramatically that a meeting of their minds—a harmony of hearts—was almost unthinkable. Historians normally write of confessionalization as a function of theology and politics; just as easily they could also describe it as a function of musical practice.

From the same angle, the confessional traditions represented by this Leipzig encounter that did not occur seem to point only toward further fragmentation. German Lutherans in the 1730s were dividing internally among the traditionally orthodox (including Bach), movements of renewal (like the Moravians), and increasingly influential proponents of rationalism (leading to Immanuel Kant). English church life would soon experience equally sharp divisions, and not only between those who embraced evangelical revival and those who found revival movements absurd, anarchic, or alienating. Even within the awakening that the Wesleys promoted, there would be those who remained in the Church of England (like Charles Wesley), those who actually or practically split off to form a separate Methodist denomination (like John Wesley), and many who embraced evangelical impulses but in Calvinistic or independent movements. For both the German-speaking and the English-speaking worlds, these ecclesiastical fissures were reflected in musical expressions that heightened the discord. In sum, the clash over musical style, taste, expression, and emotion that would have ensued in a meeting between Bach and Wesley seems to represent only the expanding confessional confusion of that age.

But there is another side to the coin. Keeping only Wesley and Bach in view, and thinking about only the German and English Protestant confessions that crisscrossed at Leipzig in July 1738, it is evident that music could be a force for uniting as well as dividing. Two footnotes to Bach, Wesley, and Leipzig in 1738 illustrate the cohesive potential of church music. The footnotes concern Bach performance in the United States and the later musical history of the Wesley family.

In the mid-eighteenth century, the pietistic disposition of the Moravians and the orthodox commitments of Bach put them on paths that diverged musically as well as ecclesiastically. Although the Moravians were always a singing movement, they looked askance at the professionalism of state-church Lutheranism, especially any perfor-mance that did not involve choirs joining multiple voices in song together. Yet from that point of divergence came a fascinating history of convergence as the Moravians spread throughout the world.[32]

That convergence may have begun in Bach's own lifetime. In years very close to when Wesley passed through Leipzig, Johann Christopher Pyrlaeus was studying theology and music at that city's university. It is possible that during this time, Pyrlaeus took in some of the performances of Bach's Leipzig Collegium Musicum. Whatever the case in Leipzig, there is solid documentation for Pyrlaeus when he joined the Moravians and then was dispatched as a missionary to America, where he helped organize the first Indian-language school for the Moravians' successful missionary work among Native Americans. In the English colonies, Pyrlaeus not only translated Moravian hymns into Mohican but in 1744 also established a Collegium Musicum in Bethlehem, Pennsylvania.[33] Within a very short time the Collegium in Bethlehem was perform-ing the works of many cutting-edge European composers, including those of Johann Christian Bach.

From the first, Moravian communities in Pennsylvania and North Carolina con-tinued the movement's commitment to choral singing. Bach's work was known to at least one of the American Moravians' early musical leaders, Daniel Gottlob Türk. Türk, however, was committed to the classical style of the post-Bach era, including compositions by J. C. Bach. That commitment led him, in a comment recorded in 1787, to dismiss J. S. Bach's *Canonic Variations on "Vom Himmel Hoch"* as merely "music for the eyes."[34]

Soon, however, more appreciative Moravians expressed a different opinion. In 1823 or 1824 Johann Christian Till, carpenter and organist of the Moravian Church in Beth-lehem, created a handwritten set of parts of Bach's Cantata 80, *Ein feste Burg*, from the Breitkopf & Härtel score published in Leipzig in 1821, presumably for performance in Central Church, Bethlehem.[35] Then at midcentury, once instrumental compositions by Bach began to appear in Boston-area concerts, it was once again Moravians who took the lead in performing Bach's church music. J. Fred Wolle, who had witnessed a

---

32. The following relies on Karl Kroeger (one-time director of the Moravian Musical Foundation), "Johann Sebastian Bach in Nineteenth-Century America," BACH 22, no. 1 (Spring–Summer 1991): 33–42; and Nola Reed Knouse's illuminating colloquium, *The Music of the Moravian Church.*

33. See "Appendix One: Biographical Sketches," in Knouse, *Music of the Moravian Church*, 281.

34. Alice M. Caldwell, "Moravian Sacred Vocal Music," in Knouse, *Music of the Moravian Church*, 90.

35. Nola Reed Knouse, "The Collegia Musica: Music of the Community," in Knouse, *Music of the Moravian Church*, 198, 284; Ralph Grayson Schwarz, *Bach in Bethlehem* (Bethlehem, PA: Bach Choir, 1998), 10–13.

performance of the *St. John Passion* while studying in Munich, returned to the United States and the Bethlehem Choral Union to mount the first full performances of Bach's choral works in America—in 1888 the *St. John Passion*, in 1892 the *St. Mathew Passion*, in 1894 portions of the *Christmas Oratorio*, and in 1900 the B Minor Mass.[36] Moravians, in other words, who had stood apart from Bach in his own day, both ecclesiastically and musically, constructed the musical bridge that brought Bach's choral music to the New World.

The footnote for John Wesley is more remarkable.[37] Although John and Charles Wesley appreciated the importance of music and so devoted much energy to publishing what they considered appropriate tunes for their own hymns, neither was particularly musical. It was quite otherwise with the two sons of Charles Wesley. Both of these sons, the younger Charles Wesley (born in 1757) and Samuel Wesley (born in 1766), were musical prodigies who became renowned for their skill on the keyboard, their compositions, and their significant roles in Anglican church music. The Bach connection for the younger Charles Wesley came through Johann Christian Bach, who in 1763 became Queen Charlotte's musical director at Britain's royal court. Besides providing keyboard accompaniment for the flute-playing King George III, J. C. Bach in 1765 established a concert series at which European visitors and local musicians performed. Charles Wesley the younger, who amazed his entire family with his precocity, is reported to have performed on the organ for Queen Charlotte herself at eighteen years of age in 1775. A few years later he took his turn as a performer at J. C. Bach's concert series. Throughout the remaining years of his life, this Wesley also devoted great energy to promoting the work of George Frideric Handel.[38]

36. "Appendix Two: A Moravian Musical Timeline," in Knouse, *Music of the Moravian Church*, 303–4. See also Paul S. Larson, *Bach for a Hundred Years: A Social History of the Bach Choir of Bethlehem* (Bethlehem, PA: Lehigh University Press, 2012); and Barbara Owen, "Bach Comes to America," in *Bach Perspectives*, vol. 5, *Bach in America*, ed. Stephen Crist (Urbana: University of Illinois Press, 2003), 1–14, esp. 13–14.

37. The following paragraphs rely on Philip Olleson, *Samuel Wesley: The Man and His Music* (Woodbridge: Boydell, 2003); Philip Olleson, ed., *The Letters of Samuel Wesley: Professional and Social Correspondence, 1797–1837* (Oxford: Oxford University Press, 2001); Peter Horton, *Samuel Sebastian Wesley: A Life* (Oxford: Oxford University Press, 2004); Nicholas Temperley and Stephen Banfield, eds., *Music and the Wesleys* (Urbana: University of Illinois Press, 2010). See also Michael Kassler, ed., *The English Bach Awakening: Knowledge of J. S. Bach and His Music in England 1750–1830* (Aldershot: Ashgate, 2004).

38. The younger Charles Wesley's connections to J. C. Bach did not, however, win over his father. In a short poem from around 1770 entitled "Modern Music," the older Charles Wesley complained that "G [for Felice de Giardini] and B [for J. C. Bach] and all / Their followers, great and small, / Have cut Old Music's throat, / and mangled every Note" (Baker, *Representative Verse*, 312).

Charles's younger brother Samuel was a real piece of work, both musically and personally. In 1784 he greatly disappointed his father and his uncle by converting, though only briefly, to Catholicism. He caused even greater consternation in his family when, after a tumultuous marriage and the birth of three children, he abandoned his wife, established a liaison with a young serving maid, and for the rest of his days lived with her and the seven children they produced.

As opposed to his clouded place in the history of second-generation Methodism, Samuel Wesley's place in English musical history is luminous. Although a few erudite Englishmen had some acquaintance with a few of J. S. Bach's works before the turn of the century, it was Samuel Wesley's discovery in about 1806 that began Bach's permanent ascent in English musical life. An opportunity to copy out Bach's *Forty-Eight Preludes and Fugues* made Samuel Wesley an enthusiastic convert. "*Saint* Sebastian Bach" he called the composer in his far-flung correspondence. In a typical rapturous letter from March 1809 he spoke of "the transcendent Merits of this marvelous Man."[39] Although Samuel Wesley's fixation dwelt primarily on instrumental works, in 1815 he also tried to publish the *Credo* from Bach's B Minor Mass, which would have been its first appearance in print. His devotion to the German master took physical embodiment when he named the first son born to his irregular union Samuel *Sebastian* Wesley, who in his turn became the most notable composer for Anglican hymnody in the mid-nineteenth century.

At the very end of his life, in 1837, Samuel Wesley was privileged to play the organ for Felix Mendelssohn. Their conversation was not recorded, but one can imagine that given Samuel Wesley's lifelong devotion and Mendelssohn's recent efforts at reviving Bach's choral work, the two may have exchanged enthusiasms for the Leipzig *Kapellmeister*.

These footnotes to the meeting that did not take place in 1738 should bring a measure of reassurance to musicologists. Yes, music can drive individuals and culturally separated movements apart, but so can it bring even discordant groups together. As a footnote to these footnotes, and as a last word, I am intrigued that in the 1994 *Evangelisches Gesangbuch* of the Evangelisch-Lutherische Landeskirche Sachsens (that is, Bach's own Saxony), where almost all of the authors and composers are German, there appears one tune by Samuel Sebastian Wesley—and that in the 2006 *Lutheran Service Book* of the Lutheran Church—Missouri Synod there are more hymn texts written by Charles Wesley (9) than hymn tunes arranged or composed by Johann Sebastian Bach (6). Which only goes to show that the power of music to create chasms can also work to build bridges.

39. Wesley to Benjamin Jacob, 3 March 1809, in Olleson, *Letters of Samuel Wesley*, 101.

Dancing in Bach's Time

Sin or Permissible Pleasure?

Joyce L. Irwin

Throughout the seventeenth century, Lutheran writers, whether they were defending or criticizing the church music of their day, agreed that dance music was unsuited to worship. In the defense of instrumental music against Calvinist-influenced attacks, theologians of the late sixteenth and early seventeenth centuries had used as a central argument the fact that a listener could tell the genus of music without necessarily hearing a text. When the principality of Anhalt took an iconoclastic turn in the late sixteenth century—a turn that was fueled by a move toward Calvinism and away from Lutheranism—the theologians of Wittenberg responded with a lengthy critique that included a defense of organ music: "Instrumental music is itself such a gift of God that it is able to move people's spirits powerfully even when human voices are not singing along. As far as the organ is concerned, if one only knows the genus, that is enough for the organist not just to be blowing empty air. But the genus is when one knows that it is spiritual songs, made for the glory of God, that are being played."[1] Clearly, to use the rhythm of a dance would confuse the listener if spiritual music is a distinct genus of music. The theologians of Anhalt had complained of the use of dance rhythms in church music, but the Wittenberg theologians denied

---

1. "Es ist die instrumentalis Musica für sich eine solche gab Gottes / das die gemüter der Menschen zubewegen krefftig / wann gleich mit Menschlicher stimme darunter nicht gesungen wird. Wenn man nur das genus weiss / so ist es (soviel die Orgeln belanget) gnug / und wird damit nicht in wind hinein georgelt. Das genus aber ist / das man weiss / es werden geistliche Lieder / die zu Gottes lob gemachet sind / darauff geschlagen" ([Theological Faculty of Wittenberg], *Notwendige Antwort Auff die im Fürstenthumb Anhalt Ohn langsten ausgesprengte hefftige Schrift* [Wittenberg: Lehman, 1597], fols. 70v–71r). For the move toward Calvinism in Anhalt, see Adolf Boes, "Lutheranism in Anhalt," in *The Encyclopedia of the Lutheran Church*, ed. Julius Bodensieck (Minneapolis: Augsburg, 1965), 1:76–77. For a reevaluation of Bach's time in Anhalt-Cöthen, see Markus Rathey, "The 'Theology' of Bach's Cöthen Cantatas: Rethinking the Dichotomy of Sacred versus Secular," *Journal of Musicological Research* 35, no. 4 (2016): 275–98.

that this occurred in Lutheran churches: "The Anhalters should not be concerned that any 'overly fleshly dance or passamezzo' (as they say) will be played in churches on our organs. There are others who are positioned to turn their attention to this and prevent it without the reproaches of the Anhalters."[2]

There were enough complaints in the seventeenth century, however, that we may conclude that the Wittenberg theologians were overconfident in their insistence that dance music would not creep into worship. The author of a very influential defense of organs, Ulm superintendent Conrad Dieterich, argued that the abuse of organ music is not a valid argument against it, as any good thing can be misused. In a statement that can be read as an implicit admission that some dance music was being heard in churches, Dieterich called this a shameful misuse that is not to be tolerated and should be punished appropriately.[3] Even so orthodox a defender of church music as Hector Mithobius warned cantors to choose only music that was devotional and serious, evoking a sense of holiness, and to avoid above all any instrumental music with secular dance rhythms, galliardic hops, or other dance modes associated with weddings or other gatherings outside of church. Likewise, organists should "avoid all unfitting and frivolous mannerisms with courantes, passamezzos and dances, in order that they not make a fool's work out of sacred, divine music and shamefully defile worship."[4]

Even by the early eighteenth century, when Friedrich Erhardt Niedt wrote that church music styles were changing like clothing fashions and it was no longer possible to say what the correct style was, he himself held the line against dance-like church music. He composed in the cantata style, he wrote, "yet everything is entirely serious and in good taste. . . . I usually put a Sonata in the beginning, but not one filled with

---

2. "Auch das kein uberfleischlicher tantz oder Passameza, des die Anhaltischen gedencken / in Kirchen auff unsern Orgeln werde gespilet / dörffen sie sich nicht bekümmern / Es sind andere darauff bestellet / (ohne jhr / der Anhaltischen / schumpffieren) solches in acht zu nehmen und zuverhüten" (*Notwendige Antwort*, fol. 71r).

3. "Thun nun das etliche auch mit den Orgeln und Instrumental Music / so ist es unrecht / ist auch solcher schändlicher Mißbrauch nit zu dulden / sondern an ihnen der Gebühr zu straffen" (Conrad Dieterich, *Ulmische Orgel Predigt* [Ulm: Meder, 1624], 33).

4. "Darum sie ja lauter andächtige / zierliche / gravitätische und Hertz-rührende Stücke / dabey eine Heiligkeit und geistreicher Nachdruck gespüret wird / auslesen und erwehlen sollen: Hergegen sich hüten für allen den jenigen Symphonien / und Stücken / welche (mit Instrumenten allein gemachet) nur weltliche / galliardische Hüpfer / oder sonst hochzeitliche Tantz-Weisen / und irrdische Lust/ (bey andern menschlichen Zusammenkunften / ausserhalb des Gottes-Dienstes gebräuchlich) in sich begreiffen. . . . Daneben auch alle ungeziemte und leichtfertige Manieren / mit Curanten / Passametzen und Täntzen zu meiden / damit sie nicht aus der heiligen / göttlichen Music / ein Narren-Werck Machen / und den Gottesdienst schändlich entheiligen" (Hector Mithobius, *Psalmodia Christiana* [Bremen: Berger, 1665], 275–76).

fanciful tricks, as if for dancing; . . . I compose Recitatives without skips or leaps."[5] In the singing of chorales, he asked cantors and other singing leaders to maintain a moderate tempo, "not to bellow such chorales too quickly, as if they were an invitation to the dance; nor to tarry too long so that one might fall asleep over them."[6]

Andreas Werckmeister, writing in 1691 on the use and misuse of church music, also emphasized the importance of fitting the music to the text and keeping appropriate tempos, but he wrote more passionately against the traditional association of slow and serious with sacred music and fast and happy with secular music. Citing the exhortations in the Psalms to sing joyfully to the Lord, Werckmeister asked, "How then can one sing cheerfully if one is supposed to sing and play a sad lament? If we are to sing cheerfully and joyfully, then an outward display of joy must also be visible, or else it is only songs of mourning."[7] It is of no consideration if some "earthly and worldly minded person" claims music in church is so happy as if it were for dancing: "It is not a dance just because a happy song of praise is being performed to the glory of God."[8] Much depends for Werckmeister on the intention and mentality of the performers and the listeners, for to the pure, all things are pure, and to the evil, all is evil.[9]

If Werckmeister came close to breaking down the distinction between church and dance music styles, Lübeck cantor Caspar Ruetz in 1752 did so more explicitly:

> Music meant for dancing must be composed in certain rhythms or cadences that are proper to the dance; these cadences are as innocent and sinless as anything in the world ever can be. If it should by chance happen that just such a rhythm as conforms to this or that style of dance should be heard in a piece of church music, would the place or the worship service be desecrated by that? If we do not want to bring into church the slightest thing that belongs to dancing, we would have to leave hands and feet or even the whole body at home.[10]

---

5. Friedrich Erhardt Niedt, *The Musical Guide: Parts 1 (1700/10), 2 (1721) and 3 (1717)*, trans. Pamela L. Poulin and Irmgard C. Taylor (Oxford: Clarendon, 1989), 258–59 (pt. 3, chap. 4).

6. Ibid., 262 (pt. 3, chap. 5).

7. "Wie kan man nun frölich singen / wenn man ein traurig Lament singen und spielen soll? Sollen wir freudig und frölich musiciren / so muß auch eine äusserliche Freuden-Bezeugung sich sehen lassen / sonst werden es lauter Trauer-Gesänge" (Andreas Werckmeister, *Der Edlen Music-Kunst Würde, Gebrauch und Mißbrauch* [Frankfurt: Calvisius, 1691], 18).

8. "Es ist doch darum kein Tantz / wenn ein lustig Lobe-Lied Gott zu Ehren musiciret wird" (ibid., 19).

9. Ibid., 18–19.

10. "Eine Music, darnach getantzet werden soll, muß in gewissen Rhithmis, oder Klang-Füssen, die dem Tantze eigen sind, abgefasset werden; diese Klang-Füsse sind so unschuldig und unsündlich, als eine Sache in der Welt immer seyn kan. Solte es sich aber einmahl von ohngefehr begeben, daß eben ein solcher Rhithmus, der mit dieser oder jener Tantz-Art überein kömmt, sich in einem Kirch-Stücke

Ruetz acknowledged and gave approval to something that had been happening for quite a while without approval. Markus Rathey has shown that composers in northern Germany in the late seventeenth and early eighteenth centuries had been creating chorale-based keyboard suites with variations on dance rhythms for domestic use.[11] It is not difficult to imagine that these suites sometimes made their way into worship, as they were said to be for spiritual delight and edification. We know from the studies of dance in Bach's music by Meredith Little and Natalie Jenne that Bach's church music utilizes dance rhythms, even if they are labeled "gavotte-like," "minuet-like," "sarabande-like," rather than as actual dances.[12] Whether this should be regarded as an unwarranted incursion of gallantry into the church, the failure to uphold religious standards, or a consistent application of Luther's theology is a question that divided Lutherans of the time. In order to gain a broader perspective, we need to go beyond the views about using dance rhythms in worship to an understanding of theological views about the legitimacy of dancing for Christians.

Formulation of the Lutheran Position on Dancing

During the period of the early church, several of the leading patristic theologians wrote against dancing. Basil of Caesarea preached against women dancing on Sundays and against mixed dancing, both of which aroused lewdness. John Chrysostom said the devil is present at dances and recalled the incident of the dancing daughter of Herodias requesting the beheading of John the Baptist (Mark 6:21–29). Both Ambrose of Milan and Augustine of Hippo warned against dancing, and the fourth-century Council of Laodicea instructed Christians not to join in dances at weddings.[13] There are other passages by these same theologians that have been used as evidence of sacred dancing in the early church,[14] but J. G. Davies more persuasively argues that these are mostly

---

solte hören lassen, solte dadurch der Ort oder der Gottesdienst verunheiliget werden?" (Caspar Ruetz, *Widerlegte Vorurteile von der Beschaffenheit der heutigen Kirchenmusik und von der Lebens-Art einiger Musicorum* [Lübeck: Böckmann, 1752], 34–35).

11. Markus Rathey, "Johann Mattheson's 'Invention': Models and Influences for Rhythmic Variation in *Der vollkommene Capellmeister*," *Dutch Journal of Music Theory* 17 (2012): 77–90, esp. 84–89.

12. Meredith Little and Natalie Jenne, *Dance and the Music of J. S. Bach*, 2nd expanded ed. (Bloomington: Indiana University Press, 2001), 299–306. See also Dominik Sackmann, *Bach und der Tanz* (Stuttgart: Carus, 2005); and Doris Finke-Hecklinger, *Tanzcharaktere in Johann Sebastian Bachs Vokalmusik* (Trossingen: Hohner, 1970).

13. J. G. Davies, *Liturgical Dance: An Historical, Theological, and Practical Handbook* (London: SCM, 1984), 20–21.

14. See, for example, Marilyn Daniels, *The Dance in Christianity* (New York: Paulist Press, 1981), 18–21; and Margaret Taylor, "A History of Symbolic Movement in Worship," in *Dance as Religious Studies*, ed. Doug Adams and Diane Apostolos-Cappadona (New York: Crossroad, 1990), 16–19.

metaphorical comparisons to heavenly joy, not reports of actual liturgical dance.[15] Nevertheless, Davies also recognizes that, in spite of disapproval by theologians and church councils, religious dancing persisted, not as an element of liturgy but as folk custom on saints' days and festivals; by the time of the High Middle Ages, he finds plentiful evidence of dancing in churches regardless of existing prohibitions.[16] Walter Salmen records not only the evidence of dancing in and around churches but also the omnipresence of dance in late medieval society, quoting a Nuremberg chronicler on the occasion of Emperor Sigismund's coronation in 1433 as saying, "All the world dances: squires, youths, maidens, and respectable women, and young fellows without number."[17] This social acceptance of dancing is the basis for Martin Luther's comments on the subject in a passage that was to serve as the basis for the orthodox Lutheran position on dance. In keeping with his belief that Christians should live in the midst of society rather than in monasteries, Luther saw no necessary conflict between social custom and faithful behavior. Commenting on the wedding at Cana, he wrote:

> Is it a sin to sing and dance at a wedding, since people say that much sin comes from dancing? I do not know whether there was dancing among the Jews; but since it is the custom of the country, just as is inviting guests, decorating, eating and drinking, and being cheerful, I do not know that I should condemn it, except its excess when it is immodest or excessive.[18] It is not the fault of dancing alone that there is sin, since also that happens at table or in the churches, just as it is not the fault of eating and drinking that some become pigs about it. Where [dancing] is modest, I leave to weddings their rights and usages; go on dancing. Faith and love are not danced away . . . as long as you are modest and moderate in them. Young children dance without sin; do the same and become a child, then dancing will not harm you. Otherwise, if dancing were a sin in itself, then we must not permit children to dance.[19]

15. Davies, *Liturgical Dance*, 36–41.

16. Ibid., 43–57.

17. Walter Salmen, "Dances and Dance Music, c. 1300–1530," in *Music as Concept and Practice in the Late Middle Ages*, ed. Reinhard Strohm and Bonnie J. Blackburn (Oxford: Oxford University Press, 2001), 162.

18. That Jewish dancing, specifically at the Cana wedding, was a controversial point in the arguments for and against dancing may be seen from Melchior Ambach, *Von Tantzen, Vrtheil, Auß heiliger Schrifft, vnd den alten Christlichen Lerern gestelt* (Frankfurt am Main: Gülfferich, 1544), sig. D1v. Ambach argued that the fact that Jews danced at weddings both in his day and in biblical times did not constitute a biblical endorsement of dancing because, as he interprets Psalm 106, Jews learned dancing from pagans. Nevertheless, Ambach credits Jews with greater discipline in dancing than was the case for Christians.

19. *Church Postil II*: Gospel for the Second Sunday after Epiphany, John 2:1–11, LW 76: 241–42. "Obs denn auch sunde sey pfeyffen und tantzen zur hochzeit, syntemal man spricht, das viel sunde vom

Noteworthy in this quotation is the distinction between dancing in the abstract and dancing in its concrete circumstances. Luther does not believe that dancing in itself is a sin, but he does admit that there may be sin associated with dancing. This is true of quite normal and necessary activities such as eating and drinking, and there can even be sin associated with going to church. Thus the criterion for judging dancing is that it be done with modesty and in moderation. This is confirmed in another passage in which Luther mentions that it is not a sin for a young man or a girl to think about a future spouse: "Indeed, to this end banquets are arranged, decent social gatherings and dances, which should by no means be condemned if they are modest and temperate."[20]

Luther did not by any means speak for all his contemporaries, however, and he showed his awareness of differing opinions in the first sentence quoted above. Late medieval and sixteenth-century German preachers of various affiliations inveighed against dancing.[21] In France there appeared numerous publications for and against dancing as both Catholics and Protestants wrestled with popular customs in need of regulation.[22] The Genevan reformers took a rigid stance in opposition to dancing, expressed most extensively by Lambert Daneau in his 1579 *Traité des danses*.[23] Toward the end of the sixteenth century, Johann von Münster, a German statesman who had embraced the Heidelberg Catechism and advocated for the Reformed confession in various northwest German territories, assembled all conceivable biblical passages and

tantz komen. Ob bey den Juden tentze gewesen sind, weys ich nicht. Aber weyl es lands sitten ist gleich wie geste laden, schmücken, essen und trinken und frölich seyn, weys ich nicht zuverdamnen, on die ubermas, so es unzuchtig odder zu viel ist. Das aber sunde da geschehen, ist des tantzs schuld nicht alleyn, syntemal auch wol uber tissch und ynn den kirchen der gleychen geschehen, Gleich wie es nicht des essens und trinckens schuld ist, das ettlich zu sewen drüber werden. Wo es aber züchtig zu gehet, las ich der hochzeyt yhr recht und brauch und tantze ymer hyn. Der glaub und die liebe lesst sich nicht aus tantzen noch aus sitzen, so du züchtig und messig drynnen bist. Die iungen kinder tantzen ia on sunde, das thu auch und werde eyn kind, so schadet dyr der tantz nicht, sonst wo tantz an yhm selbs sunde were, müst man es den kindern nicht zu lassen" (WA 17/2: 64).

20. Lectures on Genesis 24:5–7, LW 4: 251. "Quin hoc fine apparuntur convivia, congressus honesti et Choreae, quae neutiquam damnandae sunt, si sint verecundae et modestae" (WA 43: 315).

21. See Irmgard Jungmann, *Tanz, Tod und Teufel: Tanzkultur in der gesellschaftlichen Auseinandersetzung des 15. und 16. Jahrhunderts* (Kassel: Bärenreiter, 2002), 151–70. While Jungmann offers useful citations from these "Tanzprediger," it would have been more useful for our purposes to distinguish among them based on their theological stance.

22. See Marianne Ruel, *Les Chrétiens et la danse dans la France moderne: XVIᵉ–XVIIIᵉ siècle* (Paris: Honoré Champion, 2006).

23. See Ann Wagner, *Adversaries of Dance from the Puritans to the Present* (Urbana: University of Illinois Press, 1997), 27–29.

writings of classical, patristic, and Reformed writers to demonstrate the sinfulness of dancing at weddings and banquets.[24]

While Luther did not use the term *adiaphoron* or *Mittelding* for a morally neutral act, his approval of dancing in moderation in effect placed dancing in that category of neutral things or actions that can be either good or evil depending on the context. Melchior Ambach, writing against dance in 1544, had used the equivalent Latin term *res media* in arguing that dancing was not a neutral activity.[25] Similarly, Johann von Münster, in his 450-page *Godly Treatise on Ungodly Dance*, argued against equating adiaphora with Christian liberty, saying that true Christian liberty entails freedom from fleshly desires.[26] It was this book in particular that provoked Wittenberg professor Balthasar Meisner, in his twelve disputations on adiaphora, to defend dances and comedies, among other things, as theologically indifferent, that is, neither forbidden nor commanded in scripture.[27] The entire set of disputations is subtitled *Opposed to the Calvinists*, an indication of the intensity of conflict between Lutherans and Calvinists in the early seventeenth century.

Meisner begins with a survey of the history of dance and the many contexts for dancing. Not all contexts are to be approved, as when ancient Israelites danced before the golden calf or when the daughter of Herodias danced to charm Herod and entice him to give her the head of John the Baptist (Matthew 14). But these are indeed just the contexts, whereas the real sin is idolatry or lasciviousness. Considered in itself, dancing is a delight for the spirit and exercise for the body. Within certain limits, then, it is a healthy recreation. Those limits are, first, that it not take place at times designated for worship but at weddings or on other days set aside for gaiety and celebration. Second, dancing should be in public places under the watchful eye of reputable men and women. Third, the motions should be decorous, without indecent circumgyrations or lewd gestures. Finally, dancing should have an honorable purpose, which, in the words of Luther, was to teach civility in social gatherings and to train young men to honor the feminine sex.[28]

24. Cuno, "Münster, Johann," in *Allgemeine deutsche Biographie* (Leipzig: Duncker und Humblot, 1875–1912), 23:29–30.

25. Ambach, *Von Tantzen*, sig. C4v.

26. *Ein Gottseliger Tractat / von dem ungottseligen Tantz*, 2nd ed. (Hanau: Antonius, 1602), 398. First published in 1594.

27. Balthasar Meisner, *Collegii Adiaphoristici Calvinianis Oppositi: Disputatio Duodecima de Choreis et Comoediis* (Wittenberg: Gormann, 1620).

28. Ibid., fol. 3r–v.

Calvinist and Pietist Critiques of Dancing

Meisner's formulation characterized the Lutheran stance through the seventeenth century, while the Reformed position, at least as expressed by leading Dutch theologian Gisbert Voetius, solidified in opposition to dancing. Among other points, Voetius refuted the argument that because dancing is not explicitly forbidden in scripture it is therefore an adiaphoron. He observed that many ideas and practices that emerged after the writing of scripture, such as the Muslim idea of heaven, the Catholic beliefs in purgatory, transubstantiation, and the Immaculate Conception of Mary, plus various recently invented dance forms, can find no explicit refutation in scripture, but they can be shown to be unscriptural.[29] With the rise of German Pietism, the rejection of dancing became a more prominent strand among Lutherans, and it was not only dancing that was under attack but the whole idea of ethical adiaphora. Placing greater emphasis on regeneration and sanctification, Pietists held that one must turn away from worldly activities that did not lead to moral betterment. We know of the Pietist attacks on opera and on elaborate church music. These are a few of the areas in which Pietists saw nominal Christians engaging in activities that were motivated by pride, ambition, and frivolity more than devotion and service to God. Fundamentally, the Pietist view was a rejection of the viewpoint we met in the quotation from Luther that the "rights and usages" of weddings or other civil customs are not in conflict with Christian love if they are not abused.

We find in August Hermann Francke, the leader of Lutheran Pietism after Philipp Jakob Spener, for instance, a rejection of the criteria listed above for legitimate dancing. In a preface to an essay entitled "Was von dem weltüblichen Tanzen zu halten sei?" (What should one think about dancing that is customary in the world?), Francke focused his criticism above all on courtly life. Thus what Francke found unacceptable was not only those who went off to illicit clandestine gatherings or who engaged in lewd tavern dances but even—or perhaps primarily—the very cultured dances of courts. He found in courts and those who behaved after the manner of courts a "sect" that appealed to Christian freedom and the concept of indifferent things to justify their worldly activities:

> They believe that they can go along with all outward things—attend operas and comedies, feast merrily with the world and afterward get up to play, to dance and to jump around, wear all the latest styles of the world to please others and whatever other vain things they and their like carry out—and yet want to retain the name of serving

---

29. Gisbertus Voetius, "De Excelsis Mundi ad VIII Decalogi Praeceptum: Prima, Quae est de Choreis," in *Selectarum Disputationum Theologicarum* (Utrecht: Waesberge, 1667), 4:336.

God in all seriousness, giving the pretext that their hearts are not attached to these things and that one must lead a Christian life in such a way as not to be considered peculiar. They find teachers who carry out this hypocrisy with them and consider all these and similar matters to be indifferent, teaching this to the people. Through this they open wide the gate not only to hypocrisy but also to Epicureanism.[30]

Francke did grant that the bodily movements of dance were not in themselves sinful and furthermore that David's dance before the ark was a spiritual dance, that is, bodily movement expressing his joy in relation to God; but Francke thought that in his own day such a spiritual dance would only be greeted by scoffing, like that of Michal in the biblical account (2 Samuel 6:12–20). He was careful to emphasize that he was discussing dancing that was customary in the social world of his time. His clear answer to whether this was sinful is "yes": "While one may surely speculate how dancing could happen without sinful circumstances, it cannot in reality and in practice be separated from sinful circumstances in any way."[31]

Francke's reasoning takes seriously the Pauline exhortation in Colossians 3:17: "Whatsoever ye do, in word or deed, do all in the name of the Lord Jesus, giving thanks to God and the Father by him" (KJV). Similarly in 1 Corinthians 10:31: "Whether therefore ye eat or drink, or whatsoever ye do, do all to the glory of God." As we have seen, he considered it hypocrisy to think that one could be a good Christian and also dance after the manner of the world. Christians should give up worldly passions (Titus 2:11–12), and Francke could not consider dancing anything other than worldly passion: "The love of the world must not be put aside halfway but from the heart." It was easy enough to sing, "Good night, O creature / who has chosen the world, / you please me

---

30. "Sie glauben / daß sie alles wohl können äußerlich mit machen / Opern und Comoedien besuchen / lustig mit der Welt schmausen / und darnach auffstehen zu spielen / zu tantzen und zu springen / alle neue Moden der Welt zu gefallen / und doch den Namen behalten wollen / daß es ihnen ein rechter Ernst sey Gott zu dienen / vorgebende / ihr Hertz hänge nicht daran / und man müsse sein Christentum so führen / daß man nicht für singulair gehalten werde. Sie finden auch wohl Lehrer / die mit ihnen heucheln / und alle diese und dergleichen Dinge selbst für indifferent halten / und das Volck also lehren / wodurch denn nicht allein der Heucheley / sondern auch dem Epicurischen Wesen Thür und Thor aufgethan wird" (August Hermann Francke, *Werke im Auswahl*, ed. Erhard Peschke [Witten: Luther Verlag, 1969], 384). The selection is a preface to a publication of two treatises by unnamed authors entitled *Was von dem Weltüblichen Tanzen zu halten sey?* (Halle: Wetterkampf, 1697).

31. "Dieweil man wohl eine Speculation machen kan / wie das Tanzen ohne sündliche Umbstände seyn möge / aber so / wie es würcklich und in praxi ist / es von sündlichen Umbständen keines Weges separiret werden kan" (Francke, *Werke im Auswahl*, 386).

not!" from *Jesu meine Freude*, but putting the idea into practice was not so easy.[32] When one took up one's cross and followed Jesus daily, then one would forget about dancing.[33]

Clearly, if one took these two biblical verses as ethical guidelines, there was no room for morally neutral actions. The issue of adiaphora as applied to opera, comedy, dance, and elaborate church music was the subject of several lengthy volumes by Gottfried Vockerodt, the rector of the Gymnasium in Gotha from 1694 until his death in 1727. Since at least 1692 he had been closely associated with Francke, who praised Vockerodt's efforts on behalf of the Pietist cause.[34] Gotha had been somewhat predisposed to Pietism under Duke Ernest the Pious, who ruled Gotha from 1640 until 1675, but his successor Frederick I of Saxe-Gotha loved music, theater, and dancing and began to shape court life after the model of Versailles. The title of a theatrical piece performed in his honor in 1676 gives an indication of a courtly atmosphere that offended the serious moralists: "Pastorale, which was presented with singing to awaken some pleasure and diversion."[35] While one of Frederick's lasting achievements was the founding of the Gotha castle theater, the use of students to supplement the court entertainers was a major cause of tension between school administrators and court musicians.

In 1696 Vockerodt provoked a controversy by organizing a school presentation in which three pupils used Roman emperors Caligula, Claudius, and Nero as examples of an immoderate obsession with the arts and theater and a consequent inability to govern properly. Although Vockerodt's many critics regarded him as an adversary of music, he pointed to the improvement in music instruction at the school since his arrival.[36] As education must, in his view, contribute to moral betterment, the circumstances in which music is performed must be morally uplifting. If, as Pietists believed, all things must be done in faith, then he could not approve the students' participation

32. "Gute Nacht o Wesen / das die Welt erlesen / mir gefälst du nicht" (opening lines of stanza 5 of "Jesu, meine Freude," trans. Alan Ogden, http://www.schillerinstitute.org/music/jesu_meine_text.html).

33. Francke, *Werke im Auswahl*, 387.

34. See Willi Temme, *Krise der Leiblichkeit: Die Sozietät der Mutter Eva (Buttlarsche Rotte) und der radikale Pietismus um 1700* (Göttingen: Vandenhoeck und Ruprecht, 1998), 63–64n204. Vockerodt served as conrector in Halle before moving to Gotha, but there is uncertainty as to whether this move took place in 1691 or 1693 and thus as to whether Vockerodt met Francke in Halle or in Gotha. Gudrun Busch maintains that Vockerodt knew Francke when they were both in Gotha in the winter of 1691–92 ("Die Beer-Vockerodt-Kontroverse im Kontext der frühen mitteldeutschen Oper," in *Das Echo Halles: Kulturelle Wirkungen des Pietismus*, ed. Rainer Lächele [Tübingen: Bibliotheca Academica, 2001], 151).

35. "Pastorell, welches . . . zu Erweckung einiger Lust und Zeit-kürzung singend vorgestellt worden" (Busch, "Die Beer-Vockerodt-Kontroverse," 148).

36. The controversy is discussed in greater detail in my book, *Neither Voice nor Heart Alone: German Lutheran Theology of Music in the Age of the Baroque* (New York: Peter Lang, 1993), 118–26.

in unwholesome theatrical performances. The underlying theological problem was a false understanding of the meaning of adiaphora.

The concept, according to Vockerodt, had taken on a meaning that had not been intended by the writers of the Lutheran confessions. In the Formula of Concord, adiaphora are considered to be ecclesiastical rites or ceremonies that are neither commanded nor forbidden; therefore, one is free to observe or omit them.[37] In the times when Lutherans and Catholics were fighting for territory, Lutherans sometimes faced the question of whether to comply with Catholic rites; though some rites might be intrinsically indifferent, Lutherans were to resist imposition of Catholic ceremonies and to stand up for the Christian liberty of the gospel. Applying this guideline might be complicated in actual circumstances, but in any case the problem discussed in the Formula of Concord did not touch on moral behavior, only church ceremony.

Though we have seen a little of the basis for a category of moral adiaphora in Luther, Vockerodt was at least historically correct in pointing out that such a category was not included in the confessional statements. We have, however, seen it discussed and rejected by Ambach and von Münster as a justification for dancing. Thus it was clearly not a new argument in Vockerodt's time, but he regarded it as an innovation and a scandalous means of defending activities he considered immoral with the claim that they were morally indifferent:

> Those who have undertaken to go directly against the basis of evangelical belief and the symbolic books by making up a new category of indifferent matters and have stretched it to apply to time-killing pleasures like carousing, game-playing, dancing and such things have not served the evangelical religion well but instead have opened the floodgates to obvious fleshly freedom. . . . Yes, it is an irresponsible innovation that in this way there have become two categories of indifferent matters, *adiaphora ecclesiastica et politica*, indifferent matters that belong to the church and others that belong to common life, and the afore-mentioned time-killing pleasures are numbered among the latter. It is disgraceful to plead Christian freedom for works of the flesh and such activities as have no other purpose than fleshly pleasure.[38]

---

37. Formula of Concord (1577), Article X, BC-W/K 515–16, 635–40.

38. "Demnach so haben sich diejenigen umb die Evangelische Religion nicht wohl verdienet / sondern der offenbaren Fleisches-Freyheit Thür und Thor auffgethan / welche sich understanden / dem Grunde des Evangelischen Glaubens / und dem Sinne der Symbolischen Bücher schnur stracks zu wieder / eine neue Gattung der Mitteldinge zu erdichten / und die Christliche Freyheit auff kurtzweilige Lust-Handlungen / zechen / spielen / tantzen und dergleichen zu erstrecken. . . . Ja es ist eine unverantwortliche Neuerung / daß man solcher gestalt zweyerley Gattung der Mitteldinge gemacht / *Adiaphora ecclesiastica & politica*, Mitteldinge so zur Kirche / und andere / so zum gemeinen Leben gehören / und unter diese die erwehnten kurtzweiligen Lustbarkeiten gerechnet hat. Lästerlich ist es / daß man eine Christliche Freyheit in Wercken des Fleisches / und solchen Handlungen vorgegeben /

Vockerodt placed the blame for this innovation on Balthasar Meisner, specifically on the disputation dealing with dancing and comedies. Vockerodt gave Meisner credit for placing sufficient qualifications and limitations on his approval of dancing, as if Meisner himself were reluctant to consider dancing a neutral activity. And Vockerodt recognized it was the Calvinist opposition to dancing that drove Meisner to defend it, resulting in what Vockerodt regarded as a contradiction of his otherwise quite acceptable position. Nevertheless, the damage was done, and because Meisner was a respected theologian, his position is routinely cited by anyone attempting to defend this "abomination."[39] Furthermore, the new category of adiaphora that includes activities of civic life has, according to Vockerodt, become an article of faith, even if that was not Meisner's intention.[40]

The factor that enabled this approach to ethics to take hold was, as Vockerodt saw it, the rise of scholasticism and Aristotelianism among Lutherans after the Council of Trent. Thinking they had to counter Catholic theology on its own terms, Vockerodt said, they fostered a method of education based in philosophy rather than scripture. Aristotelian ethics takes moderation as the rule of virtue and excess as vice; in matters of pleasure, it is sufficient that one not take it to excess by doing either too much or too little. By means of scholastic distinctions, such philosophical thinkers weaken the basic principle of Christian life, that one must do everything through faith to the glory of God and in the name of Jesus. With invented amoral distinctions such as *immediate*, *proximate*, and *actual*, they manage to label as indifferent any action that does not obviously contradict faith or go against God's honor. Thus, Vockerodt charged, "instead of the strait gate and narrow path toward which the teaching of Christ leads, they have directed unfortunate people onto the Aristotelian middle road, that is, a sidewalk built out of indifferent things on the wide street leading to damnation."[41]

Before leaving the Pietists, we should at least touch briefly on Philipp Jakob Spener, whose *Pia Desideria* (1675) is regarded as the central statement of Pietist thinking. In contrast to Francke and especially Vockerodt, Spener mostly tried to resolve conflict instead of fomenting it. Thus his statement on dance was cited by later orthodox

---

die keinen andern Zweck / als fleischliche Lust haben" (Gottfried Vockerodt, *Erleuterte Auffdeckung des Betrugs und Aergernisses: So mit denen vorgegebenen Mitteldingen und vergönneten Lust in der Christenheit angerichtet worden* [Halle: Waisenhaus, 1699], 93).

39. Ibid., 96.

40. Ibid., 97.

41. "Also hat man an statt der engen Pforten und schmalen Weges / dahin die Lehre Christi führet / die armen Menschen auff die Aristotelische Mittel-Strasse führet / das ist / auff einen auss dem breiten Wege zur Verdammniß von Mitteldingen gebaueten Fußsteig gewiesen" (ibid., 102–3). For further background on adiaphora in post-Reformation theology, see Reimund Sdzuj, *Adiaphorie und Kunst: Studien zur Genealogie äthetischen Denkens* (Tübingen: Niemeyer, 2005).

theologians as supporting theirs, even though that is based on selective reading. He did begin his treatment of dance by saying that in the abstract there is no reason to condemn it, as movement of the body according to melody or beat is not sinful. Interestingly, to support this point of the acceptability of dance in the abstract, Spener turned not to Luther but to Reformed writers Benedictus Aretinus, William Perkins, and Lambert Daneau, all of whom wrote against dance as it was actually practiced in their time. Though from this point on Spener relied on Lutheran predecessors, he, like the Reformed, saw no reason to defend the dancing of his day; rather, there was much that was sinful that usually accompanied it. He quoted extensively from Melchior Ambach's previously mentioned work, though emphasizing that Ambach's description of dancing's sinfulness applied not to dance in the abstract but to its customary practice.[42] Spener mentioned with approval Francke's preface discussed above, agreeing that dancing was an occasion for vanity and frivolity. Still, these can occur without dancing, and if one can learn cultured bodily movement through dance as part of one's education, some benefit may occur.[43]

Of special interest to us may be a section in which Spener discussed music that was used for dancing. He reported that a certain vice *Kapellmeister* had come to him and then corresponded with him about scruples he had in relation to playing for dances.[44] Spener responded that such scruples were the workings of the Holy Spirit in him, and he should heed them. Spener recognized that taking such a stance could cause a reduction in income and possible conflict with employers or other musicians, and he did not intend to try to persuade musicians to refrain from such employment if their consciences had not convicted them. But for those such as this particular musician, Spener offered encouragement and the hope that his witness would encourage those in authority to rein in these occasions for sin.[45]

Bach and His Contemporaries

We have no reason to think that Bach was troubled by such scruples; surely by now we are all in agreement that Bach was not a Pietist. To what extent he himself played for

---

42. Philipp Jakob Spener, *Theologische Bedencken* (Halle: Waisenhaus, 1701; repr., Hildesheim: Olms, 1999), 2:485–86 (chap. 3, art. 4, sec. 30). Spener copies another long passage from Ambach on pp. 494–95, stating that the treatise is very rare.

43. Ibid., 2:502 (chap. 3, art. 4, sec. 31).

44. Probably Christian Ritter, vice *Kapellmeister* for the Swedish court. See Philipp Jakob Spener, *Briefe aus der Dresdner Zeit 1686–1691*, ed. Udo Sträter and Johannes Wallmann (Tübingen: Mohr Seibeck, 2017), 610 (no. 132, n. 3). Spener would have known Ritter from his time as court preacher in Dresden (1686–91); Ritter was court organist and deputy *Kapellmeister* under Christoph Bernhard in Dresden during the years 1683–88.

45. Spener, *Theologische Bedencken*, 2:496–502.

dances is unknown, but Christoph Wolff conjectures that in his student years Bach may have provided musical entertainment for the Ritter-Akademie in Lüneburg and perhaps also at the ducal court through the academy's dancing master, Thomas de la Selle, who was also in the court *Kapelle*.[46] Dominik Sackmann points out that even smaller courts such as Weimar and Cöthen employed dancing masters and that all musicians of the time—organists, court musicians, and town musicians alike—had the playing of dance music as one of their duties.[47] We can safely assume that Bach's incorporation of dance rhythms into his music resulted in part from his exposure to actual dancing.

Can we know anything about Bach's theological position on dancing? We could conjecture that he may have known the work of the Leipzig dancing master Gottfried Taubert, whose lengthy work *Rechtschaffener Tantzmeister* provides a thorough basis and history of dance, including its theological and biblical justification.[48] In contrast to the scholastic methodology followed by the theologians who debated biblical evidence, Taubert began with an assertion from natural theology that dance was implanted in both rational and irrational creatures by God; he refuted the position that it was invented by Satan and thus treated it as a positive good.[49] While Taubert noted briefly in chapter 2 that dance was an adiaphoron and that it was often misused in his own day, he concentrated in his early chapters on the many examples of joyful and artistic dance, both sacred and secular, that he found in the Bible and throughout history, even in the early church. The many examples of depraved, lascivious, uncouth dancing that he then related did not cast doubt on the intrinsic value of dancing but served as counterexamples to the manner of dance that he wished to teach.

There is no evidence of a direct connection between Taubert and J. S. Bach, though their time in Leipzig overlapped between 1723 and 1730. Another defense of dance,

---

46. Wolff BLM, 65–66.

47. Sackmann, *Bach und der Tanz*, 9.

48. Gottfried Taubert, *Rechtschaffener Tantzmeister, oder gründliche Erklärung der frantzösischen Tantz-Kunst, bestehend in drei Büchern* (Leipzig: Lankisch, 1717); *The Compleat Dancing Master: A Translation of Gottfried Taubert's "Rechtschaffener Tantzmeister" (1717)*, trans. Tilden Russell (New York: Peter Lang, 2012).

49. In this section Taubert offers a lengthy citation from Johann Pasch's *Beschreibung wahrer Tanz-Kunst* (Frankfurt: Michahelles and Adolph, 1707). Pasch (1653–1710) was also a famous dance master in Leipzig and encountered the Pietist objections to dancing during his time there. His work is primarily a refutation of Pietist theologian Johann Christian Lange's *Vernunfft-mässiges Bescheidenes und Unpartheyisches Bedencken über die . . . Streitigkeit vom Tantzen* (Frankfurt: Schall, 1704). For an introduction to Pasch's work, see Kurt Petermann's postscript in Johann Pasch, *Beschreibung wahrer Tanz-Kunst, nebst einigen Anmerckungen über Herrn J.C.L.P.P. zu G. Bedencken gegen das Tantzen und zwar wo es als eine Kunst erkennet wird* [1707], [*Documenta Choreologica: Studienbibliothek zur Geschichte der Tanzkunst*, vol. 16] (Munich: Heimeran, 1978).

on the other hand, was written by one of the pastors whose sermons Bach would have heard in Leipzig. Johann Gottlob Carpzov was archdeacon at St. Thomas's in Leipzig from 1714 to 1730, and his daughter was godparent to Bach's fourteenth child, Christiana Benedicta, though the baby unfortunately lived only three days.[50] Carpzov's work, entitled *Unterricht vom Spielen und Tantzen*, was published in 1743 when he was superintendent in Lübeck, thus thirteen years after he had left Leipzig, but it also contains deliberations from the ministerium of Lübeck and the theological faculty of Rostock, an indication that his position was in accordance with the prevailing Lutheran orthodox view.

For his scripture text, Carpzov used 2 Samuel 6, the story of David dancing before the ark. This, of course, is one of the positive accounts of dancing in the Bible and was routinely cited as biblical support for dancing. But Carpzov's account is quite lengthy and noteworthy for its emphasis on the outward expression of an inward joy: "He [David] applied all his powers and effort to display through such an outward dance the inner joy of his soul. The dear man is so full of joy in God that he almost forgets decorum and propriety because of it."[51] In his dance the seriousness and respectability of his regal status yield to his status as servant of God, and he becomes an instrument of God's joyous spirit.[52] While Carpzov admitted that the weddings and other celebrations of his own day were very different occasions for dancing, he nevertheless found David's example to be instructive as spiritual preparation for moderate and permissible dancing.[53]

What is permissible in Carpzov's mind, however, appears quite restrictive to our twenty-first-century mentality. The criteria of appropriate time, place, and manner are similar to Meisner's, but Carpzov's association of dance with joy seems to bring other restrictions. For instance, dancing is more appropriate for young people, who are naturally more given to joy, than for their elders, who are burdened with care and carrying a heavy cross. He seems to conflate various situations rather illogically as causing dancing to be inappropriate. First, he refers to Barzillai in 2 Samuel 19, who was so old he could not taste what he was eating and drinking or hear what the singers were singing, so dancing isn't suitable for him. Next, he explains that those who are

50. Wolff BLM, 398; on Carpzov, see also Robin A. Leaver, "Churches," in *The Routledge Research Companion to Johann Sebastian Bach*, ed. Robin A. Leaver (London: Routledge, 2017), 178–79.

51. "Er habe alle seine Kräffte und Bemühung darzu angewendet, durch solchen eusserlichen Tantz die innerliche Freude seiner Seelen an den Tag zu legen. Der liebe Mann ist der Freuden in Gott so voll, daß er bey nahe darüber das *decorum* und den Wolstand vergißet" (Johann Gottlob Carpzov, *Unterricht vom Spielen und Tantzen: In zween Wochenpredigten* [Lübeck: Böckmann, 1743], 54).

52. Ibid., 55.

53. Ibid., 59.

burdened by a heavy cross are under God's disciplining hand, and they should humble themselves and repent rather than evading God's hand with worldly joy.[54] But then Carpzov saw Germany itself as in a time of God's wrath because of wars, and thus it was a time for sackcloth and ashes, not jumping and dancing.[55] Furthermore, those who because of their office or profession are responsible for getting others to moderate their joy should not dance, lest they be a stumbling block to others. After about twelve pages of laying out unsuitable or offensive circumstances for dancing, Carpzov finally returns to a positive outlook, saying that the person who truly delights in dancing is the one who has kept God foremost and given thanks to God for this permissible pleasure, always keeping in mind how he will give an account of himself before God.[56] Returning to the example of David, Carpzov emphasizes that true joy is spiritual and that, as stated in Romans 14:17, "the kingdom of God . . . is righteousness and peace and joy in the Holy Spirit."[57]

If Carpzov sounded surprisingly close to the Pietists, this impression is modified somewhat by the other documents appended to his sermons. The statement signed by the ministerium of Lübeck recognized that not all dancing need be religious. Elaborating on the oft-cited verse in Ecclesiastes 3:4, "a time to mourn and a time to dance," the ministers say there is no basis for claiming that this refers solely to religious dancing: "The enlightened king is not speaking here at all about exercises of devotion or activities of worship but rather of those partly natural, partly moral actions of human beings that alternate in this life between being in season and out of season."[58] Similarly, the impression Carpzov gave that all weeping or mourning would be occasions for repentance is corrected; the ministers recognize that there are other "permissible" times for weeping that do not result from God's disfavor.

As for Francke's biblical guidelines, that is, that everything be done to the glory of God, the Lübeck ministers argue that even if dancing does not have the glory of God as its immediate goal, nevertheless it can be part of a life that in its totality is directed to God when one gives thanks to God for the joyous occasion for dancing and the physical ability to do so. A sentence from the statement of the Rostock theologians

54. Ibid., 62–63.

55. Ibid., 69–70.

56. Ibid., 72.

57. "Denn sie haben das Reich Gottes in sich, welches ist Gerechtigkeit, und Friede, und Freude im Heiligen Geiste" (ibid., 73).

58. "Der erleuchtete König redet hier gar nicht von Übungen der Gottseligkeit, oder Gottesdienstlichen Handlungen, sondern von denen theils natürlichen, theils moralischen Actionen der Menschen, die ihre Abwechselung, und folglich ihre Zeit und Unzeit in diesen Leben haben" ("Theologisches Bedencken vom Tantzen des Ministeriums in Lübeck" [6 July 1742], in ibid., 78).

that also accompanies Carpzov's sermons may summarize the position of the mainstream Lutheran theologians: "Insofar as the purpose is a permissible entertainment and demonstration of joy at a Christian or perhaps a wedding party, without offending our dear God or slighting his most holy honor, then such dances may rightly be considered innocent and permitted."[59]

This declaration was written as part of a deliberation on how to deal with a pastor who had caused division in his church by his stringent preaching against dance. These writings from the late 1730s and early 1740s are evidence that, while the orthodox theologians were united in defending dancing, it remained a controversial issue. Pietists clung to their position, and in 1750 the Halle orphanage press published another antidancing work, Carl Heinrich von Bogatzky's *Schriftmässige Beantwortung der Frage: Was von dem weltüblichen Tanzen und Spielen zu halten sey?* (Scriptural answer to the question: What should one think about the dancing and games that are customary in the world?). Caspar Ruetz was well aware in 1752 that his support for dance rhythms in church music would not be welcomed by all sides.

What does any of this mean for Bach scholarship? It is clear that Bach intentionally utilized dance rhythms in both sacred and secular music. Doris Finke-Hecklinger observed changes in Bach's approach from the Cöthen period to Leipzig that largely changed the character of church cantatas through the incorporation of "worldly instrumental types of movement."[60] Yet she does not regard the result as a secularization of his church cantatas; rather, by weaving together a variety of forms and rhythms, Bach rose above the distinctions of tempi and movement types.[61] In doing so, he placed himself within the open-minded orthodox party, which did not preach a rigorous separation from the world and its stylistic changes.

Nevertheless, awareness of dance rhythms in Bach's church music and of the Lutheran affirmation of the holiness of life should not lead to the conclusion that all boundaries were removed. Even Caspar Ruetz recognized that, given the vanity and lust that were inherent in the dance contexts of his time, there was no hope of restoring liturgical dance following a biblical model.[62] "Because of the corruption of Christianity in our day," Ruetz writes, dancing like David as an expression of spiritual delight "is not and cannot be introduced into worship. . . . Our composers are well aware they

---

59. "Woferne man aber ein erlaubte Vergnügung und Freuden-Bezeugung in einer Christlich–etwa Hochzeitlichen Gesellschaft zum Zwecke hat, ohne den lieben Gott zu beleidigen, und dessen heiligsten Ehre zu nahe zu treten, so wird dergleichen Tantzen billig für unschuldig und erlaubet geschätzet" ("Gründliches Bedencken der theologischen Facultät zu Rostock" [27 August 1738], in ibid., 92).

60. "Weltlich-instrumentalen Bewegungstypen" (Finke-Hecklinger, *Tanzcharaktere*, 10).

61. Ibid., 145.

62. Ruetz, *Beschaffenheit der heutigen Kirchmusic*, 37–39.

should take care not to produce any strict minuets, gavottes, bourrées, rigaudons, gigues, polonaises, angloises, passepieds, or courantes." But music that now and then utilizes dancing meter can depict and encourage the hearts of upright Christians to hop and jump.[63]

Johann Mattheson, whom Ruetz quoted at length on the positive example of ancient Hebrew dancing, also resisted a merger of sacred and secular styles. From his early works to his major theoretical work, *Der vollkommene Capellmeister*, Mattheson consistently distinguished the styles of the three main divisions of music: church, theater, and chamber.[64] Instrumental music in church, for example, should be solid and serious, not loosely organized and jesting. This does not exclude a musical liveliness that expresses joyful devotion to God, but it separates faith from frivolity: "Joy does not contradict seriousness; for then all mirth would have to consist of jesting. A cheerful disposition is best disposed for devotion; where such is not to be done mechanically or simply in a trance. Only the appropriate discretion and moderation with the joyful sounds of the clarino trumpets, trombones, violins, flutes, etc., must never be lost sight of, nor to be to the slightest detriment of the familiar commandment, which says: **Be joyous; yet in fear of God.**"[65] As for dance modes, Mattheson, consistent with Finke-Hecklinger's comments on Bach, regards the use of dance rhythms in symphonic style music as having little in common with actual dance music: "The above-mentioned dance forms [allemande, courante, sarabande, gavotte, and gigue] that are accounted as symphonic style are artfully elaborated and cannot actually be used for dancing. They only happen to have the tempo of the above dances but are *saltatione multo nobiliores* [much more noble than dancing]. An allemande for dancing

63. "Ist es zwar nicht eingeführet, und kan auch nicht, wegen des Verderbens des heutigen Christenthums, eingeführet werden, daß man beym Gottesdienste nach Art des ehemaligen Volcks aus geistlicher Wollust tantzet: so könte doch eine solche Music, die hin und wieder mit tantzenden Klangfüssen einhergehet, das Hüpfen und Springen aufrichtiger Christen Hertzen vorstellen und befördern. Unsere Componisten wissen sich wohl in acht zu nehmen, daß sie keine förmliche Menuets, Gavotten, Bourreen, Rigaudons, Giquen, Polonoisen, Angloisen, Passepieden, Couranten, zu Marckte bringen" (ibid., 41).

64. From his early works, see *Das Neu-Eröffnete Orchestre* (Hamburg: Mattheson, 1713), 113, and *Das Beschützte Orchestre* (Hamburg: [Mattheson], 1717), 139–42.

65. Ernest C. Harriss, *Johann Mattheson's "Der vollkommene Capellmeister": A Revised Translation with Critical Commentary* (Ann Arbor: UMI Research Press, 1981), 209. "Freude verwirfft keinen Ernst; sonst müste alle Lust im Schertz bestehen. Ein aufgeräumtes Gemüth reimet sich am schönsten zur Andacht; wo diese nicht im Schlummer oder gar im Traum verrichtet werden soll. Nur muß die nöthige Bescheidenheit und Mäßigung bey dem freudigen Klange der Clarinen, Posaunen, Geigen, Flöten etc. niemahls aus den Augen gesetzt werden, noch der bekannte Befehl den geringsten Abbruch leiden, da es heißt: **Sey frölich; doch in Gottes Furcht**" (Johann Mattheson, *Der vollkommene Capellmeister* [Hamburg: Herold, 1739], 83).

and one for playing are as different as heaven and earth, and the same of the others with the possible exception of the sarabande."[66] Modern interpreters of Bach would do well to keep these distinctions in mind, even as they rightfully point out the dance rhythms in Bach's music that had been overlooked in the past. To be cognizant of the dance rhythms does not entail performing the works as if to lead the audience to dance. Without an awareness of the continued distinctions among musical styles and of the acceptable standards of dance in Bach's theological circle (i.e., that dance be moderate and respectable, not frivolous and unrestrained), performers may tend to move too far in the direction of sprightliness and light-heartedness.

To be sure, the emphasis on the joyful message of faith that we saw in Werckmeister did lead to a breakdown of the distinction that identified church music as solemn and slow, though this change was resisted by many and therefore controversial. For those who resisted, the change did mark an incursion of secular styles into the church and a failure of the churches to enforce standards. A case could also be made that this process was a legitimate application of Luther's view that everyday life is holy. Even with that basic belief that all worthy human activities could be done to the glory of God, however, Lutheran writers were agreed that not all dancing was worthy. Orthodox Lutherans, including Bach, continued to distinguish a sacred application of dance rhythm from music meant for dancing, thus still maintaining, though less clearly than previously, a stylistic distinction that the listener could recognize.

66. "Obgedachte Tantz-Arten / die ad Stylum Symphoniacum gezehlet werden sind künstlich elaboriret / und mögen nicht eigentlich zum Tantzen gebraucht werden. Sie haben nur etwann das Tempo obgedachter Täntze / sind aber Saltatione multò nobiliores. Eine Allemande zum Tantzen und eine zum Spielen sind wie Himmel und Erden unterschieden / & sic de cœteris, die Sarabanden in etwas ausgenommen" (Mattheson, *Das Beschützte Orchestre*, 137–38).

A Catholic Hymnal for Use in Lutheran Leipzig

Catholisches Gesang-Buch *(Leipzig, 1724)*

Robin A. Leaver

Theological differences ran wide and deep between Lutherans and Catholics in Germany in the early eighteenth century, a continuation of the conflict of earlier centuries. But in terms of liturgical practice, especially liturgical music, the two confessions had much in common, more than perhaps they were willing to admit. For example, in the immediate aftermath of the Reformation in the sixteenth century, it is impossible to be absolutely certain what is Lutheran and what is Catholic church music, since churches on both sides of the divide could be found to be using the same music, and Catholic musicians were servicing Lutheran churches and vice versa.[1] In the seventeenth century, German Lutheran composers were enamored with Italian music, and a good many traveled to Italy to discover for themselves the music of Catholic churches. Thus, for example, Hans Leo Hassler, Heinrich Schütz, and Johann Rosenmüller, among others, experienced the music of St. Mark's, Venice, and early in the eighteenth century, Handel, for a time based in Rome, visited various Catholic churches in Florence, Naples, and Venice.[2] On the other hand, throughout the seventeenth century, a succession of Italian musicians were active in Lutheran churches, notably, the succession of *Kapellmeister* at the Saxon court in Dresden— Marco Giuseppe Peranda, Vincenzo Albrici, Carlo Pallavicino, and Giovanni Andrea

The substance of this chapter has greatly benefited from the published writings, unpublished research, and personal communications of Janice B. Stockigt, for which I gratefully record my sincere thanks.

1. See Robin A. Leaver, "The Reformation and Music," in *European Music 1520–1640*, ed. James Haar (Woodbridge: Boydell, 2006), 371–73. However, while Lutheran musicians used music composed by Catholic composers, there is almost no evidence of Catholic musicians performing music composed for Lutheran worship.

2. For German composers who studied in Venice, see Konrad Küster, *Opus Primum in Venedig: Traditionen des Vokalsatzes 1590–1650* (Laaber: Laaber, 1995).

Bontempi—who, with other Italian musicians, mostly retained their Catholicism while serving the Lutheran court chapel.[3]

In Leipzig during Bach's time, Latin motets on biblical texts by Catholic composers were heard on many Sundays in the two principal Lutheran churches, since the choirs sang from the printed part-books of Bodenschatz's *Florilegium Portense* (Leipzig, 1618–21), which included compositions by both Catholic and Lutheran composers. However, it is likely that few in the Lutheran congregations recognized the "Catholic" origins of this music. It is also a moot point regarding how many of them were aware of the few Catholic families that lived in the town or that they had their own place of worship within the town walls, since most of the yearbooks and other such literature that offered information on the life of the town and its citizens, businesses, organizations, and churches do not acknowledge Catholics' existence until late in the eighteenth century.[4] But there was a Catholic chapel in Leipzig in Bach's day that had a small regular congregation that was much expanded during the three annual fairs at New Year, after Easter, and at Michaelmas, when many visitors from all over Europe were present in the town. After outlining the background to the founding of the chapel,[5] this chapter examines the specific hymnal that was published for use by the congregation worshiping in the Catholic chapel, draws parallels between its Latin and German contents with the practice of the Leipzig Lutheran churches, and then examines the possibility of how familiar Bach might have been with the worship of this Catholic chapel.

---

3. See Mary E. Frandsen, *Crossing Confessional Boundaries: The Patronage of Italian Sacred Music in Seventeenth-Century Dresden* (Oxford: Oxford University Press, 2006). The practice continued in later generations. For example, in 1699 the Pietist pastor Christian Gerber complained of Catholic singers, mostly Italians, performing in Lutheran churches, especially in large cities and court chapels; see Joseph Herl, *Worship Wars in Early Lutheranism: Choir, Congregation, and Three Centuries of Conflict* (Oxford: Oxford University Press, 2004), 120, 200.

4. See, for example, Friedrich Gottlob Leonhardi, *Leipzig um 1800: Kommentierte und mit einem Register versehen Neuausgabe der "Geschichte und Beschreibung des Kreis- und Handelsstadt Leipzig" (1799)*, ed. Klaus Sohl (Leipzig: Lehmstedt, 2010), 79–80, 212. An exception is Anton Weitz, *Verbessertes Leipzig, oder Die Vornehmsten Dinge, so von Anno. 1698. an biß hieher Bey der Stadt Leipzig verbessert worden, mit Inscriptionibus erlautert* (Leipzig: Lanckish, 1728), 3, which has a brief reference to the inauguration of the Catholic chapel in 1710; see note 16 below.

5. Two articles by Janice B. Stockigt are invaluable for understanding the foundation and functioning of the Leipzig Catholic chapel: "The Music of Leipzig's Royal Catholic Chapel during the Reign of August II," *Understanding Bach* 11 (2016): 57–66; and "The Organists of Leipzig's Royal Catholic Chapel: 1719–1756," *Hudební věda* 2/3 (2016): 161–76. See also Paul Franz Saft, *Der Neuaufbau der katholischen Kirchen in Sachsen im 18. Jahrhundert* (Leipzig: St. Benno, 1961), 131–45; and the first chapter of Jeffrey S. Sposato, *Leipzig after Bach: Church and Concert Life in a German City* (New York: Oxford University Press, 2018).

Leipzig's Royal Catholic Chapel

Catholic theology and liturgy were replaced by Lutheran theology and practice at Pentecost 1539, when Martin Luther himself preached sermons in Leipzig churches. The university resisted the "new religion" for a few months, but by the August of the same year it too fell into line with the religious changes that had been brought about by the recent accession of Henry IV, duke of Albertine Saxony (1473–1541). Ernestine Saxony had been the cradle of the Lutheran Reformation since 1517, with its courts in Torgau and Altenberg and its university in Wittenberg, where Luther was the leading Reformer. After 1547 Albertine Saxony, with its primary court in Dresden and university in Leipzig, effectively became the political center of gravity for the whole of Saxony, since its duke served as elector of the Holy Roman Empire in Germany.[6] Thereafter all religious affairs of the Lutheran Church in Saxony were administered under the authority of the Saxon elector, who was based in Dresden. Although one controversy or another was never far away, Lutheranism in Saxony was thought to be secure, although Johann Georg II (1613–80), elector from 1656, had significant Catholic leanings that raised fears that he might convert, though he never did.[7]

That fear became a reality in 1697, when Friedrich August I, "the Strong" (1670–1733), elector from 1694, converted to Catholicism in order to assume the Polish crown (as August II). However, his claim to the Polish throne was contested. He was deposed in 1706 but was eventually reconfirmed as king in 1709. However, the Polish king continued as the Saxon elector, and that meant that while his personal faith was Roman Catholic, he remained the head of the Lutheran Church and was therefore, paradoxically, responsible as elector for issuing directives for the Lutheran Church he personally disavowed. In consequence, there had to be two governments in Dresden, one for August as elector, which was Lutheran, and the other for August as the Polish king, which was Catholic.[8] Of course, there were sensitivities and anomalies of this ar-

---

6. The division of the territories of the Saxon House of Wettin between the two brothers, Albert and Ernest, in the late fifteenth century led to rivalries that had far-reaching consequences, such as the founding of the university in Ernestine Wittenberg in competition with the older university in Albertine Leipzig. For an outline of the complexities of the ruling houses of Saxony, see Günther Wartenberg, "Saxony," in *The Oxford Encyclopedia of the Reformation*, ed. Hans J. Hillerbrand (New York: Oxford University Press, 1996), 3:489–90.

7. See Frandsen, *Crossing Confessional Boundaries*, 76–100.

8. Lutheran affairs were independently administered by the privy council but issued in the name of the elector, whose royal status was always acknowledged. For example, the new edition of *Corpus juris ecclesiastici Saxonici, Oder Churfl. Sächs. Kirchen-Schulen- wie auch andere darzu gehörige Ordnungen, Nebenst unterschiedenen Ausschreiben in Consistorial- und Kirchen-Sachen* (Dresden: Winckler, 1708), for use throughout Lutheran Saxony, was issued "Mit Kön. und Churfl. Sächs. allergnädigsten Privilegio" (with the royal and electoral Saxon's most gracious privilege).

rangement that were uncomfortable to one side or the other of the confessional divide. For example, all the arrangements of how the bicentenary of the beginning of Luther's Reformation in 1717 were to be observed in electoral Saxony were promulgated under the authority of "Augustus Rex," something that must have been hard to swallow for the Catholic king/elector, especially for the sermons that were forthcoming at that time that portrayed Catholicism as darkness and error and Luther's protest as light and truth.[9] On the other hand, when August the Strong died and his son, who had converted to Catholicism in 1712, succeeded him as Saxon elector in 1733 (and later as the Polish king), a "General Church Prayer" for the new elector and his family was published and ordered to be read from pulpits after the sermon at most services in all the Lutheran churches of electoral Saxony, something that must have engendered mixed feelings among Lutherans.[10] While Saxon Lutherans in general seemed to have tolerated Friedrich August as the Saxon elector who was also the Catholic king of Poland, they loved his wife, Christiane Eberhardine (1671–1727), because she refused to convert and had separated from her Catholic husband. She was accorded the title "Sachsens Betsäule" (Saxon Pillar of Prayer) and at her death in 1727 was honored for her Lutheran loyalty in churches throughout Saxony, not least Leipzig's university church of St. Paul in a memorial ceremony that included Bach's *Trauerode* (BWV 198), specially composed for the occasion.

In 1708 Friedrich August reconstructed the court theater in his Dresden palace as the Catholic church for his family and the Catholic courtiers.[11] The following year, 1709, when he was reconfirmed as the Polish king, he published *Ordinanciones Regis*, regulations for Catholic worship in Saxony, which were based on an earlier incomplete and undated draft by the king's father confessor, the Jesuit priest Carl Moritz Vota.[12]

---

9. Ernst Salomon Cyprian, *Hilaria Evangelica, Oder Theologisch-Historischer Bericht Vom Ander Evangelischen Jubel-Fest.* . . . (Gotha: Weidmann, 1719), 1:92–187. Bach was well aware of the sensitivities and differences between Lutherans and Catholics, since there were a number of Lutheran polemical books against Catholicism in his personal library, notably, Martin Chemnitz, *Examen Concilii Tridentini* (first published in Frankfurt am Main, 1578), Nikolaus Hunnius, *Abfall der Römischen Kirchen* (first published in Latin in Lübeck in 1632), and Philipp Jacob Spener, *Gerechter Eifer wider das Antichristliche Pabstthum* (Frankfurt am Main, 1714), which is a collection of annual Reformation Day (31 October) sermons rather than a specifically Pietistic work. See Robin A. Leaver, *Bachs theologische Bibliothek / Bach's Theological Library* (Stuttgart: Hänssler, 1983), 61–63, 176–82 (nos. 5, 49, and 48, respectively).

10. *Allgemeines Kirchen-Gebet, Wie solches in denen Chur-Sächsischen Landen ietziger Zeit ablesen wird* (Dresden: Stößeln, 1733).

11. Friedrich August Forwerk, *Geschichte und Beschreibung der Königlichen Katholischen Hof- und Pfarrkirche zu Dresden: nebst einer kurzen Geschichte der Katholischen Kirche in Sachsen vom Religionswechsel des Churfürsten Friedrich August I. an bis auf unsere Tage* (Dresden: Janssen, 1851), 10–13.

12. Stockigt, "The Music," 57–58.

In 1710 Vota was closely involved in the foundation of the royal Catholic chapel in Leipzig, which, like the Dresden court chapel, came under the administration of the Jesuit province of Bohemia.[13]

Later in 1710, Father Vota SJ reported on the founding of the chapel to Pope Clement XI in Rome in an undated letter written toward the end of the year:

> Most Holy Father. . . . The King has, with regal generosity, assigned 1,200 scudi a year to two missionaries and to the ornamentation of the church in Leipzig. He has also spent a considerable sum of money on a building suitable for the church, and on the altars. . . . The town of Leipzig has very few Catholic families, fewer than ten, but during the three fairs which are held there every year and which are among the largest and most famous in Europe, Catholics and outsiders arrive in thousands. In these periods the church fills with a great crowd attending sermons, masses, confessions, and communions. Divine offices are celebrated in the morning and in the afternoon, with Vespers and the Benediction, etc., to great edification. . . . The King has ordered that all should observe the same statutes and regulations given to his other chaplains in the church and royal chapel in Dresden.[14]

The location of the Leipzig Catholic chapel was the lower level of the tower of the Pleissenburg fortress, originally built in the thirteenth century, but it was then being used as a barracks and as a Saxon administrative building that came under the jurisdiction of the king/elector. But it was a particularly sensitive place for Leipzig Lutherans, because it was in the Pleissenburg fortress that Luther had preached at Pentecost 1539 to introduce Reformation ideals and displace Catholic theology and practice—a sermon that had condemned the "phony shrieking" (*falsch Geschrey*) of the pope, cardinals, and bishops.[15] Therefore, there was deep meaning in the fact that the day chosen for the solemn inaugural Sunday Mass in the new Catholic chapel was the Feast of Pentecost, June 8, 1710,[16] a symbolic reversal of the impact of Luther's

---

13. Brigit Mitzscherlich, "Der Neubeginn des Katholizismus in Leipzig im 18. Jahrhundert," in *Das religiöse Leipzig: Stadt und Glauben vom Mittelalter bis zur Gegenwart*, ed. Enno Büntz and Armin Kohnle (Leipzig: Universitätsverlag, 2013), 237–55; Forwerk, *Königlichen Katholischen Hof- und Pfarrkirche*, 13–14.

14. The letter is reproduced in its entirety by Augustin Theiner, *Geschichte der Zurückkehr der regierenden Häuser von Braunschweig und Sachsen in den Schooß der Katholischen Kirche im 18. Jahrhundert, und der Wiederherstellung der katholischen Religion in diesen Staaten* (Einsiedeln: Benzinger, 1843), 145–47; the English translation in Stockigt, "The Organists," 161–62, is by the late David Fairservice.

15. WA 47: 774; LW 51: 306. Luther also preached in the Thomaskirche at Pentecost 1539, but the sermon was not preserved.

16. The chapel was consecrated on Tuesday, 3 June, and the first Sunday Mass was celebrated on 8 June, the Feast of Pentecost. "Denen Herren Papisten . . . in der Festung Pleißenburg auf hohe

preaching of 1539, as a Lutheran pastor pointed out to the protesting crowd that had gathered outside the Pleissenburg at the time of the inaugural Sunday Mass.[17]

One wonders whether there was any connection between the founding of the Catholic chapel in this historic Reformation location the same year that the worship of the university church of St. Paul was expanded—which, of course, was done with due deference to the king/elector.[18] Up until this year, 1710, regular worship in St. Paul's was confined to the major festivals of the church year and other special occasions,[19] but from this time on a full range of Lutheran services were presented every Sunday, as well as on other days, in the university church. However, it is perhaps more likely that the increased opportunities for worship in St. Paul's Church were part of the general development of church life in Leipzig. From around the turn of the century there had been a continuous expansion of worship opportunities for Lutherans in Leipzig: the number of services was increased, extra seating was added to the two principal churches, and formerly disused churches were restored and reopened for use.[20] The expansion of services in the university church was clearly part of this intensification, though it might have been viewed in some way as a counteraction against the founding of the Catholic chapel that had occurred some two months before.[21]

Königl. Pohlnische Churf. Sächs. allergnädigste Special-Concession eingeräumet worden. . . . Diese von 1710. da sie am 3. Junii die erste Messe, den 8. dito aber, als am ersten Pfingst-Feyertage, die erste Papistische Predigt hielten" (The papists, with special permission of his highness the Polish king and Saxon elector, were assigned space in the Pleissenburg fortress. . . . Here in 1710 on 3 June and again on 8 June, the first Mass was held on the first day of the Feast of Pentecost, and the first papist sermon was given) (Weitz, *Verbessertes Leipzig*, 3).

17. See Saft, *Der Neuaufbau der kathlischen Kirchen*, 131–34.

18. "In dieser wurde Anno 1710. den XI. post Trinitatis, war der 13. Augusti auf allergnädigsten Königl. Pohlnischen und Churf. Sächs. Befehl der Anfang zu denen Sonn- und Festtags-Predigten gemacht" (In this [university church] in 1710, on 13 August, the eleventh Sunday after Trinity, by the command of the all-gracious Polish king and Saxon elector, sermons [that is, in this context, services in which sermons were preached] on Sundays and feast days were begun) (Weitz, *Verbessertes Leipzig*, 3).

19. See "Alt-Gottesdienst," in *Oxford Composer Companions: J. S. Bach*, ed. Malcolm Boyd (Oxford: Oxford University Press, 1999), 11.

20. See Günther Stiller, *Johann Sebastian Bach and Liturgical Life in Leipzig*, trans. Herbert J. A. Bouman et al., ed. Robin A. Leaver (St. Louis: Concordia, 1984), 40–43.

21. The creation of "new" services in addition to the "old" services in the university church led to problems at the beginning of Bach's appointment in Leipzig. These problems were resolved with Bach being responsible for the "old" services and Johann Gottlieb Görner as the director of the "new" services; see Wolff BLM, 311–12.

Leipzig's Catholic *Gesangbuch*

Non-Catholics have often misunderstood Catholic use of vernacular hymnody. Compared with Protestant worship, in which vernacular hymn singing has always been fundamental and comprehensive, the Tridentine Latin Mass made no provision for such hymnody. The conclusion frequently drawn is that singing in the vernacular was of minimal significance in Catholic worship at this time. But this ignores the fact that although the Mass has always been at the center of Catholic faith and practice, there have been other forms of Catholic worship at which vernacular congregational singing has been prominent, such as the Hours (notably Vespers), benedictions, novenas, funeral rites, and so on, as well as in domestic settings and other nonliturgical contexts. In Germany in the sixteenth century, influential Catholic hymnals were published as independent commercial ventures, notably, those of Vehe and Leisentrit.[22] These were clearly issued in direct reaction to Lutheran hymnody, though in terms of structure and layout they were nevertheless modeled on Lutheran hymnals. The first official Catholic collection of hymns was issued by the diocese of Regensburg in 1570 as an appendix to its *Obsequiale*.[23] A steady stream of hymnals for the use of German Catholics flowed thereafter, each one frequently making use of the contents of its predecessors.[24]

From the beginning of its existence, vernacular hymnody was a feature of the worship of the Catholic chapel in Leipzig, though apparently sung by a small group of singers rather than the congregation.[25] For example, at Corpus Christi (June 19, 1710)

22. [Michael Vehe], *Ein New Gesangbüchlein Geystlicher Lieder* . . . (Leipzig: Wolrab, 1537; repr., Mainz: Behem, 1567). Johann Leisentrit, *Geistliche Lieder und Psalmen / der alten Apostolischer recht und warglaubiger Christlicher Kircher* . . . (Bautzen: Wolrab, 1567; facsimile, Kassel: Bärenreiter, 1966), with later editions: Leipzig: Steinman, 1573; Dillingen: Mayer, 1575, 1576; and Bautzen: Wolrab, 1584, with the title *Catholisch Gesangbuch*; see Richard Wetzel and Erika Heitmeyer, *Johann Leisentrit's "Geistlicher Lieder und Psalmen," 1567: Hymnody of the Counter-Reformation in Germany* (Madison, NJ: Fairleigh Dickinson University Press, 2013). For the background, see Andreas Scheidgen, "Das katholische Gesangbuch im Reformationsjahrhundert," *Jahrbuch für Liturgik und Hymnologie* 48 (2009): 135–44.

23. *Cantiones germanicae, quibus singulis suo tempore Ecclesia Catholica Ratispo*, in *Obsequiale sive Benedictionale secundum consuetudinem ecclesie et dyocesis Ratisponensis* (Ingolstadt: Weßenhorn, 1570). See Klaus Gamber, ed., *Cantiones Germanicae im Regensburger Obsequiale von 1570; Erstes offizielles katholisches Gesangbuch Deutschlands* (Regensburg: Pustet, 1983).

24. See Wilhelm Bäumker, *Das katholische deutsche Kirchenlied in seinen Singwesen von den frühesten Zeiten bis gegen Ende des siebzehnten Jahrhunderts* (Freiburg: Herder, 1883–1911; repr., Hildesheim: Olms, 1962); Dominik Fugger and Andreas Scheidgen, *Geschichte des katholischen Gesangbuchs* (Tübingen: Francke, 2008).

25. On music in the early years of the Leipzig Catholic chapel, see Clemens Harasim, *Die Kirchenmusik an der Propsteikirche zu Leipzig*, ed. Helmut Loos (Leipzig: Schröder, 2015), 1–24; for chant books obtained between 1711 and 1713, see ibid., 13.

after sung Mass the priest sang *Pange lingua*, "to which the singers responded *in choro* with the organ. After the first verse they sang some beautiful new German hymns."[26] On Exaltatio S. Crucis, since the regular singers were away, the Mass was spoken, not sung, but the Italian priest "sang a German hymn with other singers."[27] What these hymns were or what they sang from is unknown.

A few years later, according to the careful accounts of the Jesuits who were in charge of the Catholic chapel in Leipzig,[28] a hymnal was compiled for the use of the congregation. Under the date, March 13, 1715, it is reported that Christoph Zunckel, printer in Leipzig,[29] had supplied 1,000 copies of "ein Catholisches Gesangbuch," of which 216 had been distributed; therefore, 739 copies were available for future use.[30] No copy of this edition has been located, but it was given a brief notice in a Lutheran theological journal, published in Leipzig in 1717, where the title is given as *Catholisches Gesang-Buch zum Gebrauch der Römisch-Catholischen Gemeinde in Leipzig. 1715*.[31]

In 1710, according to Father Vota's letter to the pope (see above), there were fewer than ten Catholic families resident in Leipzig. If one assumes that four or five members of each family had a copy of the hymnal, then they would account for approximately 40 to 50 copies; therefore, around 160 copies were obtained by visitors to the Leipzig fairs—and probably also by some non-Catholic Leipzigers—during 1715–16, the first year of the hymnal's publication. Over the next two years, a further 300 or so copies were sold, since in 1718 it is reported that there were still "more than 400 copies"

---

26. *Diarum Missionis Lipsiensis . . . erectae primum Annon 1710 Die 3 Junÿ in arce Pleissenburg*. Microfilm copy held in Diözesanarchiv des Bistum Dresden-Meissen. Entry under the date 19 June 1710: "Sacerdos intonavit Pange lingua, cantores responderunt in choro cum organo, post primam stropham cecinerunt pulchros cantos Germanicos novos."

27. "Cum abfuerint musici praecipui non fuit Cantata Missa post concionem, sed lecta et Domini Itali cecinerunt cum aliis cantum Germanicum" (ibid., 14 September 1710).

28. D-BAUd, I, *Kirchenrechnungen 1710–1745*, D D. I. 004, Band 142 (Alt signatur 12/3 Band I).

29. [Christian Friedrich Gessner and Johann Georg Hager], *Die so nöthig als nützliche Buchdruckerkunst und Schriftgießerey* [1] (Leipzig: Gessner, 1740), 130; Johann Heinrich Zedler, *Grosses vollständiges Universal-Lexicon aller Wissenschaften und Künste* (Leipzig: Zedler, 1731–54), 64: col. 45.

30. *Kirchenrechnungen 1710–1745*, entry under the date 13 March 1715; see Stockigt, "The Music," 60.

31. *Unschuldige Nachrichten von alten und neuen Theologischen Sachen . . . Auff das Jahr 1717* (Leipzig: Braun, 1717), 429–30. A later Lutheran source records the title of the 1715 edition, which is identical with that of the 1724 edition (see below): Jacob Wilhelm Feuerlein, *Bibliotheca Symbolica Evangelica Lutherana* (Nuremberg: Schwartzkopf, 1768), 345. It is possible that it took time for Lutherans to become aware of the Catholic *Gesangbuch*, since in 1718, that is, not long after the review had appeared in *Unschuldige Nachrichten*, the Leipzig consistory discussed its troubling existence; D-Dla, 10025 Geheimes Konsilium, Loc. 6636/03 Haupt Buch 1718 etc., fol. 260r, under the date 30 September 1718.

remaining, amounting to a capital value of "more than 16 thlr."[32] The implication is that these 400 copies were dispersed over the following five years (averaging around 80 per year), because in 1724 a new edition was published:

> Catholisches Gesang-Buch Auf unterschiedliche Zeiten und Feste des gantzen Jahres eingerichtet, Und Aus andern gebräuchlichen Catholischen Gesang-Büchern[.] Zusammen getragen, Samt Den Sonn- und Fest-Tags-Vespern und Complet, Zum Gebrauch Der Catholischen Gemeinde in Leipzig. Anno M D CC XXIV. 12°. 266 numbered, and 10 unnumbered pages.[33]

That it is a reprint rather than a new edition is confirmed by the fact that in the 1717 review of the original edition of 1715 there is a list of eighteen first lines of German hymns that are given with their page numbers, which in every case are identical with the pagination of the 1724 edition.[34] Although no printer is named, it was probably Christoph Zunckel, who had printed the first edition, and the print run is likely to have been 1,000, the same as the first edition. However, there is apparently no reference to the cost of these hymnals in the chapel accounts, as there had been for the first edition. Further, the 1718 note in these accounts, indicating that the remaining 400 copies of the first edition represented a significant capital investment,[35] suggests that the financial burden of this second edition was borne elsewhere. Perhaps the printer, Zunckel, took the financial risk in the hope that copies could be sold to the many Catholics who visited the annual Leipzig fairs. On the other hand, funds from the Catholic Dresden court may have been made available for this second edition of the hymnal. This becomes a stronger possibility when the year 1724 is taken into account, since it marked the bicentenary of the publication of the first Lutheran hymnals, 1524–1724. Bach was then in his second year in Leipzig, focusing on the Lutheran

---

32. "NB Wegen des Anno 1715 gedruckten Gesang-Buchs müßen der Capellen noch restitiret werden 15 thlr. 20 gr. dafor bleiben noch über 400 exemplar deselben buchs das stück zu 1 gr. machet mehr als 16 thlr." (NB For the hymnal printed in 1715, the chapel still needs to be repaid 15 thlr. 20 gr. In return, more than 400 copies of this book still remain, each worth 1 gr., which equals more than 16 thlr.) (*Kirchenrechnungen 1710–1745*, undated entry under the year 1718). Sixteen *Thaler* was approximately the monthly salary of a pastor (see Wolff BLM, 540), or the cost of transporting the new organ from Annaberg to the Leipzig Catholic chapel in 1720 (see Stockigt, "The Music," 64).

33. Only one copy has been located, in the Wernigerode Hymnal Collection, Staatsbibliothek, Berlin, shelf mark: Wernigerode Sammlung Hb 3062; see Bäumker, *Das katholische deutsche Kirchenlied*, 3:55. There was a later edition, essentially a reprint with the same title (Erfurt: Kauffmann, 1740); see Bäumker, *Das katholische deutsche Kirchenlied*, 3:65–66.

34. This, of course, only accounts for the hymnal section, but it seems extremely unlikely that the 1715 edition would have omitted the Mass Ordinary and other Latin liturgical hymns and psalms.

35. See note 32 above.

chorale tradition with his chorale cantatas, almost certainly composed to observe this important bicentenary. Thus in the same way that Pentecost 1710 was carefully chosen for the first Sunday Mass in the Catholic Chapel, the liturgical day on which Luther inaugurated the Reformation in Leipzig, it seems likely that the new edition of the Catholic hymnal was issued in 1724 to assert the practice of Catholicism as against that of Lutheranism.

The hymnal made a significant contribution to the worship of the Catholic chapel. In 1717 it was reported that "the hymns and prayers which are customarily sung or said at the beginning and end of the day have been printed and distributed to the congregation and resound more magnificently now that the voices of the younger and the older are enjoined."[36] Two years later (1719), twenty-four copies of the hymnal were bound at the expense of the chapel, probably for the use of the royal family and their courtiers when they were in Leipzig.[37]

Unlike most Lutheran hymnals, this Catholic hymnal has no preface, but on the reverse of the title page, in Latin and German, is Psalm 46 [47]:7–8: "Psallite Deo nostro . . . , psallite sapienter. Singet unserm Gott zu Ehren, und mit Verstand" (Sing to our God with praise and with understanding).

The hymnal is structured in two main sections. The first contains mostly German hymn texts (see appendix 1), and the second contains the texts of Latin liturgical chants, psalms, and hymns (see appendix 2). In many respects, the volume parallels two Leipzig Lutheran liturgical handbooks: the *Leipziger Kirchen-Andachten* (Leipzig, 1694) and the *Leipziger Kirchen-Staat* (Leipzig, 1710).[38] The title page of the former declares that its first part is a "prayer book, or the order of the whole public worship throughout the church year," and the second part is a "songbook in which are all the hymns, together with an appendix of Latin hymns and collects";[39] the title page of the latter is similar.[40] The structure of the Catholic hymnal is opposite in that the

---

36. "Cantiones et orationes sub initium ac finem diei sero? decantari solitae, typis mandatae interque auditores distributae, unitis minorum et majorum vocibus resonant solemnius" (*Archivum Romanum Societatis Iesu Fondo Vecchia Compagnia, Rome, Provinciae Bohemia* [hereafter cited as ARSI, Boh.], 131:21).

37. *Kirchenrechnungen 1710–1745*, undated entry under the year 1719.

38. It is interesting to note that this liturgical handbook was published the same year that the university church significantly expanded its services and that the Catholic chapel came into use.

39. *Leipziger Kirchen-Andachten / Darinnen Der Erste Theil Das Gebetbuch / Oder Die Ordnung des gantzen öffentlichen Gottes-Dienstes durchs gantze Jahr / . . . Der Ander Teil Das Gesangbuch / In welchem Alle Lieder / nebst einem Anhang der Lateinischen Hymnorum und Collecten . . .* (Leipzig: Würdig, 1694).

40. *Leipziger Kirchen-Staat / Das ist Deutlicher Unterricht vom Gottes-Dienst in Leipzig / wie es bey solchem so wohl an hohen und andern Festen / als auch an denen Sonntagen ingleichen die gantze Woche über gehalten wird . . . und denen verordneten Teutsch- und Lateinischen Gesängen . . .* (Leipzig: Groschuff, 1710).

vernacular hymns form the first section, and the liturgical chants, psalms, and hymns form the second section. It also does not include the extensive additional devotional material found in the Lutheran handbooks. But it is clear that Catholics and Lutherans in Leipzig sang a similar repertoire in both German and Latin.

Catholic or Lutheran?

The brief notice of the publication of the first edition that appeared in the Lutheran theological journal of 1717 is somewhat barbed:

> Catholisches Gesang-Buch zum Gebrauch der Römisch-Catholischen Gemeinde in Leipzig. 1715. . . . The Roman-minded in Leipzig have unfortunately used their parochial rights to arbitrarily usurp themselves, as one can see in this title, what we have known for a long time and is demonstrated in this Gesangbuch, in which one can find the following Evangelical-Lutheran hymns:[41]

[4] *Christum wir sollen loben schon*
[5] *Der Tag der ist so Freudenreich*
[7] *Gelobet seyst du Jesus Christ*
[15] *O Traurigkeit, O Hertzeleid*
[19] *O Lamm Gottes unschuldig*
[20] *O Mensch, bewein dein Sünde groß*
[22] *Christus, der uns selig macht*
[37] *Nun bitten wir den heiligen Geist*
[39] *Komm, heiliger Geist, Schöpfer mein*
[41] *Gott der Vater wohn uns bey*
[42] *Wir glauben all an einen Gott*
[43] *Allein Gott in der Höhe sey Ehr*
[52] *Diß sind die heiligen zehen Gebot*
[58] *Warum betrübst du dich mein Hertz*
[59] *Sag, was hilfft alle Welt*
[62] *Kommt her zu mir, spricht Gottes Sohn*
[73] *Aus meines Hertzen Grunde*
[75] *Christe, der du bist Licht und Tag*[42]

The claim is that the congregation of the Catholic chapel was singing Lutheran hymns. With one exception ([59] *Sag, was hilfft alle Welt*), all could be found in the basic Leipzig

---

41. "Es haben die Römisch-Gesinnten in Leipzig sich leider heraus genommen die parochial-Rechte eigenmächtig zu usurpiren, wie man aus dem Titel dieses uns zwar langsam bekannt gewordenen Gesang-Buchs siehet." The numbers in the listing are those assigned in appendix 1.

42. See note 31 above.

Lutheran cantional, Vopelius's *Neu Leipziger Gesangbuch* (Leipzig, 1682),[43] on which various subsequent Leipzig collections of hymns were based, including the *Leipziger Kirchen-Andachten* and the *Leipziger Kirchen-Staat*. However, the list is incomplete and could, for example, have included the following hymns, which are also to be found in the Vopelius hymnal:

[8] *In dulci jubilo*
[9] and [12] *Ein Kind geborn zu Bethlehem*
[13] *Da Jesus an dem Creutze stund*
[26] *Christus ist erstanden*
[33] *Erstanden ist der heilig Christ*
[36] *Gen Himmel aufgefahren ist*

But the claim that the *Catholisches Gesang-Buch* contained "Lutheran" hymns is not entirely true. Certainly, they were regularly sung in Lutheran worship, but in origin they were based on Latin Catholic hymns, either folk hymns already circulating before the Reformation in vernacular versions or translations made during the Reformation period. Leipzig Catholics reading the 1717 Lutheran notice of their hymnal would no doubt have asserted that the opposite was in fact the case: that Lutherans not only were singing versions of Catholic hymns but in some cases were doing so following the Catholic practice of alternating Latin and German stanzas:

[9] *Puer natus in Bethlehem / Ein Kind gebohrn* = Vopelius, 41–42
[33] *Surrexit Christus Hodie / Erstanden ist der heilig Christ* = Vopelius, 296–97
[36] *Coelos ascendit hodie / Gen Himmel aufgefahren ist* = Vopelius, 377–79

Further, a similar list could be constructed of Latin hymns that could be found in Vopelius's *Neu Leipziger Gesangbuch* and in the Leipzig hymnals based on it, demonstrating that Lutherans sang Latin Catholic hymns.[44]

When the individual hymn texts of the *Catholisches Gesang-Buch* in the 1717 listing are examined, it becomes clear that they are not exactly the same as in the Lutheran sources. One or two of the texts are mostly the same, but the others are different

---

43. Gottfried Vopelius, *Das Neu Leipziger Gesangbuch / Von den schönsten und besten Liedern verfasset* (Leipzig: Klinger, 1682). See Jürgen Grimm, *Das Neu Leipziger Gesangbuch des Gottfried Vopelius (Leipzig, 1682)* (Berlin: Merseburger, 1969).

44. Identified by an asterisk (*) in appendix 2. It is a short list because of specific Catholic theology expressed in many of the Latin hymns. However, the repertoire of Latin hymns in Vopelius included texts that were not found in the *Catholisches Gesang-Buch*, such as *Veni repemptor gentium*, *Ascendit Christus hodie*, and *Veni sancte Spiritus*.

versions, some of them quite different.[45] So it seems that whoever compiled the list was somewhat superficial in drawing conclusions from the familiar first lines without carefully reading the complete texts. But the 1717 reference to the hymnal is correct in that the congregations of the two confessions in Leipzig were at least singing versions of the same hymns and that they both were singing the same melodies. Like most Lutheran hymnals, the *Catholisches Gesang-Buch* contained no music, though melodies for two of the texts are specifically named.[46] For the rest, the assumption is that the associated melodies were well known. The realization that there was a common repertoire of melodies sung by both Lutheran and Catholic congregations in Leipzig sheds new light on Bach's organ chorale preludes. The assumption that such settings were of interest only to Protestants is obviously invalid.

Bach and the Royal Catholic Chapel in Leipzig

The new edition of the *Catholisches Gesang-Buch . . . zum Gebrauch der Catholischen Gemeinde in Leipzig* was published in 1724, that is, during Bach's second year in Leipzig. The inventory of the books he owned, drawn up after his death, records only a massive eight-volume anthology of hymns in Bach's possession.[47] None of the practical hymnals he would have needed both privately and professionally were listed. Similarly, Bibles and prayer books do not appear in the listing. The feeling is that such books that Bach must have owned were distributed among the family members before the inventory of his effects was compiled. Thus we remain in the dark with regard to the extent and scope of his hymnal collection. But at one time or another he must have at least had copies of the hymnals that were necessary in his positions in Arnstadt, Mühlhausen, Weimar, and Leipzig, as well as the hymnals he would have sung from in his schooldays in Eisenach, Ohrdruf, and Lüneburg. During his first professional appointment as organist in Arnstadt, he worked alongside the deacon, Johann Christoph Olearius, who was an avid collector of hymnals, and he may have encouraged Bach to follow his example, only on a smaller scale.[48] Thus it is unknown whether or not Bach

---

45. Further research into the sources of these texts and tunes needs to be undertaken in order to trace their origins and transmission in various Catholic hymnals, not only the earlier anthologies of Vehe and Leisentrit (see note 22 above) but also the hymnals that appeared in the generation before the Leipzig *Catholisches Gesang-Buch* was compiled, such as those published in Cologne (DKL 1694[11], 1696[08], 1697[10, 21], 1701[07]), Mainz (DKL 1697[12], 1700[02, 13], 1704[18], 1705[07], 1709[03]), and Würzburg (DKL 1693[03], 1700[11], 1701[10], 1704[14], 1708[10], 1709[09], 1710[16]), among others.

46. See appendix 1, [32] and [52].

47. See Leaver, *Bachs theologische Bibliothek*, 188–90 (no. 52).

48. See Robin A. Leaver, "The Organist Encounters the Hymnologist: J. S. Bach and J. C. Olearius in Arnstadt," *Understanding Bach* 7 (2012): 21–28.

owned a copy of the Leipzig Catholic hymnal, though he must have been aware of the Catholic chapel and its worship and that its congregation sang from its own hymnal.

Whenever the king/elector visited Leipzig—staying in the Apel House,[49] which belonged to a prosperous silk merchant, because the Lutheran town council would not allow the Catholic king to build a palace within the town—he and his family attended worship in the royal Catholic chapel in the Pleissenburg fortress. Since Bach was an official of the Leipzig Lutheran churches, it is unlikely that he would have formally attended worship in the Catholic chapel, though it remains a possibility.[50] On the one hand, there were theological and political differences between the two confessions. Lutheran-Catholic friction was generally kept out of sight, but it was only slightly below the surface of everyday life. From time to time it became publicly contentious, such as the Lutheran protest at the time of the inaugural Catholic Mass celebrated in the chapel in 1710,[51] or the inflammatory anti-Luther sermon the newly arrived Jesuit priest preached in March 1723, which resulted in a riot and the recall of the priest to Dresden.[52] On the other hand, Bach's responsibilities in the Leipzig churches on Sundays and festivals meant that there was little opportunity for him to observe the worship of the Catholic chapel. Nevertheless, notwithstanding the sensitivities between the two confessions or the demands the Leipzig appointment made on his time, as *Director Musici Lipsiensis* Bach would have been aware of the elector/king's movements whenever he was in Leipzig, including his attendance at the Catholic chapel. So there may well have been times when Bach was an observer in the Catholic chapel, especially when the king/elector was in Leipzig.

Over the years there were increasing connections between Bach and the respective king/elector, apparently beginning in 1725 with his appeal to the king, the first of others Bach would make, for a resolution of his dispute with the university over the

---

49. See Robert L. Marshall and Traute Marshall, *Exploring the World of J. S. Bach* (Urbana: University of Illinois Press, 2016), 91–92.

50. At the time of the inaugural Mass in 1710 it was pointed out that since the Pleissenburg fortress was also an arsenal, the large protesting crowds presented a possible danger. It was therefore decreed that only Catholics would be admitted to the chapel, and no more than forty at any one time (Saft, *Der Neuaufbau der kathlischen Kirchen*, 134). How long this restriction was in force is unclear. In later years, Lutherans are known to have observed Catholic worship in the Leipzig chapel. For example, in 1733, during the three days of mourning marking the death of August II, so many people wanted to attend that only Catholics were permitted to attend the services (see note 62 below). The implication is that on other occasions Lutherans were not barred from being present at Catholic worship. Similarly, in 1739 Lutherans were present in the chapel for the Corpus Christi procession (see note 72 below).

51. See note 16 above.

52. See Janice B. Stockigt, *Jan Dismas Zelenka: A Bohemian Musician at the Court of Dresden* (Oxford: Oxford University Press, 2000), 280–81; and the forthcoming article on the incident also by Stockigt.

direction of music for the "old" and "new" services,[53] and continuing with his composing of celebratory cantatas in honor of the king and members of his family.[54] It also
seems likely that Bach would have been aware of the organists and other musicians
attached to the chapel.

There is reference to an organ being used during the first year of the chapel's existence: "cantores responderunt in choro cum organo."[55] This was probably a small
Positiv organ. In 1719 plans were made for a single-manual organ with pedal to be
built for the chapel. Each year an annual letter was sent to Rome, reporting on the
activities of the chapel during that year. The 1719 letter includes the following note:
"Furthermore, to avoid confusion in the singing of the congregation and to create
greater harmony among the musicians during services an organ was commissioned
by the mission at the cost of 120 Imperials. It was installed in the royal chapel on 6
December and soon will achieve a perfect sound."[56] The report was somewhat opti-
mistic, since there was a dispute between the two organ builders, and the instrument
was not finally installed and playable until the late spring of 1720.[57] It was a rather
modest instrument, which was appropriate, since the chapel itself was not large, with
a capacity of perhaps not more than one hundred. The organ had just six stops—Principal 4', Gedakt 8', Gedakt, 4', Quint 3', Octav 2'—with a double rank Mixtur and
pedal board coupled to the manual.[58]

Beginning in June 1719, the records of the chapel include references to the succession of appointed organists who either also served as sacristan or taught in the Catholic
elementary school:[59]

1719–22   Augustin Uhlig (1703–73) was the first chapel organist. He came from
Sonnenberg in northern Bohemia and was clearly a gifted musician.
It seems that this position in Leipzig was considered to be part of the
Dresden court musicians. When he left Leipzig in 1722 it was to join
the *Kapellknaben* as organist. The *Kapellknaben* was the ensemble of
instrumentalists, singers, and organists of the Catholic court chapel in
Dresden. In 1732, before the disbanding of the *Kapellknaben* in 1733,
after the death of Friedrich August I (August II), he became a violinist
in the revered Dresden *Hofkapelle*.

53. See BDOK 1:30–45, nos. 10–12; BDOK 2:155–56, no. 202; NBR, 118–25, nos. 119–20.

54. See table 10.5 in Wolff BLM, 362.

55. See note 25 above.

56. *ARSI, Boh.* 133, 12, cited in Stockigt, "The Music," 62.

57. See Stockigt, "The Music," 62–64; Mitzscherlich, "Der Neubeginn des Katholizismus," 245.

58. Stockigt, "The Music," 61–62; Harasim, *Die Kirchenmusik*, 14.

59. This and the following paragraphs are indebted to Stockigt, "The Organists," 161–76. The Catholic
school was in a private house in the Burgstraße; see Harasim, *Die Kirchenmusik*, 16.

1723–24	Johann Georg Gruß (uncertain dates) also came from Sonnenberg in northern Bohemia.
1722–25	Joseph Tiederle (uncertain dates). In 1725 Tiederle, like Uhlig, left Leipzig to become a violinist in the *Kapellknaben* of the Dresden court chapel.
1726–31	Johannes Petrus Griesel (uncertain dates) also came from Bohemia. After his departure in 1731 an anonymous Lutheran schoolteacher played the organ for four weeks, against the objection of one of the Jesuit priests.[60]
1731–35	Antonio Harnisch (uncertain dates) served as a teacher in the Catholic school, as well as being organist.
1735–36/37	Emanuel Harnisch (uncertain dates) was presumably a relative of his predecessor.
1736–67	Joseph Rainaldi (uncertain dates). It seems likely that he was the son of a Leipzig-based Italian merchant, probably one of the two sons of "Herr Rainaldi" baptized in the Catholic chapel (one in July 1719 and the other in June 1722), and he almost certainly attended the Catholic elementary school in Leipzig. It therefore seems likely that he was taught by one of the earlier organists of the chapel. In the year before his appointment as organist, there is a record that he and the organist Emanuel Harnisch were paid for playing horns at a requiem Mass. From 1745 he is listed among the musicians attached to the Leipzig Catholic chapel: "Josephus Rainaldus, Organist der Königl. Capelle zu Leipzig."[61]

What is clear is that the music of the Catholic chapel was of a particularly high standard, as is obvious from the various organists who continued their careers as instrumentalists at the court in Dresden. This was to be expected, since members of the Polish royal and Saxon electoral family made frequent visits to Leipzig and attended Mass in the chapel, and such visits increased in significance after the marriage in 1719 of the Saxon electoral prince to the Hapsburg archduchess Maria Josepha. For example, the death of Friedrich August I (August II) in February 1733 was observed in the chapel over three days, with extra musicians brought in from Bohemia to augment the Leipzig musicians for the solemn obsequies. On the first day the congregation was too large to be accommodated within the chapel and was not restricted to Catholics, since it was reported that members of the Leipzig senate and students from the university were also in attendance.[62]

---

60. "Organistae Lutherano Ludi-Magistro obstante nostro pro 4 hebdom. organum luserit. 3. Tlr."

61. HStCal 1745, 26.

62. See Janice B. Stockigt, "Die 'Annuae Literae' der Leipziger Jesuiten 1719–1740: Ein Bach Dokument?," BJ 78 (1992): 79.

Bach's admiration for the musicians of the Dresden court was implicit in his "Ent-wurff" of August 1730, his petition to the town council for raising the musical standards of Leipzig:

> German musicians are expected to be capable of performing at once and *ex tempore* all kinds of music, whether it come from Italy or France, England or Poland, just as may be done, say, by those virtuosos for whom the music is written and who have studied it long beforehand, indeed, know it almost by heart. . . . [O]ne need only go to Dresden and see how the musicians there are paid by His Royal Majesty. It cannot fail, since the musicians are relieved of all concern for their living, free from *chagrin* and obliged each to master but a single instrument; it must be something choice and excellent to hear.[63]

Bach had personal contacts with the Dresden *Hofkapelle*, notably, Zelenka and almost certainly Pisendel, Buffardin, Quantz, and Weiß, among others.[64] The records of the Leipzig Catholic chapel indicate that the organists and other musicians were also in close contact with the court musicians in Dresden. Did these musicians of the Catholic chapel in Leipzig provide Bach with supportive encouragement at a time when he was receiving only discouragement from Leipzig officialdom? Further, on the death of August II in 1733, was there any mutual encouragement in connection with Bach's petition to the new king/elector, Friedrich August II (August III), for court recogni-tion, since many court musicians were then taking the opportunity to petition for their own status and well-being?[65] Were the former Leipzig chapel musicians Uhlig and Tiederle in any way involved in Bach's decision to present to the king his settings of the Latin liturgical texts that were fundamental in the Catholic Mass? Of course, in the absence of documentary evidence answers can only be speculative; nevertheless, these important questions need to be asked.

Bach had to wait three years before his petition was granted, but that granting came at a most fortuitous time, since in August 1736 the acrimonious and lengthy conflict between Bach and the rector of the Thomasschule, Johann August Ernesti, had just broken out. But a few months before the document was signed there is an intriguing entry in the Catholic chapel's records. The king/elector and queen/electress were in Leipzig for the Michaelmas fair in 1736:

63. NBR, 150, no. 151; BDOK 1:63, no. 22.

64. See Ortrun Landmann, "The Dresden Hofkapelle during the Lifetime of Johann Sebastian Bach," *Early Music* 17 (1989): 17–30; and Stockigt, *Jan Dismas Zelenka*, passim.

65. Szymon Paczkowski, "The Role and Significance of the Polonaise in the 'Quoniam' of the B-minor Mass," in *Exploring Bach's B-minor Mass*, ed. Yo Tomita, Robin A. Leaver, and Jan Smaczny (Cambridge: Cambridge University Press, 2013), 60–61.

On the feast of St. Michael [Saturday, September 29], when their Most Serene Stars entered the city, night itself . . . was turned to day and shone with festive lights. . . . Nor did the chapel, however humble, lack its own splendour. On the following Sunday [September 30] Her Serene Highness [Maria Josepha] first attended a Mass which the Royal Father Confessor, at our earnest request, sang with assistants. Her Highness then attended a second Mass, said [but probably means "sung"] by the . . . Bishop of Posen. Then a sermon [was] given by one of our priests to a distinguished congregation. Finally, upon the arrival of His Most Serene Highness [August III], she attended with singular devotion a third Mass said . . . by His Excellency the Apostolic Nuncio, Camillo Paulucci Merlini. During the Mass, a virtuoso organist delighted the royal ears with sweet-sounding pieces.[66]

Who was this organ virtuoso? Clearly, it was someone other than Emanuel Harnisch, who was the chapel's organist at the time.[67] Janice Stockigt has suggested that the organist may have been Bach.[68] The chapel sources rarely, if ever, give the names of musicians, so the fact that the organist is unnamed is not exceptional. Similarly, Bach as a Lutheran would not necessarily have been barred from playing in the chapel. As is referred to above, in 1731 a Lutheran (also unnamed) was engaged to play the chapel organ for four weeks.[69] What may be of singular significance is that this took place just a few weeks before the document appointing Bach as *Hof-Compositeur* to the Dresden court was signed, on November 19, 1736, responding to Bach's petition made three years before. The king initialed the document, which was signed by the Saxon prime minister, Count Heinrich von Brühl, a significant donor to Leipzig's Catholic chapel.[70] If the organist was Bach on this occasion, then his displayed skills may have had some effect on the official granting of his long-overdue request just a few weeks later. Beginning in 1738, the annual court calendar recorded Bach's name, the fifth in the list of sixty-one members of the *Hofkapelle*, which from 1745 also included (but much later in the annual publication) the name of Joseph Rainaldi, organist of the Leipzig Catholic chapel.[71]

66. *ARSI*, *Boh*. 154:13; Stockigt, "Die 'Annuae Literae,'" 79–80.

67. Joseph Rainaldi was not appointed until October 1736.

68. Stockigt, "Die 'Annuae Literae,'" 80.

69. See note 60 above.

70. BDOK 2:278–79, no. 388; NBR, 188, no. 190. In 1734 Brühl donated to the chapel his and his wife's wedding garments, which were made of pure silver thread; see Janice B. Stockigt, "The *Annuae Literae* of the Leipzig Jesuits, 1719–1740," in *Bohemia Jesuitica 1556–2006*, ed. Petronilla Cemus and Richard Cemus SJ (Prague: Nakladatelsvi Karolinum, 2010), 2:1106.

71. HStCal 1738, 14; HStCal 1745, 26.

In 1738 the Leipzig chapel was extended and renovated, the organ was moved (possibly enlarged?), new furnishings were installed, and a balcony for the royal and electoral family was newly constructed. The chapel now had three entrances, and one of them provided public access.[72] Thus it is reported that in 1739 the Corpus Christi procession within the chapel was observed by Lutherans (*Lipsiae heterodoxi*).[73]

In the last few years of his life, Bach was working on a complete setting of the Ordinary of the Latin Mass, what has become known as the B Minor Mass, combining (and revising) the Missa, that is, the Kyrie and the Gloria, which in 1733 he presented to King August II in Dresden; the Sanctus, originally composed in 1724; to which he added the Symbolum Nicenum, Ossana, Benedictus, and Agnus Dei, newly recomposed, in order to create a complete setting of the Ordinary of the Mass. All parts of the Ordinary were common in Lutheran worship but not in the same way as Catholics celebrated Mass. Although Lutherans used the Latin texts of the Ordinary at major festivals, they did not always employ all these liturgical texts at every celebration. Indeed, while the Saxon *Kirchen Ordnung* refers to the singing of the Latin Agnus Dei, the text was not included, and it is likewise absent from Vopelius and other Leipzig liturgical sources.[74] Bach certainly knew of Catholic settings of the complete Mass Ordinary in both print and manuscript, and he had access to the complete liturgy of the Catholic Mass in one of his books.[75] But Leipzig's royal Catholic chapel gave him the possibility of hearing how such musical settings of the Catholic Mass functioned liturgically according to the sequence published in the *Catholisches Gesang-Buch . . . zum Gebrauch der Catholischen Gemeinde in Leipzig.*[76]

72. ARSI Boh. 157:61–62; Stockigt, "The *Annuae Literae*," 2:1112 (Document 7); see Harasim, *Die Kirchenmusik*, 15.

73. ARSI Boh. 158: 62–63; Stockigt, "The *Annuae Literae*," 2:1110 (Document 3).

74. See Robin A. Leaver, "Bach's Mass: 'Catholic' or 'Lutheran'?," in Tomita, Leaver and Smaczny, *Exploring Bach's B-minor Mass*, 30–32.

75. Erdmann Neumeister included the complete Catholic Mass in German translated by Balthasar Bebel, originally published as *Bericht von der Meße* (Straßburg, 1684), as the introduction to his Eucharistic sermons: *Tisch des Herrn* (Hamburg: Kißner, 1722); see Leaver, *Bachs theologische Bibliothek*, 171–73 (no. 46).

76. See appendix 2.

APPENDIX I

Catholisches Gesang-Buch, Leipzig, 1724

HYMNAL

A Latin first line appearing after a German first line, with a vertical line in between (|), indicates that Latin and German stanzas are alternated. Page numbers appear in the right-hand column.

Hymns, Mostly German

Catholische Advents-Gesänge

Catholische Weihnachts-Gesänge

Fasten-Gesänge

Oster-Gesänge

Himmelfahrts-Gesänge

Pfingst-Gesänge

Von der Hoch-Heiligen Dreyfaltigkeit

Vom zarten Fronleichnam Christi

Catechismus-Gesänge

In Allerhand Anliegen

APPENDIX 2

Catholisches Gesang-Buch, Leipzig, 1724

LATIN LITURGICAL CHANTS, PSALMS, AND HYMNS

The liturgical section of the hymnal contains the Latin texts of the Ordinary of the
Mass and the Psalms, canticles, hymns, and other chants for the offices of Vespers and
Compline. Most occur within the provisions for the festivals and saints' days throughout the ecclesiastical year. Many Psalms, hymns, and antiphons have multiple usage,
to be sung on different days and for different celebrations. Instead of repeating the
full text for each occasion, every text appears once and then is referred to by its page
number(s) when it is required to be sung on another day or occasion. Rather than give
these items in the order they occur within the hymnal, they are given here as follows:
items of the Ordinary appear in liturgical sequence, the Psalms are arranged in biblical
order (following Vulgate numbering), and the hymns are listed alphabetically. Page
number(s) appear in the right-hand column. An asterisk (*) indicates a Latin hymn
that is found in the first section of mostly German hymns, where (with one exception)
the German and Latin stanzas are alternated. In these cases, the number assigned in
the first section of the hymnal immediately follows the first line.

Mass Ordinary

Kyrie	156
Gloria in excelsis Deo	157
Credo in unum Deum	158
Sanctus	160
Agnus Dei	160

Office Canticles

Psalms

Hymns

Liturgical Music for a New Elector

Origins of Bach's 1733 Missa Revisited

Janice B. Stockigt

O n February 1, 1733, Saxon Elector Friedrich August I (1670–1733; as king of Poland titled August II, "the Strong") died in Warsaw. His sole legitimate son, Electoral Prince Friedrich August (1696–1763), then succeeded as Saxon Elector Friedrich August II. Upon succession, the new elector received many petitions and musical gifts, including a Missa, BWV 232[I]—the Kyrie and Gloria from the Mass Ordinary—which Johann Sebastian Bach deposited in Dresden together with a petition dated July 27, 1733. Bach sought the protection of the most powerful patron in the land with this musical offering, a work that could be performed in either Lutheran or Catholic liturgy. Musical settings of the *Kyrie e Gloria* were not only heard in the Lutheran liturgy in Leipzig but also widely used in the Catholic liturgy, as is witnessed in the repertoire of Dresden's Catholic court church.[1] Further, the structure and musical styles employed by Bach for the Missa of 1733 are closely related to models heard in Dresden's first post-Reformation Catholic church. Explored here are Bach's connections with the Dresden court and its repertoire and the possibility that the Missa, BWV 232[I], or part of it, was heard at the *Erbhuldigung* service in Leipzig in 1733.

Bach, Zelenka, and the Dresden Court

It is well established that the Missa demonstrates that by 1733 Bach was well acquainted with the type of Italian Mass settings that were performed in the Catholic court church of the Dresden palace. The structure and musical styles employed by Bach in the Missa are closely related to models regularly heard in the Dresden court

I acknowledge with gratitude the assistance and advice given by Jóhannes Ágústsson, Susanne Haring, Samantha Owens, Frederic Kiernan, and Robin A. Leaver (especially with regard to liturgical matters). All translations from Latin were prepared by the late David Fairservice.

1. See, for example, George Stauffer, *Bach: The Mass in B Minor* (New York: Schirmer, 1997).

church, especially "number" settings coming from Naples.[2] Such Masses were either composed or possessed by musicians of this church, including the Masses written by and held in the collection of Jan Dismas Zelenka (1679–1745), a composer known to and admired by Bach. In response to the eleventh question posed by Johann Nikolaus Forkel for his biography on Johann Sebastian Bach, C. P. E. Bach wrote: "In his last years he [Johann Sebastian Bach] esteemed highly: Fux, Caldara, Händel, Kayser [Keiser], Hasse, both Grauns, Telemann, Zelenka, Benda, and in general everything that was worthy of esteem in Berlin and Dresden. Except for the first four, he knew the rest personally."[3]

The relationship between Bach and Zelenka seems to have developed in the 1730s, and it was probably based upon a mutual reverence for the music of polyphonic masters of the past, as well as an appreciation of contemporary developments. Sectarian differences would have been of little or no significance in their relationship. This association came at a time when both Bach in Leipzig and Zelenka in Dresden had simultaneously, and each in his own way, embarked upon a program of composition to provide a complete repertoire to serve the church year of their respective confessions. From the time of the death of Dresden *Kapellmeister* Johann David Heinichen on July 16, 1729, and February 3, 1734, when Johann Adolph Hasse arrived to take up this position, Zelenka was the acting *Kapellmeister* of the Dresden court. His tasks included responsibility for the royal musical library, and it might have been Zelenka who came to supply Bach with Dresden sources that either were in Bach's possession or else were used as the basis of works. Bach's copies of Italian sacred music (made mainly between the late 1720s and the early 1740s) as listed by Kirsten Beißwenger,[4] include works still held in Dresden: Antonio Caldara's *Magnificat* in C;[5] Antonio Lotti's *Missa*

2. See Janice B. Stockigt, *Jan Dismas Zelenka: A Bohemian Musician at the Court of Dresden* (Oxford: Oxford University Press, 2000), 138–39.

3. NBR, 400, no. 395.

4. Kirsten Beißwenger, *Johann Sebastian Bachs Notenbibliothek* (Kassel: Bärenreiter, 1992); see also Beißwenger, "Other Composers," in *The Routledge Research Companion to Johann Sebastian Bach*, ed. Robin A. Leaver (London: Routledge, 2017), 237–64.

5. Beißwenger, *Bach's Notenbibliothek*, I/C/1, copied 1740–42. Caldara's *Magnificat* setting in C Major (D-Dl, Mus. 2170-D-2, 3) once was in the possession of Dresden *Kapellmeister* Johann David Heinichen, whose cover note states that the work should be transposed into D ("Transponiert in d♯"), presumably to accommodate the tuning of Saxon trumpets.

Sapientiae;[6] Palestrina's *Missa sine Nomine*;[7] and Pergolesi's *Stabat Mater*.[8] Another work in Bach's possession, a setting of the Sanctus in D Minor (BWV 239), recently has been identified as having its basis in the Gloria from a Missa by Antonio Caldara, a work in Zelenka's collection that he reorchestrated in circa 1727 to suit Dresden conditions and "stretched" to become a *missa tota*.[9] (A *Kyrie e Gloria* could be "stretched" into a *missa tota* either through the creation of new movements from existing sections of the setting or by new composition.)[10] Zelenka composed the Credo and titled the work *Missa Providentiae*.[11]

The royal chapel was established in 1708 by August II in the former theater of the Dresden palace, and it served both August II and his son who, in 1737, four years after his election as king of Poland, had plans drawn up for a much larger building.[12] On June 29, 1751, the *Hofkirche* was consecrated.[13] On an order from August II, another royal Catholic chapel, sometimes referred to as the *Schloßkirche*, was established in 1710 in a room at the base of the tower of the Pleißenburg fortress in Leipzig.[14] Both the

6. Beißwenger, *Bachs Notenbibliothek*, I/L/2, copied 1732–35, D-Dl, Mus. 2159-D-4. Reworked by Jan Dismas Zelenka for Dresden and listed as no. 30, page 7 (recent pagination) into his *Inventarium rerum Musicarum Ecclesiae servientium*, D-Dl, Bibl.-Arch. III Hb 787d, http://digital.slub-dresden .de/fileadmin/data/425379515/425379515_tif/jpegs/425379515.pdf.

7. Beißwenger, *Bachs Notenbibliothek*, I/P/2, copied ca. 1742, D-Dl, Mus. 997-D-16. This Mass is listed on page 5 of Zelenka's *Inventarium* as being notated in his "Collectaneorum Musicoru[m]. libri 4 de diversis Authoribus," a collection of works copied in Vienna between 1717 and 1719. See D-Dl, Mus. 1-B-98.

8. Beißwenger, *Bachs Notenbibliothek*, II/P/3, D-Dl, Mus. 3005-D-1a, Mus. 3005-D-1b. Reworked by Bach as *Tilge, Höchster, meine Sünden* (BWV 1083), 1746–47.

9. I am very grateful to Bruno Musumeci, who communicated his identification of the author of the apocryphal Sanctus (BWV 239); see the forthcoming article in BJ.

10. These reworkings are termed "gestreckte Messen" by Wolfgang Horn, who describes this procedure as a Kyrie and Gloria (sometimes with Credo) being enhanced or made complete with an added Sanctus and Agnus Dei by using material from existing parts, often in the manner of parody, sometimes with new composition; Wolfgang Horn, *Die Dresdner Hofkirchenmusik 1720–1745: Studien zu ihren Voraussetzungen und ihrem Repertoire* (Kassel: Bärenreiter; Stuttgart: Carus, 1987), 149–89, identifies "gestreckte Messen" in Zelenka's collection.

11. D-Dl, Mus. 2170-D-7.

12. Friedrich August II was elected king of Poland on 5 October 1733 and crowned at Cracow on 17 January 1734.

13. Today this is the cathedral of the Catholic Diocese of Dresden-Meissen.

14. See Janice B. Stockigt, "The Music of Leipzig's Royal Catholic Chapel during the Reign of August II," *Understanding Bach* 11 (2016): 57–66.

Dresden and Leipzig churches were open for public worship, and although Dresden acquired a great collection of sacred Catholic music, as seen in the catalog drawn up in 1765,[15] little is known about the music collection of Leipzig's church until later in the eighteenth century.[16]

With one exception, the instrumental and vocal scoring of the 1733 Missa reflected Dresden practices of the 1730s. Bach certainly would have heard the voices of two of the young male castrati who had been specially trained in Italy for the revival of the Dresden opera,[17] and he would have known the vocal qualities of two older castrati of the Dresden court. In September 1731 Bach and Wilhelm Friedemann traveled to Dresden to attend a performance of *Cleofide*, an opera by Johann Adolph Hasse.[18] The two younger singers were male soprano Ventura Rochetti (known as Venturini), who sang the role of "Gandarte" in the 1731 production of *Cleofide*, and male alto Domenico Annibali, who sang the role of "Alessandro." Although male soprano Giovanni Bindi (trained in Italy by Porpora) also arrived in Dresden in 1730, he did not sing in this production. The older altos were Nicolo Pozzi ("Timagene"), who had been in Dresden since 1724, and Antonio Campioli ("Porus"), who previously had taught the castrati in Venice, then joined the vocal ensemble for this 1731 production. The capabilities of each singer might have been in Bach's mind when composing the solo and ensemble movements of the Missa. From this visit of 1731 Bach also would have heard a revitalized *Hofkapelle* and the particular strengths of its instrumentalists, many of them personally known to him. The instrumental ensemble was led by Johann

---

15. "Catalogo (Thematico) [*sic*] della Musica di Chiesa (catholica [*sic*] in Dresda) composta Da diversi Autori—secondo l'Alfabetto 1765," compiled by Joannes Georg Schürer, MS. D-B, Mus. ms. theor. Kat. 186.

16. See Clemens Harasim, *Die Kirchenmusik an der Propsteikirche zu Leipzig: Von ihren Anfängen bis heute*, ed. Helmut Loos (Leipzig: Schröder, 2015).

17. On the training of these singers, see Jóhannes Ágústsson, "The Secular Vocal Collection of Jan Dismas Zelenka: A Reconstruction," *Studi vivaldiani* 13 (2013): 3–52.

18. While Hasse did not finally settle in Dresden as *Kapellmeister* until February 1734, on 20 July 1731, shortly after he arrived to direct *Cleofide*, the Bavarian ambassador to Saxony reported that the king had officially declared Hasse to be the new *Kapellmeister*. See Janice B. Stockigt and Jóhannes Ágústsson, "Reflections and Recent Findings on the Life and Music of Jan Dismas Zelenka (1679–1745)," *Clavibus unitis* 4 (2015): 7–48, here 25. On 15 August 1731 the diary of the Dresden Jesuits (*Diarium Dresdae*) reported that the "novus Capellae Magister D. Haas" had produced the music for the sung Mass; see Wolfgang Reich, "Exzerpte aus dem Diarium Missionis S.J. Dresdae," in *Zelenka-Studien II: Referate und Materialien der 2. Internationalen Fachkonferenz Jan Dismas Zelenka (Dresden und Prag), 1995*, ed. Wolfgang Reich and Günter Gatterman (Sankt Augustin: Academia Verlag, 1997), 356.

Georg Pisendel,[19] and principal positions were filled by Pierre-Gabriel Buffardin and Johann Joachim Quantz (flutes), Johann Christian Richter (oboe), the Schindler brothers, Johann Adam and Andreas (horns), Arcangelo Rossi (violoncellist), and Johann Samuel Kayser (contra bassist: Käyser, Kaiser, Keyser). The continuo section included *Cammer-Lautenist* Sylvius Leopold Weiß, two or more bassoonists led by Johann Gottfried Böhme, and players of the violoncello and string bass; probably Christian Petzold played second keyboard to the director, Hasse.

To this ensemble a number of younger players were formally admitted in 1732, although they probably had played for the 1731 performances of *Cleofide*. Their inclusion in the *Hofkapelle* was due to intervention by the electoral prince, who, from autumn 1730, took a personal interest and a large degree of responsibility for the membership of the court's musical ensembles. A memorandum he wrote in 1731 noted that, due to the departure from Dresden ensembles of one singer (Andrea Ruota) and four dancers (Jeanne Houlondel, known as "la France"; Bartelome Derval; Louis Dupré; and François St. Denis), the large sum of 2,500 *Thaler* would become available for the *Hofkapelle*. The prince stated that because the majority of the *Hofkapelle* musicians had become incapacitated, new players could be employed.[20] Those nominated to enter the *Hofkapelle* included six violinists (two of them were the earliest organists of Leipzig's *Schloßkapelle*: Augustin Uhlig and Josef Tiederle),[21] one violist, a cellist, a contrabass player, an oboist, and a bassoonist. Three of these musicians came from the *Capelle* of Count Wackerbarth: oboist and chalumeau player Johann Wilhelm Hugo, bassoonist Johann B. Linke, and cellist Arcangelo Califano.[22]

---

19. Pisendel (1687–1755), who had been acting concertmaster since the death of Volumier (7 October 1728), was formally named concertmaster in a document signed by August II dated 1 October 1731, with salary backdated to 1 February 1730; see Kai Köpp, *Johann Georg Pisendel (1687–1755) und die Anfänge der neuzeitlichen Orchesterleitung* (Tutzing: Schneider, 2005), 448–49, nos. 43 and 44.

20. "Ces 2500 thl. [Thaler] pourois [!] etre employes a mettre L'orquestre en etat qu'il en a grand besoin la pluspart etant invalide" (D-Dla, 10026 Geheimes Kabinett [Geh. Kab. hereafter], Loc. 383/5, *Französische Comoedianten und Orchestra betr. Ao 1721–33*, fol. 224a).

21. From 1719 to 1722 the Bohemian musician Augustin Uhlig was the first organist of the Leipzig *Schlosskapelle*. Josef Tiederle (Titterle), also from Bohemia, served in Leipzig's *Schlosskapelle* in 1724 and 1725. Both moved from Leipzig into the music ensemble of Dresden's Catholic court church (the *Kapellknaben*), Uhlig as organist and Tiederle as violinist; see Janice B. Stockigt, "The Organists of Leipzig's Royal Catholic Chapel: 1719–1756," *Hudební věda* 2/3 (2016): 161–76.

22. On the ensemble of Count Wackerbarth, see Szymon Paczkowski, "Christoph August von Wackerbarth (1662–1734) and His 'Cammer-Musique,'" in *Music Migration in the Early Modern Age: Centres and Peripheries—People, Works, Styles, Paths of Dissemination and Influence*, ed. Jolanta Guzy-Pasiak and Aneta Markuszewska (Warsaw: Liber Pro Arte, 2016), 109–26.

The Missa as Homage to the New Elector?

The wording on the title page of Bach's Missa, while not unambiguous, at least suggests that in July 1733 the elector either had been shown a copy of the work or else had heard it:

> Sr. Königl[ichen] Hoheit und ChurFürstl[ichen] Durchl[aucht] zu Sachßen bezeigte mit inliegender Missa . . . seine unterthänigste Devotion der Autor J.S. Bach.[23]

> With the enclosed Missa . . . the author J. S. Bach demonstrated his most humble devotion to His Royal and Electoral Serene Highness of Saxony.

Bach's use of the past tense led Arnold Schering to propose that before delivery in Dresden of the Missa and the accompanying petition, dated July 27, 1733, the elector had prior knowledge of this work.[24] Schering suggested that this occurred during the new elector's visit to Leipzig in April 1733 for the *Erbhuldigung* (homage) ceremonies that followed the death of August II and the succession of his son Friedrich August as elector of Saxony. The traditional formalities were held in major Saxon centers. They began with a grand official entrance into the city, continued with speeches of welcome, church services (one in which the homage sermon was preached), and the taking of oaths from leaders and subjects in return for the confirmation of privileges, and ended with a major feast (*Tafel*).

In order to assess the possibility that Bach's Missa could have been heard by the elector before the work was deposited in Dresden, Michael Maul recently reexamined Schering's suggestion that a performance had been given during the elector's *Erbhuldigung* visit to Leipzig in April 1733.[25] Various alternative suggestions have been made, such as the possibility of a liturgical performance in Dresden on Sunday, July 26, the day before the presentation,[26] although that is unlikely, since it was a day listed in the

---

23. Autograph dedication on the cover of the Missa BWV 232[I], D-Dl, Mus. 2405-D-21.

24. Arnold Schering, "Die Hohe Messe in h-moll: Eine Huldigungsmusik und Krönungsmesse für Friedrich August II," BJ 33 (1936): 6–14.

25. Michael Maul, "Das *Kyrie* der *h-Moll-Messe*: Eine genuine Musik für die Leipziger Erbhuldigung?," in *Bachs Messe h-Moll: Entstehung, Deutung, Rezeption*, ed. Michael Gassmann (Kassel: Bärenreiter, 2014), 9–22; see also Manuel Bärwald, "Eine unbekannte Leipziger Erbhuldigungskantate aus dem Jahr 1733," BJ 99 (2013): 359–74; and Peter Wollny, "Neuerkenntnissen zu einigen Kopisten der 1730er Jahr," BJ 102 (2016): 76–78.

26. Apart from church services for the feast of St. Anne (which always was published as a red-letter day in the Gregorian calendar, observed by the Dresden court), on that day in 1733 the "Hof Journal" of the Dresden court noted that a *Cour* was held to celebrate the name day of Saxon princess Maria Anna. See D-Dla, 10006 Oberhofmarschallamt (OHMA hereafter), O 1, Nr. 3, *Dresdner Hoftagebücher,* 1732–34: "Journal 1733," fol. 57a. Moreover, shortly before, on 13 July, the electress of Saxony (Maria Josepha) had given birth to Saxon prince Carl Christian Joseph Ignaz Eugen Franz Xaver.

Saxon *Hof- und Staats-Calender* to be held *in Galla* at the Dresden court.[27] Another conjecture is the suggestion of a concertizing performance made in connection with Bach's trip to Dresden. Since such conjectures have their problems, Schering's argument, based as it is on a specific event, needs to be reconsidered. Although extensive reporting of the *Erbhuldigung* events held in Leipzig is given in the 1735 publication of the *Hof- und Staats-Calender*, primary sources held in Dresden report on the planning for the elector's visit to Leipzig, especially the records of the office of the high marshal (*Oberhofmarschallamt*).[28] This office faced immense organizational challenges for the multifaceted events associated with the homage ceremonies, especially the Lutheran church services, which traditionally were splendid occasions held in the presence of the incoming elector. Planning in 1733 was particularly difficult because between the death of August II in Poland on February 1 and the Dresden exequies and visits to Leipzig, Wittenberg, Torgau, Bautzen, and Freiberg, Holy Week and Eastertide had to be observed. Moreover, post-Reformation planning schedules had been created for Lutheran electors, and Friedrich August II was a convert to Catholicism.

Undoubtedly the *Oberhofmarschallamt* in 1733 would have needed to confront the question of how the new elector would demonstrate to Saxony's Lutheran population the seriousness with which he regarded his conversion. Unlike his father, who had avoided major sectarian difficulties (due largely to a somewhat pragmatic attitude to his change of religion: only a Catholic could become a candidate for election to the Polish throne), Friedrich August II was a devout and committed convert. During the first week of July 1711, August II and his fourteen-year-old son, Prince Friedrich August, visited the Clementinum, Prague's great Jesuit college, which came to be associated with so many Jesuits who served in the royal chapels of both Dresden and Leipzig.[29] Entries made into the *Diarium* of the Clementinum reveal that the prince arrived there on July 1,[30] followed by his father on July 4.[31] Meetings then were held,

---

27. HStCal, July 1733 [6v].

28. D-Dla, 10006 OHMA, D, Nr. 8, *Kurfürst Friedrich August II. Erbhuldigung, Dresden, 1733*; Nr. 9, *Kurfürst Friedrich August II. Erbhuldigung, Leipzig, 1733*.

29. Soon after their establishment the Catholic churches of Dresden and Leipzig came to be administered by the Jesuit Province of Bohemia. The annual letters from Dresden and Leipzig ("Literae annuae") to the general of the Society of Jesus in Rome are held in the Roman Jesuit Archives (ARSI), Bohemia (Bohemiae [Boh.]). Paginated.

30. *Diarium Clementem*, 1 July 1709: "Venit Praga[m] Princeps Electoralis Saxoniae." "Diarium collegii Societatis Jesu ad sanctum Clementem Vetero-Pragae 1699–1714," fol. 193v.

31. *Diarium Clementem*, 4 July 1709, fol. 193v: "Tota die in armis expectabat Guarnison Rege Polonia . . . Rex venit vesperi" (The garrison, fully armed, waited all day for the king of Poland . . . The king arrived in the evening).

at which time a Catholic court (*aula catholica*) was assembled for the prince. On July 7, Father Kogler, a Jesuit from the Province of Austria who was to become the prince's future theologian, also arrived at the Clementinum. On that same day the Lutheran court, which had come to Prague, was sent back to Dresden.[32] Following another three-hour meeting on July 8, August II and his son left for Dresden with the *aula catholica*, whose members traveled via a different route.[33]

At Bologna during his Grand Tour the prince renounced the Lutheran faith and embraced the Catholic religion on November 27, 1712.[34] In 1719 he married the imperial archduchess Maria Josepha, a union that August II appears to have hoped for as early as 1705.[35] With Maria Josepha, Austrian Piety—that distinctive Habsburg religious expression characterized by Eucharistic devotion, veneration of the Cross,

32. *Diarium Clementem*, 7 July 1709, fol. 193v: "Et hodie . . . P. Antonii Kugler ex Austriaca Prov[icinci] á, futurus Theologus Principis Electoralis Saxoniae, cui his diebus formata est Aula Catholica. Haeretica vero remissa Dresdam" (Father Antonio Kugler [Kogler, Kögler] from the Province of Austria called on us. He is the future theologian to the electoral prince of Saxony, for whom a court has been formed in these days. The heretical [Lutheran] court has been sent to Dresden). Fr. Anton[ius] Kögler SJ (d. 1721, Dresden) became the confessor and companion to the electoral prince; see Bernhard Duhr, *Geschichte der Jesuiten in den Ländern deutscher Zunge im 18. Jahrhundert* (Munich-Regensburg: Manz, 1928), 4:496. Monthly payments were made to "Pater Kogler" between October 1717 and March 1719, when the electoral prince was living in Vienna during his courtship of an Austrian archduchess; D-Dla, 10026 Geh. Kab., Loc. 763/8, *Des Königlichen Prinzen Herrn Friedrich August, Hoheit, Hofkassenrechnungen, 1719, 1722, 1725, 1734*, fol. 42a–b.

33. On the conversion of Saxon electoral prince Friedrich August, see Horn, *Die Dresdner Hofkirchenmusik*, 21–23. Apart from a confessor, the court of Friedrich August probably included a *Hofmeister*, secretary, cashier, quartermaster (*fourier*), wardrobe master (*garde-robbe*), wig maker (*peruquier*), chamber servants, laundry maid, and a servant responsible for the heating (*Stubenheitzer*); information based upon the court of the son of August III and Maria Josepha, Electoral Prince Friedrich Christian as reported in the HStCal, 1738, 50.

34. See Stockigt and Ágústsson, "Reflections," 9.

35. The dynastic ambitions of August II are discussed in ibid., 13. As early as May 1705 August II had written a memorandum titled "Project ins fahl das Haus Estreich absterben sohltes" (Plan in the event of the House of Austria dying out), in which he outlined how he or his son the electoral prince might succeed to the imperial crown. In June 1716 the papal legate to Saxony, Father Giovanni Battista Salerni SJ, before whom Saxon prince Friedrich August renounced his Lutheran faith and converted to Catholicism at Bologna in 1712, was also in Vienna. Father Salerni wrote to the Roman Curia expressing the view that if an alliance between the Habsburgs and House of Wettin could be arranged, Catholicism would enter Saxony without protest or fuss. On 8 September 1716 August II wrote to Emperor Charles VI stating his interest in having his son marry one of the emperor's two nieces: Archduchess Maria Josepha (born 1699—the official Habsburg heir until the birth of Maria Theresa on 13 May 1717) or Archduchess Maria Amalia (born 1701). The king also emphasized that such an alliance would strengthen Catholicism in Saxony.

and adoration of Mary as Queen of Heaven—entered Saxony.[36] Thus, the planning of the elector's *Erbhuldigung* visits in 1733 presented a delicate situation and the probable reason for the blurred official reporting of the Leipzig and other *Erbhuldigung* visits, a vagueness also evident in the accounts published in the *Hof- und Staats-Calender*.

For the *Erbhuldigung* rituals held in Dresden, however, the published reports in the *Hof- und Staats-Calender* suggest that no difficulties were faced. There, on the morning of April 15, the ceremonies began with a Lutheran service in the Protestant court church in Dresden. There is no record of any member of the electoral family being present when the *Oberhofprediger*, Bernhard Walther Marperger, preached the homage sermon that he had authored (on the text of Psalm 28:8–9); it was to be read throughout Saxony at every *Erbhuldigung* service with no changes to the text.[37] Following this, at 9:30 a.m., homage ceremonies began in the Parade Hall (Riesen-Saal) of the Dresden palace and continued outside the Dresden Gewandhaus in the Judenhof, and again in the palace, after which a great feast was held.

Three days (a *triduum*) of exequies for August II then began in Dresden's Catholic court church. The *Hof- und Staats-Calender* reported that "their Highnesses [Elector Friedrich August II and Electress Maria Josepha], their children, and the complete court attended the Dresden court's Catholic church for services at which moving mourning music [*beweglichen Trauer-Musik*] was heard."[38] These Dresden events of April 15 were reported in the annual letter of the Dresden Jesuits to the general of the Society of Jesus in Rome:

Apparatu igitur lugubri solennes pro Augusti anima Inferiae triduò sunt celebratae. Priùs tamen decimô septimô Calendas Maji matutino tempore in foro jusjurandum Cives praestiterunt, tandem à prandiis Matutinum cum Laudibus ex officio Defunctorum initium sumpsit, sedente in faldistorio in elatiori Baptisterii loco, Reverendissimo, Perillustri, ac Amplissimo Domino Martino Graf ordinis Cisterciensis Neocellensi Praelato Infulato cum Levitis quaternis, et octonis Ministris. Matutinum in Choro erat decantatum, alternos Sacerdotibus versus prosequentibus in Capella inferiùs, primi Nocturni Lectiones in tono Lamentationum Jeremiae lugubrè decantârunt Musici Itali, reliquae à sub-diacono, Diacono, et Pontifice sunt continuatae.[39]

---

36. On Austrian Piety (Pietas Austriaca), see Friedrich W. Riedel, *Kirchenmusik am Hofe Karls VI (1711–1740)* (Munich: Katzbichler, 1977), 26–29.

37. HStCal, 1735, sig. F1v. The text was not very subtle, given that the recently deceased royal elector was known as "August der Starke": "Der Herr ist ihr Starke" ("The Lord is their strength, and he is the saving strength of his anointed. Save thy people, and bless thine inheritance: feed them also, and lift them up for ever" [Psalm 28:8, KJV]).

38. HStCal, 1735, sig. D3r.

39. "Annuae Literae Missionis Dresdensis ad Annum 1733," ARSI, Boh. 150, 27–34, at 29–30.

The funeral ceremonies were performed for the soul of Augustus with a *triduum*. Before this, however, on the morning of April 15 the citizens swore a public oath, and only in the afternoon did Matins begin with Lauds from the Office of the Dead. The mitred Martin Graf, solitary prelate of the Cistercian order in Neuzelle, with four priests and eight servers, was seated on a faldstool in the upper part of the baptistry. Matins was sung in the choir [*in Choro*], with priests giving responses in the body of the chapel. The Italian musicians mournfully sang the lessons of the first nocturne in *tono Lamentationum Jeremiae* [reference to the style of the music, which the writer must have regarded as being similar to Zelenka's Lamentations and Responsories for Holy Week (zwv 47)], and the other readings were continued by the subdeacon, deacon, and priest.

Zelenka composed the Invitatory, three Lessons, and nine Responsories for the Office of the Dead (zwv 47) for Matins held on April 15. On April 16 the exequies continued. This was the occasion when Zelenka's Requiem Mass (zwv 47) was performed.[40] Zelenka's entry of this work into his *Inventarium* is accompanied by these words: "Raptissime composit[um]," an indication that the planning of the services for this *triduum* had been hurried. The instrumentation of this Requiem Mass (which includes two trumpets with timpani and two horns and a four-part string ensemble with a full woodwind section) reveals that the ban on the performance of solemn music, which had been prohibited throughout Saxony until July 2 (Feast of Visitation of B.V.M.), was not observed in Dresden's Catholic court church.

At this same time a *triduum* was held in Leipzig's royal Catholic chapel, where, as in Dresden, a *castrum doloris* (the elaborate structure covering a bier) had been erected.[41] The annual letter from the Leipzig Jesuits reported that such was the throng of people who attended the services in the Catholic *Schloßkapelle* (including those of the senatorial order and graduates) that the chapel proved too small to hold them.[42] For these Leipzig services, three musicians were brought from Bohemia, and the sum of sixteen *Thaler* was paid to six military musicians, presumably from Leipzig.[43] The organist of

---

40. "Die Exequiarum subsequente horâ 9 pro Concione funebri dixit P. Superior, quâ finitâ Neo Cellensis Praelatus cum adstitibus suis sub lugubri Orchestrae Regiae ode pontificavit, sub finem incensatus est Sarcophagus," ARSI, Boh. 150, 29.

41. An illustration of the castrum doloris in the Dresden Catholic court church is published in the HStCal, 1735, opposite sig. D3v. A similar representation is published by Stockigt and Ágústsson, "Reflections," illustration 5, p. 27. Members of the electoral family are seated to the right of the structure. The mitred Martin Graf from Neuzelle is seated to the left on a faldstool surrounded by priests and servers. The musicians in their gallery are just visible behind the coffin. This illustration represents the exequies held on 15 April.

42. "Annuae Literae Missionis Lipsiensis ad annum 1733," ARSI, Boh. 150, 35.

43. Financial records of the Leipzig Jesuits, 1733, "Rationes," I. 004, Band 142 (previous signature 12/3, Band I), Kirchenrechnung 1710–45, D-BAUd, DADM.

the Leipzig *Schloßkapelle* in 1733 was Antonio Harnisch, yet another Bohemian musician who later came to hold significant positions with the music ensembles that served both Dresden's Catholic court church and the imperial chapel in Dresden-Neustadt.[44]

Immediately after the Dresden *Erbhuldigung* ceremonies and the *triduum*, *Oberhofmarschall* Graf von Löwendahl traveled to Leipzig to make the necessary arrangements for the *Erbhuldigung* to be held there. The elector left Dresden for Leipzig at 3:00 p.m. on April 19, traveling via Hubertusburg, the court's hunting castle at Wermsdorf. Before he and his entourage entered the city on April 20, a camp was set up where the elector changed clothes and prepared for the splendid ceremonial entry into Leipzig.[45]

As Arnold Schering considered that the service in the St. Nicolai Church could have been the occasion when Bach's Missa might have been heard by the elector, Michael Maul investigated accounts of the service in this church on April 21, when the homage sermon was preached. Those reported as being present in the church included the privy councilors, *Oberhofmarschall* von Löwendahl, and cavaliers of the Dresden court. The duke of Weissenfels and the generals were in the *Fürstenstand* (electoral pew), the knights were in the gallery opposite the pulpit, and university representatives were in the chancel. No direct reference to the elector's presence in the Nicolai Church on this day is given in the lengthy accounts of this visit to Leipzig.

The *Hof- und Staats-Calender* reported that at 10:00 a.m. on that day there was a gathering in the electoral antechamber (presumably of the Apel House, where Friedrich August II was accommodated), where oaths of allegiance were given, after which he was carried in a sedan chair to the stock exchange (*Kauffmanns-Börse*). The elector then went to the town hall, where further homage was received, then to the balcony erected in front of the town hall at the marketplace to accept homage from the citizens and subjects of the region who had gathered there.[46] He remained in Leipzig for the remaining days of the Easter Fair before returning to Hubertusburg. Some members of his court, however, then traveled to Wittenberg to prepare for the next stage of the *Erbhuldingung* visits.

In the planning of the elector's Leipzig visit, the Leipzig authorities made requests to Dresden for details. Responses, however, were vague. The Dresden Ober-Consistorium finally sent details on April 13, just one week before the Nicolai church service was held. The preworded homage sermon was delivered by Leipzig's Superintendent Salomon Deyling, who was obliged to read it without change.[47] At this time the following order of service was received in Leipzig:

44. On Antonio Harnisch, see Stockigt, "The Organists," 172–73.

45. HStCal, 1735, sig. G1v.

46. HStCal, 1735, sig. G1v–G2v.

47. This sermon is referred to above; see note 37.

Ordnung des Gottes-Diensts bey der Erbhuldigungs-Predigt.

1.) Komm heiliger Geist Herre Gott.

2.) Kyrie.

3.) Allein Gott in der Höh sey Ehr.[48]

4.) Collecte pro Pace . . . und abzulesen Psalm 28. ganz.

5.) Ich dancke dir demüthiglich.

6.) Glaube [Wir glauben all an einen Gott]

7.) Predigt aus Psalm 28. v. 8. 9. und vor dem Vater Unser: Beschirm die Policeyen, bau unsers Fürsten Thron.

8.) Es woll uns Gott genädig seyn.

9.) Collecte pro Magistratu . . . und Seegen.

10.) Verleih uns Frieden gnädiglich.[49]

The reference to "Kyrie" here does not necessarily imply the absence of "Gloria." In various contemporary Lutheran sources "Kyrie" means "Missa," both the Latin Kyrie and Gloria, and in many hymnals the two items appear as one essential unit. For example, in Vopelius's *Neu Leipziger Gesangbuch* (1682), both are included together under the one heading "Missa, oder das Kyrie Eleison."[50] Bach echoes this meaning in his outline of the Advent liturgy on the covers of Cantatas 61 and 62 with "Kyrie, so gantz musiciret wird."[51] It was therefore usual for the complete Missa to be given, either in chant or in concerted settings, the Gloria following on from the Kyrie. For such an important occasion that marked both the death of the previous Saxon elector and the accession of his successor, to whom homage was due, a suitable concerted Missa was required. Thus Bach's Missa BWV 232[I] would have been an appropriate and superlative expression of both mourning (Kyrie) and celebration (Gloria). Its significant length was in keeping with the importance of the occasion, and the use of trumpets and timpani were not out of place in a service that included a strong element of mourning for the deceased elector, since Zelenka's Requiem Mass (ZWV 47) for Augustus II, performed

48. This hymn would have been preceded by the chant intonation of *Gloria in excelsis Deo*, just these four words, not the complete text. Even though four of the five hymns were penned by Luther, they were confessionally neutral in that they were based on either pre-Reformation Latin texts or a biblical psalm.

49. "Von Seiten der Hofbehörden erstellter Ablaufplan," D-Dla Geheimer Rat, Loc. 8733/5 (Erb-Huldigung zu Dresden, Leipzig, Wittenberg, Torgau und Freyberg, von Ihr. Königl. Hoheit dem Durchlauchtigsten Churfürsten zu Sachßen in eigene Person eingenommen. *Ao.* 1733), Band 2, fol. 54r, as cited in Maul, "Das *Kyrie* der *h-Moll-Messe*," 15.

50. Gottfried Vopelius, *New Leipziger Gesangbuch* (Leipzig: Klinger, 1682), 421–23.

51. BDOK 1:248–49, 251, nos. 178, 181.

in Dresden on April 16, 1733, had employed both. However, it could be argued that the performance of Bach's Missa as part of the *Erbhuldigung* service in the Nicholaikirche would have been unlikely, since the tradition of the Leipzig churches was that if the Latin *Gloria in excelsis Deo* was sung, it was not customarily followed by the singing of the Gloria hymn, *Allein Gott in der Höh sei Ehr*, and vice versa. If this is so, then the fact that the *Erbhuldigung* service calls for the singing of the Gloria hymn would seem to imply that there was no Latin Gloria. But two primary factors undermine this conclusion: first, the Leipzig practice is not as obvious as it might appear; and second, the liturgical form of the *Erbhuldigung* service did not originate in Leipzig.

For most of the seasons of the church year in the Leipzig churches, if the Latin Gloria was presented in a concerted setting, it would not normally be followed by the singing of the German Gloria hymn. In many ways, the liturgical practice was conditioned by the Thomasschule tradition with regard to Choir I and Choir II. When Choir I was performing a concerted setting of the Gloria in one of the two principal churches, Choir II would be leading the congregation in the Gloria hymn in the other church. Thus an either/or alternation between the Latin and German Glorias was the norm Sunday by Sunday for most of the church year.[52] But there was an exception. During Lent and Holy Week the Latin Gloria was followed by the vernacular Gloria hymn: the choir chanted monophonically the complete Latin Gloria, and the congregation followed it by singing *Allein Gott*.[53] The Gloria hymn following the Latin Gloria in the 1733 *Erbhuldigung* service was therefore not without precedence in the Leipzig churches.

The 1733 liturgical form for the *Erbhuldigung* service held in the Nicholaikirche was not drawn up by the Leipzig clergy. It had been compiled by the *Oberhofprediger* in Dresden, Bernhard Walther Marperger (see above), and the liturgy was to be observed not only in Leipzig but also in Wittenberg, Torgau, Bautzen, and Freiberg, wherever the *Erbhuldigung* ceremony was held. In 1730 Marperger's predecessor, Johann Andreas Gleich (1666–1734), outlined the details of the principal service on Sundays and feast days in the Lutheran court church in Dresden:

---

52. See Günther Stiller, *Johann Sebastian Bach and Liturgical Life in Leipzig*, trans. Herbert J. A. Bouman et al., ed. Robin A. Leaver (St. Louis: Concordia, 1984), 89–90.

53. Johann Christoph Rost, "Nachricht, Wie es, in der Kirchen zu St: Thom: alhier, mit dem Gottesdienst, jährlichen sowohl an Hohen Festen, als andern Tagen, pfleget gehalten zu werden" (manuscript, begun in 1716, in the archive of the Thomaskirche, Leipzig; no shelf mark), fol. 10r: "Gehet d. Priester ad altare und singet *Gloria* & darauf respondiret Chorus & dann wird *Allein Gott in der Höh sey Ehr*"; and fol. 21r: "Wird das latienische Kyrie gesungen, mit dem dritten [Kyrie] gehen sie hinaus an altar bethen & wird *Gloria* intoniret & Chorus resp. *Et in terra pax* & hernach *Allein Gott in der Höh sei Ehr*."

Fest und Son[n]tags, da die *Musicali*schen Capelle in der Churfl-Schloß-Kirchen gehalten wurde, sang man 1) einen *Introitum*, oder *Motette*, 2) das Kyrie *Musicali*sch, 3) darauf derjenige Hoff-Prediger, so die Aufwartung vor dem Altar hatte, das *Gloria in Excelsis Deo* anstimmte, und der Chor antwortet: *Et in terra pax.* . . . . 4) Darauf die Collecte vom Hoff-Prediger gesungen, und die gewöhnliche Epistel gelesen wurde. 5) Hernach stimmte man mit der Gemeinde ein teutsch Lied darzwischen an. 6) Alsdenn wurde das Evangelium gelesen, und der Hoff-Prediger *intonirte* vor dem Altar: *Credo in unum Deum.* Darauf die Capelle mit stattlicher *Music* das völlig *Symbolum* Lateinische *continuirte.* 7) Ward der Glaube teusch [*Wir glauben all an einen Gott*] gesungen.[54]

On festivals and Sundays, the musicians of the electoral court church sing 1) an introit, or motet, 2) the Kyrie in a figural setting, 3) thereafter the court preacher, standing before the altar, intones *Gloria in excelsis Deo*, and the choir answers, *Et in terra pax.* . . . . 4) Then the court preacher sings the collect and reads the customary epistle. 5) Then is sung a German hymn together with the congregation. Then is read the gospel, and the court preacher before the altar intones *Credo in unum Deum.* The Capelle continues, with solemn music, the complete Creed in Latin. 7) Then is sung the Creed in German [Wir glauben].

The regular practice of the Lutheran court church in Dresden therefore was that, following the "Kyrie *Musicali*sch," the Gloria was always sung in Latin and that the hymn *Allein Gott* neither replaced it at this juncture nor alternated with it week by week—though no doubt it was sung from time to time elsewhere in the liturgy. The Dresden court church was attended by high-powered Lutherans of the Saxon court, such as members of the privy council who oversaw the concerns of the churches in Saxony. Thus the worship had a significant Latin content. The starting point for the *Erbhuldigung* service was therefore this order for the Dresden court church in which the Latin Missa, Kyrie and Gloria, was a regular feature. However, since the *Erbhuldigung* service was also to be repeated in parish churches, as well as in the Dresden Lutheran court church, the congregational Gloria hymn was directed to follow the Latin *Gloria in excelsis Deo*—in the same way that the Latin *Credo in unum Deum* was customarily followed by its vernacular equivalent, *Wir glauben.* Further, the *Erbhuldigung* service was not the weekly celebration but a special occasion that had not been observed since 1694, a gap of almost forty years.

After Leipzig the next station of the *Erbhuldigung* was Wittenberg, where, on May 11, the homage sermon was delivered between 7:00 a.m. and 9:00 a.m. in All Saints, the

---

54. *Johann Andreas Gleich, Vorbericht / In sich fassend Die Reformations-Historie Chur-Sächs. Albertinischer Linie [I], Wie auch allerhand glaubwürdige Nachrichten von der Chrfl. Sächs. Schloß-Kirche zu Dresden, Ingleichen dem darinnen angeordneten Gottesdienste, und Hoff-Ministerio* (Dresden and Leipzig: Sauereßig, 1730), 58–59.

university church in Wittenberg castle, by the provost, Professor Christoph Heinrich Zeibig.[55] For this event, the Dresden office of the high marshal reminded the Wittenberg councilors to attend in good numbers! Following the service, officials from the offices of Wittenberg, Gräsenhannichen, and Commern gathered in the castle hall for homage formalities in the presence of the elector, after which hats were flung in the air to shouts of "Vivat." A *Tafel* (banquet) then was held. On this same day the elector left at about 4:00 p.m. for Torgau, the next *Erbhuldigung* station, arriving there on the evening of May 11.[56] The next morning he viewed the horse studs, and on the following day, May 13, he received a formal welcome to the city. The service in the castle church commenced at 7:00 a.m. with the homage sermon, read by Superintendent Michael Linda. At midday the elector attended a lunch but remained only until 2:00 p.m. before leaving for Dresden, because in that year the Feast of the Ascension of Our Lord (Himmelfahrt) fell on May 14.[57]

For this feast, it will be seen that it was necessary for Zelenka and Pisendel to return from Bautzen—the next place in the cycle of *Erbhuldigung* ceremonies—on May 13, as their presence was required for the music in Dresden's Catholic court church.[58] Careful planning for the elector's homage visit to that city had been under way for some time. Upon the elector's order, the Dresden Jesuit superior, Father Nonhardt, had written to the dean of the Collegiate Convent of St. Petri and apostolic administrator of Upper Lusatia, Johann Josef Ignaz Freyschlag von Schmidenthal (1669–1743), in Bautzen to introduce the elector's "well-born and virtuoso *Kapellmeister*," Zelenka. On this letter in Latin from Father Nonhardt, the date "10 May 1733" is written (which might imply the date on which the letter was received).[59] Zelenka, together with Pisendel, had offered to advise on the placement of musicians in the chancel of Bautzen's St. Petri Dom, where a select group of musicians from the elector's *Hofkapelle* was to perform. As space was limited, a plan for a performance area had been prepared by the *Oberlandbaumeister* of the Dresden court, Matthäus Daniel Pöppelmann, who already

55. HStCal, 1735, sig. G3v, which mistakenly gives the date of the Wittenberg homage sermon as 17 May.

56. HStCal, 1735, sig. G4r.

57. HStCal, 1735, sig. G4r. In the Gregorian calendars published in the HStCal, this feast always is printed as a red-letter day.

58. These two musicians had been sent to Bautzen to advise on the placement of royal musicians in the biconfessional St. Petri Dom in preparation for a performance of the *Te Deum laudamus* that was to be given for the elector during the next stage of the *Erbhuldigung* tour. See Janice B. Stockigt and Jóhannes Ágústsson, "The Visit of Members of the Dresden *Hofkapelle* to Bautzen," *Clavibus unitis* 5 (2016): 1–12, here 4.

59. Father Nonhardt's letter is reproduced as illustration 2 in ibid., 3.

had visited Bautzen at the beginning of May.[60] This electoral visit to Bautzen in Upper Lusatia (Oberlausitz) is of great importance, because in the extensive published accounts of the elector's *Erbhuldigung* visits, this is the only occasion on which he is reported to have entered a church. Bautzen was the principal city of a group known as the Sechs-Städte, a confederation of the fortified cities of Görlitz, Kamenz, Lauban, Lobau, and Zittau, all with differing languages (Sorbian or German) and religious affiliations (Catholic or Protestant). Following the Reformation, a mainly peaceful coexistence was maintained between the two religions in Upper Lusatia,[61] and Bautzen's St. Petri Dom became (and remains) a biconfessional church: Lutherans occupy the nave; Catholics worship in the chancel.

On May 18 twenty-one instrumentalists and nine singers from Dresden's *Hofkapelle* traveled to Bautzen for the Te Deum performance on May 19. Many of those musicians who recently had been admitted to the *Hofkapelle* were included among those sent there. Zelenka's name is given at the head of the list of singers, and it is likely that from that position he directed the performance of his own 1731 Te Deum (ZWV 146), a work set for SSATB soloists and SATB chorus with full orchestral accompaniment.[62] On May 19 the elector, who had left Dresden early that morning, was greeted at the gate to the city with a speech given by the *Oberamtshauptmann*, Count Friedrich Caspar Gerßdorff, on behalf of the nobility of Upper Lusatia. Friedrich August II and the entourage then moved into Bautzen, where he was welcomed by members of the council and deputies from the Sechs-Städte. After the ceremonial presentation of keys the procession moved to the St. Petri Dom. At the outer wall of the church the

60. On 12 May, during the visit of Zelenka and Pisendel, the Bautzen Council (Senatis Budißen) met to debate whether Pöppelmann's planned extension, which involved raising the floor level of a section of the chancel, should be allowed as a temporary measure as proposed by Dean von Schmidenthal. This suggestion was not accepted. (Pöppelmann also was responsible for alterations to Bautzen's Ortenburg castle, where the elector was to be accommodated and traditional ceremonies were to be held during the *Erbhuldigung* visit.) On 16 May the Bautzen *Bürgermeister* received a communication from the elector demanding alterations to be made in time for his upcoming *Erbhuldigung* visit. This led to an agreement being reached on the alteration, albeit a temporary one. See ibid., 4–5.

61. Noted by Dr. Rüdiger Laue, who published an informative essay titled "Musik bei Huldigungen der böhmischen Könige und Sächsischen Kurfürsten in der Oberlausitz als Ausdruck der sichtbaren und hörbaren Macht," in the program of the festival, *Lausitzer Musiksommer* (2010), no pagination. This essay provides a historic overview of the music heard at homage visits to Upper Lusatia.

62. The instrumental ensemble comprised six violins (led by Pisendel), two violas, two cellos, one *Contrebass*, two oboes, two flutes, two bassoons, two horns (*Waldhörner*), "Tiorba," and organ. For this performance, it is probable that two of the Dresden court's royal trumpeters (and timpani) also were in St. Petri. Of the eight royal trumpeters who accompanied the elector to Bautzen, only six are reported as playing the marches during the procession into the city; see Stockigt and Ágústsson, "The Visit," table 1, p. 6.

elector was met by twenty-three Catholic clerics in vestments, who accompanied him through the churchyard to the entrance to St. Petri. There a speech of welcome was given in Latin before entering the church. The *Hof- und Staats-Calender* reported:

> Und folgends von vorgedachten Herren von der Ritterschaft und der Cathol. Geistlichkeit, durch den Lutherischen Theil der Kirche in das Chor derselben, so die Catholicken inne haben, und wohin auch die Ministri und Hof-*Cavaliers* folgten, geführet wurden; In selbiger war auf der Evangelischen Seite ein *Baldachin* aufgeschlagen, und unter selbigen ein Stuhl gesetzet; dessen sich aber Ihro Königl. Hoheit nicht bedienten, sondern das *Te Deum Laudamus*, so unter Trompeten- und Pauken-Schall, auch annehmlicher *Musique* der aus Dresden anhero gekommenen *Capell-Musicorum* und *Castraten* abgesangen worden, stehende mit anhöreten.[63]

> [His Royal Highness] then was led by members of the knighthood and the Catholic clerics through the Lutheran part of the church to the choir [chancel] of the same, which the Catholics hold, and the ministers and *cavaliers* of the court followed. In the church, a baldachin had been set up on the Lutheran [*Evangelische*] side and a chair placed under it. However, His Royal Highness chose not to sit down. Instead, he remained standing to listen to the *Te Deum laudamus*, which was sung, accompanied by trumpets and timpani, and the pleasant *musique* of the chapel musicians and castrati who had come here from Dresden.

Performance of the Te Deum had historic precedence for *Erbhuldigung* ceremonies held in Bautzen: in the sixteenth century, when Bautzen was under Bohemian rule, the Te Deum was sung in 1538 by a choir during the Mass held in St. Petri on the occasion of the homage visit of Ferdinand I, king of Bohemia.[64]

Following the 1733 performance, the elector rode to the Ortenburg castle, where, according to tradition, deputies of the Bautzen Council presented wine and food. At 6:00 a.m. on May 20 the homage sermon was read in St. Petri by the pastor, Johann Christoph Lange, in the presence of the nobles, council, and citizens in the Lutheran part of the church. The *Hof- und Staats-Calender* reported that the elector then was met by the Catholic clerics in the foyer, and the procession then entered the "Catholischen Chore" for the Mass.[65] The somewhat vague *Hof- und Staats-Calender* report leaves it unclear as to whether the elector was present in the (Lutheran) nave or in the (Catholic) chancel of St. Petri for the homage sermon. According to the *Hof- und Staats-Calender*,

---

63. HStCal, 1735, sig. H1r.

64. StA Bautzen (Archivverbund Stadtarchiv und Staatsfilialarchiv Bautzen): U III Chronik Bautzen 1400–1599, 665, cited in Laue, "Musik bei Huldigungen," note 5.

65. HStCal, 1735, sig. H1v. Laue, "Musik bei Huldigungen," indicates that for the Mass the elector was carried into the church in a *chaise-a-porter* (sedan chair).

he then intended to listen to another homage sermon, as his predecessors had done, but, due to rain, this was canceled, and the knighthood and council were dismissed.

A great many people had gathered in the homage hall of Ortenburg castle for the giving of oaths, after which the elector sat for the meal. But because Pentecost was approaching, he did not partake in the traditional feasting. In 1733 Pentecost Sunday (Whitsun) fell on May 24. On this day, which always was celebrated as a *Galla-Tag* (gala day, special celebration) in the Dresden Catholic court church, indulgence (*Ablaß*) was given. In annual editions of the *Hof- und Staats-Calender*, this notice is published below the *Galla-Tage* lists:

> (NB. Es ist zu *observiren*, daß alle heilige Zeiten, als Ostern, Weynachten, Neu-Jahrs Tag, Pfingsten, das grosse Neue-Jahr, allezeit Galla ist, wie auch das Frohn-Leichs-nams-Fest.)

> (NB: It is to be observed that all holy times, such as Easter, Christmas, New Year's Day, Pentecost, the Great New Year, are always held in Galla, as is also the feast of Corpus Christi.)

At the end of the same page a second instruction always is given:

> Wo in dem Gregorianischen Calender bey einem Tage † stehet, da ist zu mercken, daß an solchem Tage in der Königl. Catholischen Hof-Capelle vollkommener Ablaß ist.

> Where, in the Gregorian Calendar a † stands next to a day, it is to be noted that on such a day a complete indulgence [is given in] the royal Catholic court church.[66]

The *Hof- und Staats-Calender* reported that on Thursday, May 21, Friedrich August II left Bautzen at 5:00 a.m. to return to Dresden.[67]

The elector's final *Erbhuldigung* visit was to Freiberg.[68] The *Hof- und Staats-Calender* reveals that he originally had planned to go there on June 3 but then changed the date to June 9. The reason for this becomes clear in the annual Jesuit letter from Dresden to Rome: the elector wished to be in Dresden for the Corpus Christi (Theophoria) procession on June 4, which the Jesuits reported as giving particular spiritual comfort:

> Cui successit peculiari Singulorum solatio Theophoriae Octava quotidianis Litaniis de SSo Eucharistico Sacramento decantatis devotionem teneriorem terminavit. Festum ipsum hoc praecipuum censet maximè ac solemne, quòd intrà Capellam processum

---

66. These observances must have given Saxon Lutherans cause for concern, since Luther's Reformation began as a protest against Catholic theology and the practice of indulgences.

67. HStCal 1735, sig. H2v.

68. HStCal 1735, sig. H2v.

instituerit ad quatuor Stationes Aula comitante longè celeberrimum, non absque frequentiore populi multitudine ingentique aedificationis exemplo.[69]

The octave of Theophoria followed, which gave particular spiritual comfort. Daily litanies of the Eucharistic Sacrament were sung. This feast is the one that he [the elector] considers to be the most important and solemn, as he has instituted by far the most impressive procession to the four stations within the chapel. The court accompanies the procession with a large number of people present: the effect is highly edifying.[70]

On June 8 the elector finally left for Freiberg. On the following day the homage sermon was given at 7:00 a.m. in Freiberg's great cathedral, where many of his Lutheran ancestors are interred. The report of his activity for that day begins only at 10:00 a.m., when it is stated that he left his room to go to the homage hall. On June 10 he visited the silver mines and returned to Dresden in time for the conclusion of the Corpus Christi octave on the following day, when the *Diarium Missionis* of the Dresden Jesuits noted that royal music was heard in the Catholic court church. Perhaps Zelenka's *Missa Eucharistica* (zwv 15, dated "1733") was composed for this octave?

As to the question of whether or not a presentation of Bach's Kyrie and Gloria bwv 232[I] took place at the *Erbhuldigung* service in Leipzig's Nicolai Church, it could be concluded that Bach would have composed the work in the previous week for performance on April 21, 1733. The fact that the Kyrie has a reduced instrumentation suggests that a performance of the Kyrie alone (without the Gloria) was a distinct possibility. Two factors support these speculations. The first concerns the order of service for the Bautzen homage service held in 1681 for Saxon Elector Johann Georg III. The instructions for this service read:

Im Nahmen Jesu

Alß S.r Churfürstl. Durchl. zu Sachßen, Herzog *Johann Georg der dritte*, am 24. Febr. / 6 Martÿ die Huldigung zu Budißin einnahm, wurde vorher der Gottesdienst mit Orgelschlagen, Singen und Predigen folgender gestalt gehalten, und zwar hierzu umb 7. Uhr eingelautet: So bald nun S.r Churfürstl. Durchl. in die Kirche kam, wurde angefangen zu singen.

When His Electoral Serene Highness of Saxony, Duke *Johann Georg III*, accepted the oath of allegiance in Bautzen on February 24 / March 6, the church service held at 7:00 began with organ playing, singing, and preaching; the order was as follows: as soon as His Electoral Serene Highness arrived at the church, the singing commenced.

---

69. arsi, Boh. 150, 27–28.

70. Religious processions in the open air had been prohibited by August II. By 1733 the Corpus Christi procession took place between four altars in the Catholic court church.

1. Vater Unser im Himmelreich
2. *Kyrie. Figuraliter musici*ret, und das *Gloria* von dem Altar *intonirt,*
3. Allein Gott in der Höh sey Ehr
4. *Collecta.* Allmächtigen Herr Gott, ein Beschützer alle die, und abgelesen das 23. Capitel an die Römer.
5. Nun lob mein Seel den Herren.
6. Wurde abgelesen der 20.ste Psalm.
7. *Motet: Psalm:* 20.
8. Wir glauben all an einen Gott.
9. Predigt. Und vor dem Vater Unser: Es woll uns Gott genädig seyn.
10. Herr Gott Dich loben wir.
11. Danck. *Collecta* und Seegen.
12. Verleih uns Frieden gnädiglich.[71]

Thus, the basis of at least one Lutheran homage service during the *Erbhuldigung* ceremony in Bautzen in 1681 included organ playing and performance of a figural setting of the Kyrie during the period of mourning for the predecessor. This was followed by the pastor intoning the incipit *Gloria in excelsis Deo*, but instead of the choir continuing with *Et in terra pax*, the congregation sang *Allein Gott in der Höh sei Ehr.*[72]

The second factor relates to the great length of Bach's Kyrie I, a setting that takes at least nine to ten minutes to perform. This is far longer than the usual performance times of Kyrie I settings from the collection of Dresden's Catholic court church. Thus Kyrie I alone might have been heard as a single item within the order of homage service in the Nicolai Church, and if so, this could perhaps explain the duration of Bach's setting.

On November 19, 1736, the title Bach had hoped for was received, and from 1738 "Bach, Joh. Seb. : Kirchen Compositeur *Tit.*" was listed close to the top of the membership of "Die Königl. Capelle und Cammer-Musique" published in the *Hof- und Staats-Calender*. His name was preceded only by the administrative director of the *Hofkapelle*, Herr Heinrich August von Breitenbauch, *Capell-Meister* Hasse, *Poet* Stefano Pallavicini, and church composers (*Kirchen Composit[eurs]*) Jan Dismas Zelenka and Tobias Butz. The petition Bach submitted with the Missa was among the many pleas

---

71. D-Dla, 10006 OHMA, D, Nr. 4, *Kurfürst Johann Georg III, Erbhuldigung, 1681: Actus der Erb-Huldigung der Stände der Marggrafft und OberLausitz zu Budißin 1681*, fols. 165a–174a, at 173b–174a.

72. When the 1733 liturgical order is compared with the earlier order of 1681 a notable omission becomes apparent. The 1681 liturgy called for the singing of *Herr Gott dich loben wir*, Luther's distinctive vernacular version of the Te Deum, sung antiphonally by choir and congregation, which on such occasions would also have been accompanied by trumpets and timpani. The 1733 order omits it in favor of Luther's biconfessionally neutral version of Psalm 67, *Es wolle uns Gott genädig sein*. Interestingly, in Bautzen the day before the *Erbhuldigung* service, Zelenka directed a concerted setting of the Latin Te Deum in the presence of the new elector.

presented to the new elector from musicians of the Dresden court.[73] There is no sign that the 1733 Dresden set of parts were used for performance. Nor is the work entered among the collection of music held by the Dresden *Hofkirche* that was cataloged after the Seven Years' War by Johann Georg Schürer in 1765. The earliest known listing of these materials is found as an entry into the incomplete inventory believed to have been of Maria Josepha's collection.[74] Under the title "Musica di Chiesa di varii Autore" Bach's Missa is the opening listing: "1. Missa â 18 voc.—Bach."[75] The work subsequently was entered into the catalog of Maria Josepha's husband, August III.[76] It then went into the music catalog of their grandson Saxon Elector Friedrich August III (King Friedrich August I of Saxony from 1807 until 1827).[77] Thus, for generations, Bach's offering remained in the personal collections of Saxony's ruling family. Today Bach's Missa is a highly prized holding among the many musical treasures of the Sächsische Landesbibliothek—Staats- und Universitätsbibliothek, Dresden.[78]

The accession of Friedrich August as Saxon elector in 1733 required the public pomp and circumstance of the *Erbhuldigung* ceremonies in prominent Saxon cities. The liturgical context within which this was done required that there should be appropriate music of sufficient gravity. Such was Bach's Missa (BWV 232[I]), which may have graced the ceremony in the St. Nicholas Church in Leipzig, a work that bridged the confessional divide between Catholic and Lutheran. It was a divide nevertheless, as Saxons had to acknowledge that the new elector, though personally a Catholic, was nominally head of the Lutheran Church, a reality that the new elector seems to have made emphatic in Bautzen by ensuring that he remained in the Catholic chancel of the biconfessional cathedral.

73. Petitions from Dresden musicians, dancers, and actors presented to the Dresden court are held in D-Dla, 10026 Geh. Kab., Loc. 383/1, *Varia, Das Theater, die Italienische Oper, die musicalische Capella und die Musik betreffend 1680–1784*.

74. Incomplete catalog of the music collection of Maria Josepha, without title: MS. D-Dl, Bibl.-Arch. III Hb 787c. The title page and opening sections of this inventory now are missing. Until her death Maria Josepha took ultimate responsibility for the collection of music of the Catholic court church.

75. The sacred works listed below the entry of Bach's Missa are "Missa a 4—Putz" (Tobias Buz [or Butz], a composition student of Zelenka and church composer to the Dresden court); "Oratorio Dio sul Sinai—Kelleri" (Fortunato Chelleri); "Litanias de Oᵐ Sanctis—Zelenka"; "Missa à 5—[Francesco] Feo"; "Missa à 5—[Francesco Nicola] Fago"; "Missa à 5—Sarri" (Domenico Sarro); "Missa Mortuorum—[Antonio] Lotti"; "Maria Santissima de'dolorè, Principe d'Ardore" (Don Giacomo Francesco Milano).

76. "Catalogo della Musica, e de'Libretti di S. M. Augusto III," D-Dl, Bibl.-Arch. III Hb 787h.

77. "Catalogo della Musica, e de'Libretti de S. M. Augusto III. la quale si trova nella Bibliotecca [*sic*] Musicale Friedrich August III," D-Dl, Bibl.-Arch. III Hb 787i.

78. D-Dl, Mus. 2405-D-21.

Bach's *Christmas Oratorio* and the Mystical Theology of Bernard of Clairvaux

Markus Rathey

The first part of Johann Sebastian Bach's *Christmas Oratorio* culminates in a setting of the Lutheran hymn stanza "Ach mein herzliebes Jesulein" (Oh, my beloved little Jesus). The lines of the four-part setting are interrupted by fanfares from the trumpets and drums, which contrast markedly with the calm vocal sections. The sonic contrast in the closing stanza of part 1 of the oratorio brings together the two major theological themes of this first section: the royal office of Christ, symbolized by the regal trumpets, and the mystical union between the believer and Jesus, expressed in the words of the hymn.[1] Even though the words and the melody were written by Martin Luther and are part of the popular Christmas hymn *Vom Himmel hoch, da komm ich her*, the text of this particular stanza seems closer to a more modern form of piety that emphasizes an emotional response to the biblical narrative of the birth of Christ. The text of the hymn asks the "beloved little Jesus" to make his bed in the heart of the believer, suggesting a degree of intimacy with the divine son that is not present in the biblical story.

Later generations of scholars and listeners had problems with the multilayered and multifaceted character of the libretto for the oratorio. The biblical text is repeatedly interrupted by reflective poetry in recitatives, arias, and hymn stanzas. These interpolated texts oscillate between topics such as the mystical unity between bride and bridegroom, the longing of the believer for the coming of Christ, death, and the final Day of Judgment. Performances of the oratorio in the early nineteenth century often

---

1. For a more detailed discussion of these different facets of the *Christmas Oratorio*, see Markus Rathey, *Johann Sebastian Bach's "Christmas Oratorio": Music, Theology, Culture* (New York: Oxford University Press, 2016), 80–82. All translations of texts from Bach's *Christmas Oratorio* are based on Michael Marissen's translation in *Bach's Oratorios: The Parallel German–English Texts, with Annotations* (New York: Oxford University Press, 2008). Translations of theological sources from the seventeenth and eighteenth centuries are my own unless indicated otherwise.

made significant cuts that emphasized the biblical story by eliminating what seemed to be baroque digressions from the actual plot.[2] Some interpreters have occasionally explained the different textual layers in the libretto (and in Bach's music) as an amalgamation of different theological traditions—Lutheran orthodoxy and Pietism. In his study of the *Christmas Oratorio*, Ignace Bossuyt suggests that orthodox Lutheran thought influenced the use of the unaltered biblical text in the oratorio, while the emotional arias and recitatives exhibited influences of the Pietist movement. While Bossuyt concedes that Bach himself was not a Pietist, "this did not, however, prevent the occasional appearance of Pietistic concepts in some texts, as, for instance, in the symbolism of the bride and bridegroom (representing the soul and Christ), with their fervent longing to be united, and the intimate, loving and emotionally-charged relationship with Jesus found particularly in some of the chorales of Paul Gerhardt, the so-called 'Ich-Lieder,' texts written in the first person . . . and other free texts."[3]

Pietism, Orthodoxy, and Mystical Language

It is beyond the scope of this essay to provide a detailed discussion of the differences (and connections) between Lutheran orthodoxy and Pietism in early eighteenth-century Germany. In short, Pietism was a reform movement within the Lutheran Church (with equivalent movements in other branches of Protestantism) that "sought to bring reformation to the Reformation . . . [by promoting] a practical Christianity marked by personal transformation, programs for social betterment, hopes for Christ's kingdom on earth, and calls for an end to denominational strife. Born-again laypeople . . . became agents of their own spirituality, meeting in non-church settings to pray, read and discuss the Bible, and to encourage one another in their faith."[4] The Pietist movement often made use of the intimate language Bossuyt describes because it helped emphasize Pietism's focus on the individual and her relationship with God; however, what is now often identified as "Pietist language" was also employed by other religious camps, including Lutheran orthodox theologians. One example mentioned above by Bossuyt is the poet Paul Gerhardt (1607–76). While Gerhardt's religious poetry is highly emotional and strikes a very individualistic tone, the poet was a staunch Lutheran and would probably have objected to any characterization of his work as diverging from Lutheran doctrine and tradition.

2. See Rathey, *Bach's Christmas Oratorio*, 384–86.

3. Ignace Bossuyt, *Johann Sebastian Bach: "Christmas Oratorio" (BWV 248)*, trans. Stratton Bull (Leuven: Leuven University Press, 2004), 31.

4. For examples of other movements, see the contribution of Mark Noll to this volume. The quote is from Douglas H. Shantz, *An Introduction to German Pietism: Protestant Renewal at the Dawn of Modern Europe* (Baltimore, MD: Johns Hopkins University Press, 2013), 1.

This is not to single out Bossuyt and his interpretation of the theological profile of Bach's *Christmas Oratorio*. Rather, he follows an older trend of historical scholarship that constructed a strict dichotomy between Pietist and orthodox theologies, depicting Pietism as emotional and orthodox Lutheranism as "intellectually rigid and spiritually dead."[5] More recently, scholars of Protestant church history have increasingly questioned this view.[6] Johann Anselm Steiger summarizes: "The old Protestant Orthodoxy has been seriously neglected in scholarly research right up to the present day [1996], so that between the investigation of the Reformation period and of Pietism there yawns a huge gulf. One still frequently hears the sparrows singing from the rooftops the old scholarly caricatures: Protestant Orthodoxy was stubbornly dogmatic and dead and placed little value on piety and the ministry."[7]

Just as the branch of Lutheran orthodoxy in which Bach grew up and lived did in fact value piety, it also did not leave the field of emotional language to the Pietist movement alone. In fact, both religious camps tapped into the same well of theological metaphors, which predated them both.[8] In a recent study on Martin Luther's theological roots, the German church historian Volker Leppin begins his introduction with the question, "Am Anfang war . . . Luther?" (In the beginning was . . . Luther?) and ends with the provocative statement, "Am Anfang war: die Mystik" (In the beginning was: mysticism).[9]

---

5. Shantz, *German Pietism*, 38.

6. An interpretation of Bach's *Christmas Oratorio* that takes these recent changes in the interpretation of Lutheran mysticism into account is the introduction in Meinrad Walter, *Johann Sebastian Bach—"Weihnachtsoratorium"* (Kassel: Bärenreiter, 2006).

7. Johann Anselm Steiger, "Einleitung," in *Melancholie, Diätetik und Trost: Konzepte der Melancholie-Therapie im 16. und 17. Jahrhundert* (Heidelberg: Manutius, 1996); English translation cited after Shantz, *German Pietism*, 38.

8. In his dissertation from 1958, theologian and musician Wolfgang Herbst demonstrated the impact of medieval mysticism on Lutheran orthodox theology and on Johann Sebastian Bach in particular. Since the dissertation was only published as a typescript, the study remained mostly unnoticed by Bach scholars. See Herbst, "Johann Sebastian Bach und die lutherische Mystik" (PhD diss., Friedrich-Alexander-Universität Erlangen, 1958). For a comprehensive overview on Bach and the mysticism reception of seventeenth-century Lutheranism, see Elke Axmacher, "Mystik und Orthodoxie im Luthertum der Bachzeit?," in *Theologische Bachforschung heute: Dokumentation und Bibliographie der Internationalen Arbeitsgemeinschaft für Theologische Bachforschung, 1976–1996*, ed. Renate Steiger (Berlin: Galda & Wilch, 1998), 215–36.

9. Volker Leppin, *Die fremde Reformation: Luthers mystische Wurzeln* (Munich: Beck, 2017), 9–10. A short English summary of Leppin's observations is available in Leppin's articles "Luther's Roots in Monastic-Mystical Piety" and "Luther's Transformation of Medieval Thought: Discontinuity and Continuity," in *The Oxford Handbook of Martin Luther's Theology*, ed. Robert Kolb, Irene Dingel, and L'Ubomír Batka (Oxford: Oxford University Press, 2014), 49–61, 115–24.

Lutheran theology in the seventeenth and eighteenth centuries, in both the orthodox and Pietist camps, borrowed language from medieval mystical theologians such as Bernard of Clairvaux (1090–1153), Johannes Tauler (ca. 1300–1361), and others.[10] While interest in these theologians intensified in the early seventeenth century, Martin Luther's theology and devotional language had already been influenced by their work. The Reformation was not only a break with medieval traditions but also, to some degree, a reinterpretation and reevaluation of those traditions. As Leppin shows, especially Luther's early theology was influenced by mystical writers, and the Reformer particularly valued Bernard's interpretation of the Song of Songs and the image of bride and bridegroom, which is essential to Bernard's theology of mystical unity.[11] Luther also held fourteenth-century theologian and preacher Johannes Tauler in high esteem and edited the anonymous *Theologia Deutsch*, a mystical text from the fourteenth century, to which he added his own preface.[12] Lutheran theologians in the seventeenth and eighteenth centuries even tried to co-opt Bernard as a proto-Lutheran. An example is a theological dissertation by Annaberg superintendent Georg Heinrich Goetze published in Leipzig in 1701 with the title *De Lutheranismo D. Bernhardi*.[13] Leipzig professor Jacob Thomasius even stated in 1682 in his *Historisches Spruch-Buch* that Bernard of Clairvaux had been in some regards "a good Lutheran."[14]

10. For a short overview of Luther's Bernard reception, see Theo M. M. A. C. Bell, "Luther's Reception of Bernard of Clairvaux," *Concordia Theological Quarterly* 59 (1995): 245–77. For a more extensive study, see Franz Posset, *Pater Bernhardus: Martin Luther and Bernard of Clairvaux* (Kalamazoo: Cistercian Publications, 1999). While Posset's book is a valuable resource, he often glosses over the differences between Luther's and Bernard's theologies and makes the medieval theologian appear more "Lutheran" than he actually was. On Tauler, see the fundamental study by Steven E. Ozment, *Homo Spiritualis: A Comparative Study of the Anthropology of Johannes Tauler, Jean Gerson and Martin Luther (1509–1516) in the Context of Their Theological Thought* (Leiden: Brill, 1969).

11. Bernard summarizes programmatically his interpretation of the Song of Songs in the first sermon of his cycle on this biblical book: "And so, divinely inspired, he [Solomon] sang the praises of Christ and the Church, of the gift of holy love and the mystery of eternal union with God. And at the same time he expressed the longing of the holy soul, its wedding song; and exulting in the Spirit, he composed a joyful song" (Bernard of Clairvaux, *Selected Works*, trans. and foreword by G. R. Evans [New York: Paulist Press, 1987], 213). On Bernard's theology, see Leppin, *Die fremde Reformation*, 47.

12. Leppin, *Die fremde Reformation*, 39–43.

13. Georg Heinrich Goetze, *De Lutheranismo D. Bernhardi, schediasma theologicum: In conventu ordinario, qvu Annaeanus dicitur . . . ad d. XXVII. Julii anno MDCCI. exhibitum . . .* (Dresden: Miethen, 1701).

14. "Man wird aber hin und wieder dergleichen Erzehlungen und Sprüche mehr von und aus *Bernhardo* finden / daraus herhellet / daß er in diesem Stück gut Lutherisch gewesen" (One can occasionally find stories or phrases from and about Bernard that make clear that he was a good Lutheran in this regard [i.e., his theology of repentance]) (Jacob Thomasius and Johann Christoph Meelführer, *Historisches Spruch-Buch / Darinnen Hundert vornehme Sprüche aus Gottes Wort Alten und Neuen Testaments mit schönen Historien zu mercken anmuthig gemacht . . .* [Leipzig: Lanckisch und Scholvien, 1682], 384).

Numerous Lutheran theologians in the sixteenth, seventeenth, and eighteenth centuries shared this appreciation of Bernard and Tauler.[15] Not only did some of their theological ideas influence Lutheran theology and hymnody,[16] but poetic texts from this tradition found their way into devotional books as well. Most influential were two extensive poems that were at some point attributed to Bernard himself: the hymn *Jesu dulcis memoria*, a meditation on the sweetness of Jesus, and the *Oratio rhythmica* "*Membra Jesu Nostri*," a meditation on the limbs of the crucified Christ. While it is known today that neither of the texts was written by Bernard directly, both preserve Bernardian thinking and reflect his mystical theology.[17] Both texts became popular in the Latin original but also (and even more) in German translations. *Jesu dulcis memoria* was frequently set to music by Protestant and Catholic composers in the seventeenth century, among them Heinrich Schütz, Johann Rudolph Ahle, and Samuel Capricornus.[18] The most important setting of the meditation *Membra Jesu Nostri* is, of course, Dietrich Buxtehude's composition with the same name (BuxWV 75). The seventeenth-century poet and theologian Paul Gerhardt furnished a popular German rendition of the poem. While most of the poem is not in use anymore, the meditation on the head of the suffering Christ became one of Gerhardt's most cherished hymns,

15. Bernard's impact on sixteenth-century theology is mediated through several channels. Luther himself was familiar with Bernard's writings; but Bernard's mystical theology also influenced a new form of piety in the fourteenth century, the *devotio moderna* around Dutch theologian Geert Groote and his *Brüder des gemeinsamen Lebens* (Brethren of the common life). The important mystical text by Thomas à Kempis (1380–1471), *The Imitation of Christ*, grew out of this movement, and Luther's own mentor, Johann von Staupitz (1460–1524), had been strongly influenced by the *devotio moderna* as well.

16. Two of the most prominent examples are Philipp Nicolai's hymns *Wie schön leuchtet der Morgenstern* and *Wachet auf, ruft uns die Stimme*, published in 1599. Both hymns make extensive use of Bernardian ideas of intimacy and devotion. In Bach's chorale cantatas based on Nicolai's hymns (BWV 140 and 1, respectively) these aspects are even further developed and expanded.

17. The *Oratio rhythmica* was written by thirteenth-century Cistercian abbot Arnulf of Leuven, while the author of *Jesu dulcis memoria* is still unknown. Mary E. Frandsen has explored how medieval devotional texts were used and set to music at the electoral court in Dresden during the seventeenth century. Her findings reflect the general use of these texts in Protestant Germany; see Frandsen, *Crossing Confessional Boundaries: The Patronage of Italian Sacred Music in Seventeenth-Century Dresden* (New York: Oxford University Press, 2006), 101–71.

18. See the series of articles by Werner Braun on the reception of this text: "'Jesu dulcis memoria' in Tonsatzreihen zwischen 1600 und 1650: Katholische Autoren," in *Mittelalter und Mittelalterrezeption: Festschrift für Wolf Frobenius*, ed. Herbert Schneider (Hildesheim: Olms, 2005), 173–90; and "'Jesu dulcis memoria' in Tonsatzreihen zwischen 1600 und 1650: Evangelische Autoren," *Jahrbuch für Liturgik und Hymnologie* 44 (2005): 163–73. For Heinrich Schütz's settings in particular, see Markus Rathey, "Christoph Kittels Bearbeitung von Schütz' 'O süßer Jesu Christ' (SWV 427)—Funktion und Anspruch," *Schütz-Jahrbuch* 28 (2006): 141–55.

O Haupt voll Blut und Wunden (O sacred head, now wounded), the famous "Passion Chorale" Bach used several times in his *St. Matthew Passion* (BWV 244).

Unio Mystica

The popularity of these two texts in seventeenth-century Lutheranism are only the most visible signs of the continuing presence of mystical (and especially Bernardian) thinking in early modern Protestantism.[19] When the text of the alto aria in the *Christmas Oratorio*, "Bereite dich Zion," asks Zion to ready herself for "the Most Handsome, the Most Beloved," it is the Bernardian understanding of the Song of Songs that provides the theological basis for this view of the arrival of Jesus. The same applies when the "Daughter Zion" and the "Believers" engage in a dialogue at the beginning of the *St. Matthew Passion* to welcome the bridegroom (Jesus), who is about to suffer as the sacrificial lamb.[20]

While Luther had already appreciated Bernard's theology, it was the early seventeenth-century theologian Johann Arndt who borrowed most heavily from his medieval predecessor.[21] Arndt's influence on the development of Lutheran devotion in the seventeenth and early eighteenth centuries cannot be overestimated. His *Von wahrem Christenthumb* (translated into English as *True Christianity*), first published in 1605 and later reissued and expanded, was the most important and influential devotional text for more than a century and a half—indeed, Bach owned a copy of this work.[22]

---

19. Susan McClary is probably too pessimistic when she states that "Bernard's moment had passed" and that it required a new "wave of mystics" in the sixteenth and seventeenth centuries to emphasize the "direct spiritual and even quasi-physical contact with Jesus" (*Desire and Pleasure in Seventeenth-Century Music* [Berkeley: University of California Press, 2012], 134–35). An early revival of Bernardian piety can also be seen in the *devotio moderna* of the fourteenth and fifteenth centuries; from there it had a direct impact on Luther and the Catholic Reformation in the sixteenth century. In fact, McClary's perceptive analysis of Heinrich Schütz's *Anima mea liquefacta est* from 1629 (ibid., 148–58) could easily be supplemented with theological sources by Protestant theologians such as Johann Arndt and Johann Gerhard, among others.

20. For the impact of Bernardian piety and the theology of love in the *St. Matthew Passion*, see Markus Rathey, *Bach's Major Vocal Works: Music, Drama, Liturgy* (New Haven, CT: Yale University Press, 2016), 107–37.

21. See Johannes Wallmann, "Johann Arndt und die protestantische Frömmigkeit: Zur Rezeption der mittelalterlichen Mystik im Luthertum," in *Frömmigkeit in der Frühen Neuzeit: Studien zur religiösen Literatur des 17. Jahrhunderts in Deutschland*, ed. Dieter Breuer (Amsterdam: Rodopi, 1984), 50–74.

22. Excerpts from Arndt's voluminous book have been published in Johann Arndt, *True Christianity*, trans. Peter Erb (New York: Paulist Press, 1979); see especially the fifth book, devoted to the unity of bride and bridegroom in mystical thinking (241–72).

Church historian Martin Brecht calls Arndt aptly "the most influential Lutheran since the Reformation."[23]

One aspect Arndt borrowed from Bernard is the strong emphasis on the love of Christ and the intimate relationship between Christ and the believer, both of which Bernard had especially developed in his *Sermons on the Song of Songs*. The following passage is paradigmatic of Arndt's focus on divine love: "It is not knowledge that makes the Christian but the love of Christ. . . . The scholarly study of the Scriptures without love and a holy Christian life is simply worthless."[24] While Arndt criticized practices in contemporary Lutheran theology, he remained firmly within a Lutheran framework by tying the demand for divine love and a Christian life to the Lutheran theology of scripture.

The influence of Bernard of Clairvaux is especially present in Johann Arndt's *Paradiesgärtlein*, a devotional book published in 1612 and often bound together with his *Von wahrem Christenthumb*.[25] Arndt explores the theological ramifications of Bernard's Jesus-centered mysticism and the longing of the soul for the heavenly bridegroom. The goal, both for Bernard and for Arndt and his followers, was the unification with Christ, the *unio mystica*.

Arndt was occasionally criticized for promoting "Catholic" ideas, and in 1620 he published a treatise that reiterated that, in his view, the idea of mystical unity had to be related to the Lutheran theology of scripture, summarized by the term *sola scriptura*. In his *De Unione Credentium cum Christo Capite Ecclesiae* (About the union of the believers with Christ, head of the church), Arndt demonstrates that his views are in complete accordance with Lutheran dogma. Arndt published in the same year a German translation, which, although it was originally written as an apologetic text and for an academic audience, was subsequently incorporated into his *Von wahrem Christenthumb*, thus becoming an integral part of the canon of Protestant devotional literature in the seventeenth century. In these writings, Arndt argues that the goal of human life is unification with God but that this unification was mediated through God's word (the Bible) and the sacraments: "In the word and in the holy sacraments is laid down the true memory of the name of God. That is why he is unified with us through the word and the sacrament; which was confirmed by the Savior through the

23. Martin Brecht, "Das Aufkommen der neuen Frömmigkeitsbewegung in Deutschland," in *Der Pietismus vom siebzehnten bis zum frühen achtzehnten Jahrhundert*, Geschichte des Pietismus, vol. 1, ed. Martin Brecht (Göttingen: Vandenhoeck und Ruprecht, 1993), 150.

24. Arndt, *Von wahrem Christenthumb* (1605); English translation cited after Shantz, *German Pietism*, 27.

25. See Ferdinand van Ingen, "Die Wiederaufnahme der Devotio Moderna bei Johann Arndt und Philipp von Zesen," in *Religion und Religiosität im Zeitalter des Barock*, 2 vols., ed. Dieter Breuer (Wiesbaden: Harrassowitz, 1995), 2:474.

beautiful and lovely saying: He who loves me will keep my word and my father will love him and we will come to him and dwell with him (John 14:13)."[26] Arndt explores this idea further, employing the image of a wedding and of a bride and bridegroom. While this idea has scriptural roots (Ephesians 5:32), it was particularly influenced by Bernard of Clairvaux's reading of the Song of Songs:

> The unification of the Lord Christ with the faithful soul is caused by the spiritual marriage and wedding. When the bridegroom arrives, the holy soul [*Seele*] is happy and pays exact and diligent attention to his presence as his joyful, heart-refreshing, and holy arrival drives away darkness and night. The heart has sweet joy, the soul melts for love, the spirit is full of joy, the affects and desires turn fervent, the love is ignited, the soul [*Gemüt*] rejoices, the mouth praises and extols and utters vows, and all the powers of the soul [*Seele*] rejoice in and because of the bridegroom. She [the soul] is full of joy, so I say, because she has found the one who loves her and because he has taken her as a bride. She honors him. O what love! O what burning desire! O what conversations full of love! O what a chaste kiss, when the Holy Spirit descends, when the consoler overshadows, when the highest illuminates, when the word of the father is there, when Wisdom talks truth, and when love embraces her warmly.[27]

In other words, while the mystical union, the *unio mystica*, is the goal, it cannot be accomplished by human activity, like devout contemplation; instead, it is mediated through the church, which administers the sacraments and interprets the word of God.

---

26. "Im Wort aber und H. Sacramenten ist das rechte Gedächtniß des Namens GOttes gestiftet. Darum wird er auch durch das Wort und Sacrament mit uns vereiniget. Welches unser Heyland mit dem schönen und lieblichen Spruch bekräftiget: Wer mich liebet, der wird mein Wort halten, und mein Vatter wird ihn lieben, und wir werden zu ihm kommen und Wohnung bey ihm machen[,] Joh. 14,13" (Johann Arndt, *Sechs Bücher vom Wahren Christenthum . . . Nebst dessen [Arndt's] Paradieß-Gärtlein* [Altdorff: Zobel, 1735], 634 [= book 5, chap. 3, § 3]).

27. "Durch die geistliche Ehe und Vermählung geschiehet die Vereinigung des HErrn Christi mit der gläubigen Seele. [/] Wenn der Bräutigam kommt, so freuet sich die H. Seele, und giebt genaue und fleißige Achtung auf seine Gegenwart; denn durch seine fröhliche, Herz-erquickende und H. ankunft vertreibet er die Finsterniß und die Nacht. Das Herz hat süsse Freude, es fliessen die Wasser der Andacht, die Seele schmelzet vor Liebe, der Geist freuet sich, die Affecten und Begierden werden inbrünstig, die Liebe wird entzündet, das Gemüth jauchzet, der Mund lobet und preiset, und thut Gelübde, und alle Kräfte der Seelen freuen sich in und wegen des Bräutigams. Sie freuet sich, sage ich, daß sie den gefunden hat, welcher sie liebet, und daß der sie zur Braut auf- und angenommen, welchen sie ehret. O welche Liebe! O welch ein feuriges Verlangen! O welche liebreiche Gespräche! O wie ein keuscher Kuß, wann der H. Geist herab kommt, wann der Tröster überschattet, wann der Höchste erleuchtet, wann das Wort des Vatters da ist, die Weißheit redet, und die Liebe freundlich sie umfänget" (ibid., 641–42 [= book 5, chap. 7, § 1]). On Bernard's reading of the Song of Songs, see E. Ann Matter, *The Voice of My Beloved: The Song of Songs in Western Medieval Christianity* (Philadelphia: University of Pennsylvania Press, 1990).

The chorale stanza "Wie soll ich dich empfangen," written by seventeenth-century poet and theologian Paul Gerhardt and incorporated into the opening section of Bach's *Christmas Oratorio*, exemplified this connection between divine indwelling and the word of God evoking the image of the "torch," which was a common metaphor for the word of God (referring to Psalm 119:105, "Your word is a lamp for my feet"):[28]

Wie soll ich dich empfangen	How shall I receive you,
Und wie begegn' ich dir,	And how shall I meet you,
O aller Welt Verlangen,	O desire of all the world
O meiner Seelen Zier?	O ornament of my soul?
O Jesu, Jesu setze	O Jesus; Jesus, set
Mir selbst die Fackel bei,	The torch next to me yourself,
Damit, was dich ergötze,	So that whatever brings you enjoyment
Mir kund und wissend sei.	May be manifest and known to me.

Lutheran orthodox theologians such as Johann Andreas Quenstedt (1617–88) could thus embrace the idea of divine love and mystical unity within a framework of Lutheran theology and ecclesiology. Quenstedt summarizes the widely accepted view in his *Theologia Didactico-Polemica*, published in the year of Johann Sebastian Bach's birth:

> The mystic unification of the faithful with God is an act of active grace by the Holy Spirit through which the substance of the justified and believing man (both his soul and his body) is unified with the substance of the most Holy Trinity and the body [flesh] of Christ, mediated through faith, which was ignited by the word (in particular the gospel) and the use of the holy sacraments; [this unification] is true, real, and most close, but also unmixed, unlocal, and without spatial extension for the very purpose that God, after consummation of this spiritual community, may be known and continuously present and that he may cause holy actions; the believers, however, who are joined with God and their savior for the glory of the divine majesty, can be sure of the life-giving power and all blessings of Christ, the most present grace, and the fatherly love that are granted through this community; and they can remain in the state of God's children and the unity of faith and love, together with the other parts of the mystical body, and be blessed forever.[29]

---

28. See, for instance, Marissen, *Bach's Oratorios*, 5n8.

29. "Unitio fidelium cum DEO mystica est actus gratiae Spiritus S. applicatricis, quo substantia hominum justificatorum atque fidelium anima & corpore substantiae SS. Trinitatis, & carnis Christi, mediante fide, verbo imprimis Evangelii & Sacramentorum usu accensa, vere, realiter & arctissime, impermixtibiliter tamen, illocaliter & incircumscriptive conjungitur, ut facta spirituali communicatione, DEus familiariter & constanter praesens sancta operetur; Fideles autem DEO & Redemptori suo ad gloriam Majestatis divinae conjuncti, per mutuam immanentiam vivificae facultatis & omnium

This emphasis on the unity between Christ, the bridegroom, and the believer, the bride, in Lutheran theology explains the presence of these ideas at the beginning of the *Christmas Oratorio*.[30] The third and fourth movements, an accompagnato recitative and the subsequent aria, describe waiting for the Savior with metaphors of spousal affection and love.[31] In the accompagnato recitative, the alto proclaims, "Nun will mein liebster Bräutigam" (Now will my most beloved bridegroom), and the following aria advises Zion (here the church) to ready herself for the arrival of Christ, the bridegroom, who is, as the text states, the most handsome and most beloved.[32] The following chorale stanza, "Wie soll ich dich empfangen," continues this train of thought and anchors the idea even more in a Lutheran theology of scripture.

In the fourth part of the *Christmas Oratorio*, Bach composes two interesting movements for soprano and bass that further explore the ardent love of the bride for the bridegroom.[33] These recitatives (nos. 38 and 40) frame the famous echo aria "Flößt, mein Heiland." The movements are formally chorale tropes in which the soprano sings a hymn text (with Bach's own melody) while the bass sings a recitative with a

---

Christi beneficiorum participes facti, de praesentissima gratia, amoreque paterno & subsecutura gloria certiores redditi in statu filiorum DEI atque unitate fidei & charitatis, cum reliquis corporis mystici membris perseverent, aeternumque salventur" (Johannes Andreas Quenstedt, *Theologia Didactico-Polemica, sive Systema Theologicum, in Duas Seciones, Didacticam et Polemicam, Divisum* [Wittenberg: Quenstedt und Schumacher, 1685], 3:622v). Cf. Karsten Lehmkühler, *Inhabitatio: Die Einwohnung Gottes im Menschen* (Göttingen: Vandenhoeck und Ruprecht, 2004), 153–54.

30. The strong emphasis on an emotional relationship between Christ and the believer had its counterpart in an increasing interest in the emotional qualities of music in the seventeenth century and the numerous attempts to grapple with the emotional power of music from a scientific perspective. See Daniel Garber, "Disciplining Feeling: The Seventeenth-Century Idea of a Mathematical Theory of the Emotions," in *Structures of Feeling in Seventeenth-Century Cultural Expression*, ed. Susan McClary (Toronto: University of Toronto Press, 2013), 19–34; see in the same collection of essays the reception of some of these theories: Penelope Gouk, "Clockwork or Musical Instrument? Some English Theories of Mid-Body Interaction before and after Descartes," 35–59.

31. For a broader overview of bridal imagery in Bach's vocal works, see Lucia Haselböck, *Du hast mir mein Herz genommen: Sinnbilder und Mystik im Vokalwerk von Johann Sebastian Bach* (Vienna: Herder, 1989), 164–78.

32. For a thorough study of concepts of mystical love and the influence of medieval mysticism in seventeenth- and eighteenth-century Lutheranism, see Isabella van Elferen, *Mystical Love in the German Baroque: Theology, Poetry, Music* (Lanham, MD: Scarecrow, 2009).

33. The relationship between these movements and Lutheran mysticism has also been discussed by Walter Blankenburg, "Mystik in der Musik J. S. Bachs," in *Theologische Bach-Studien I*, ed. Walter Blankenburg and Renate Steiger (Stuttgart: Hänssler, 1987), 47–66.

different text;[34] however, the combination of soprano and bass is also typical of Bach's love duets. In addition, abundant use of voice leading in parallel motion further evokes stylistic characteristics of baroque love duets.[35] In the following excerpt from the libretto, the text of the hymn is printed in bold letters:

Jesu, du mein liebstes Leben,	**Jesus, you, my most beloved life,**
Meiner Seelen Bräutigam,	**My soul's bridegroom,**
Komm! Ich will dich mit Lust umfassen,	Come! With delight I will embrace you,
Mein Herze soll dich nimmer lassen.	My heart shall never leave you.

Bach's setting (example 1) captures the emotional tone of the text through a dense texture combined with parallel voice leading and occasional expressive chromatic progressions. The train of thought is continued in recitative no. 40, which again invokes the ardent desire for the presence of Christ in the human heart:

Wohlan, dein Name soll allein	Well then, your name alone shall
In meinem Herzen sein.	Be in my heart!
. . . .	. . . .
So will ich dich entzücket nennen,	These are what I, in a trance, will call you,
Wenn Brust und Herz zu dir vor	When [my] breast and heart burn in love
Liebe brennen.	for you.

We can see how this idea relates back to the first part of the *Christmas Oratorio*, where the alto urges Zion to welcome the beloved bridegroom. It also points forward to the final hymn setting of part 1, where the text asks the believers to prepare their hearts for the coming of Christ and to make the heart a manger for the newborn Son of God.

Bernard of Clairvaux's theology of mystical unity appears here as the underlying idea for the interpretation of the Christmas narrative. The believer has awaited the coming of Christ, the bridegroom, ardently. When he finally arrives in the manger in Bethlehem, she opens her heart and lets him enter.

The Threefold Coming of Christ

While Bernard's theology of divine love may explain some of the images in the text of the *Christmas Oratorio*, the influence of Bernardian theology (and its later reception in Lutheran theology) goes even deeper and has, as we will see, even an impact on the

---

34. For a discussion of this movement, see Markus Rathey, "Drama and Discourse: The Form and Function of Chorale Tropes in Bach's Oratorios," in *Bach Perspectives*, vol. 8, *J. S. Bach and the Oratorio Tradition*, ed. Daniel R. Melamed (Urbana: University of Illinois Press, 2010), 59–62.

35. See George Stauffer, *The Mass in B Minor: The Great Catholic Mass* (New Haven, CT: Yale University Press, 2003), 57.

Example 1. J. S. Bach, *Christmas Oratorio*, bwv 248[IV]/38, mm. 10–13.

structure of the oratorio. Mystical unity is the result of divine presence in the human heart. For Bernard and other theologians, however, this is only one of the ways in which Christ manifests his presence in the world. Indeed, Bernard differentiates between three modes of Christ's presence, which form a sequence in salvation history.[36] He explains that Christ comes three times: the first time he came to gather and save the lost (see Luke 19:10), which constitutes the incarnation and historical birth of Jesus.

36. See Jean Leclercq, *St. Bernard et l'esprit cistercien*, 3rd ed. (Paris: Éditions du Seuil, 1975), 30.

The second time he comes not in incarnate form but spiritually into the heart of the believer. Bernard stresses that those who love God, obey his word, and prepare their hearts for his presence will be rewarded with Christ's entrance into their hearts.[37] This second coming is what is commonly described by the idea of *unio mystica*, the mystical presence of Christ in the believer's heart. Finally, Christ will come on the Day of Judgment at the end of times. As Ulrich Knöpf has shown, the framework of a threefold coming of Christ forms the basis for Bernard's concept of salvation history, in which the personal encounter with Christ represents the center of his theology of salvation.[38] While the historical events of Christ's first and last comings are important, their immediate existential relevance is only revealed through his mystical and spiritual presence in the believer's heart.

The idea of a threefold coming of Christ can be found in the writings of other mystical theologians as well. In a sermon for Christmas, Johannes Tauler applies a similar framework. However, he differentiates between an inner-Trinitarian "birth," Christ's incarnation, and the culmination in the *unio mystica*. The return of Christ at the end of times is, at least in this Christmas sermon, not part of Tauler's framework:

> Today Holy Christendom commemorates a threefold birth, which should so glad-den and delight the heart that, enraptured with joyful love and jubilation, we should soar upward with sheer gratitude and bliss. . . . The first birth, and the most sublime, is that in which the Heavenly Father begets His Son within the divine Essence, yet distinct in Person. The second birth we commemorate is that of maternal fruitfulness brought about in virginal chastity and true purity. The third birth is effected when God is born within a just soul every day and every hour truly and spiritually, by grace and out of love.[39]

While Tauler's threefold structure makes room for the Johannine idea of Christ's presence with the Father since the beginning of the world, Bernard's concept of the threefold coming of Christ focuses more on the modes of human encounter with the divine: in his historical incarnation, his spiritual presence, and his return for judgment. It was Bernard's and not Tauler's framework that was adopted by Luther and later Lutheran theologians. Already in his first lectures on the Psalms from 1514, Martin Luther applied a threefold framework to his interpretation of divine presence, sum-

---

37. Cf. Michael Stickelbroeck, *Mysterium Venerandum: Der trinitarische Gedanke im Werk des Bernhard von Claixvaux* (Münster: Aschendorf, 1994), 246.

38. Ulrich Köpf, *Religiöse Erfahrung in der Theologie Bernhards von Clairvaux* (Tübingen: Mohr Sie-beck, 1980), 228; Köpf refers to Bernard's important Advent sermon "In adventu Domini" (in Migne, *Patrologia Latina*, [Opera omnia] S. Bernardi abbatis primi Clarae-Vallensis opera omnia, accurante Jacques Paul Migne, Patrologia Latina, vol. 183 [Turnhout: Brepols, 1995; reprint of the edition Paris, 1854], 35–56).

39. Johannes Tauler, *Sermons*, trans. Maria Shrady (New York: Paulist Press, 1985), 35.

marized in the formula "Triplex est adventus eius" (His advent is threefold). Luther differentiated between the incarnation, an *adventus spiritualis* (coming in the spirit), and Christ's return at the end of times.[40]

Lutheran theologians in the sixteenth, seventeenth, and early eighteenth centuries adopted this view in their dogmatic treatises and devotional texts. Even the structure of the *Schemelli Gesangbuch*, for which Bach provided several settings (and probably some melodies) in 1736, follows this sequence when the hymns for the beginning of the ecclesiastical year appear in the following categories:

6. Von Christi Zukunft ins Fleisch	6. About the coming of Christ into the flesh
7. Von der Geburt JEsu Christi	7. About the birth of Jesus Christ
8. Von Christi Zukunft ins Herz	8. About the coming of Christ into the heart
9. Von Christi Zukunft zum Gericht	9. About the coming of Christ for judgment[41]

The threefold coming of Christ, while agreed upon among most theologians of the time, appears in different terminologies. The Lutheran theologian Joachim Lohner differentiates in 1586 between an *adventus redemptionis* (coming for redemption), an *adventus sanctificationis* (coming for sanctification), and an *adventus judicii* (coming for judgment).[42] A generation later, Conrad Dieterich used a similar framework. While his terminology differs from that of Lohner, the underlying concept is essentially the same: an *adventus carnis* (coming in the flesh), an *adventus mentis sive gratiae* (coming in the spirit or in grace), and an *adventus majestatis sive gloriae* (coming in majesty or in glory).[43] Not only do the two theologians apply the same framework as Bernard, but both reference the medieval mystic as a source in the margins of their texts. These references show that even in times of massive denominational conflict, Lutheran theologians were free to refer to Bernard of Clairvaux as a source and justification for theological concepts.[44]

40. Martin Luther, *Dictata super Psalterium*, 1513–16, WA 4: 344; cf. Renate Steiger, *Gnadengegenwart: Johann Sebastian Bach im Kontext lutherischer Orthodoxie und Frömmigkeit* (Stuttgart: Frommann-Holzboog, 2002), xvii; see also Ulrich Asendorf, *Heiliger Geist und Rechtfertigung* (Göttingen: Vandenhoeck und Ruprecht, 2004), 201.

41. *Musicalisches Gesang-Buch herausgegeben von George Christian Schemelli . . .* (Leipzig: Breitkopf, 1736; facsimile, Hildesheim: Olms, 1975), Erstes Register [no pagination; following p. 654].

42. Joachim Lohner, *Methodicae Dispositiones Evangeliorum Dominicalium* (n.p., 1586), fol. B 2.

43. Conrad Dieterich, *Analysis evangeliorum dominicalium* (Leipzig: Schurer, 1630), 7.

44. Cf. Elke Axmacher, "Die dreifache Zukunft des Herrn: Wie soll ich dich empfangen?," in *Johann Arndt und Paul Gerhardt: Studien zur Theologie, Frömmigkeit und geistlichen Dichtung* (Tübingen: Francke, 2001), 95.

While Lohner and Dieterich wrote their works for an academic audience, the idea of a threefold coming also appears in seventeenth-century sermons. Johann Gerhard (1582–1637), one of the most influential Lutheran theologians in the first half of the seventeenth century and who was also closely connected to Johann Arndt, reminded the congregation in a sermon for the first Sunday in Advent of the three ways in which Christ comes into the world:

> The first is the coming of Christ **in the flesh**, as he took on human nature when the time was fulfilled. . . . The other coming is the **spiritual coming**, as the Lord Christ offers us through the word grace and wants to begin in our hearts his kingdom of grace. . . . The third coming is now the coming **for judgment**, as He will come at the end of the world with great power and glory in the clouds, to judge the living and the dead. . . . These are the three kinds of the coming of Christ; the first has already passed, the other one still happens daily, the third still has come to pass. The first one leads to the second, as Christ has become man and has in his assumed manhood done the work of salvation so that he may distribute such blessings through the word and that he may assemble a church. The second one leads to the third, since we do believe in Christ and serve him in his kingdom of grace so that we can stand the judgment at his last coming and be accepted into his kingdom of glory.[45]

Here Gerhard outlines the three modes of Christ's coming in salvation history. He emphasizes that the second coming is the present and existential realization of the first coming and the precondition of the third. As we have discussed earlier in connection with Arndt's view of *unio mystica*, Gerhard also emphasizes that the second coming of Christ is mediated through the Word of God and through the Church and not as an

---

45. "Erstlich ist die Zukunft Christi **ins Fleisch**, wie Er nämlich in die Fülle der Zeit wahre menschliche Natur angenommen . . . Die andere Zukunft ist die **geistliche Zukunft**, da nemlich der HErr Christus durchs Wort uns seine Gnade anbeut und in unsern Herzen sein Gnadenreich anfangen will. . . . Die dritte Zukunft ist nun **zum Gericht,** da Er nemlich einmal am Ende der Welt kommen wird mit großer Kraft und Herrlichkeit in den Wolken des Himmels zu richten die Lebendigen und die Todten. . . . Dieß sind die dreierlei Arten der Zukunft Christi, der erste ist vergangen, die ander geschieht noch täglich, die dritte ist noch zu gewarten. Die erste siehet auf die andere, denn darum ist Christus Mensch geworden und hat in seiner angenommenen Menschheit das Werk der Erlösung verrichtet, auf daß Er solche Wohlthaten durchs Wort austheile und ihm eine Kirche sammle. Die andere siehet auf die dritte, denn darum glauben wir an Christum und dienen ihm in seinem Gnadenreich, auf daß wir einmal in der letzten Zukunft Christi zum Gericht vor ihm bestehen mögen und ins Reich der Herrlichkeit aufgenommen werden" (Johann Gerhard, *Postille das ist die Auslegung und Erklärung der sonntäglichen und vornehmsten Fest-Evangelien über das ganze Jahr . . . Nach den Original-Ausgaben von 1613 und 1616. Vermehrt durch die Zusätze der Ausgabe von 1663* [Berlin: Schlawitz, 1870], 1:11–12).

independent divine revelation. Gerhard and other contemporary theologians called this dwelling in the heart *inhabitatio* (indwelling) or used the German term *Gnadengegenwart*, a concept that has its roots in the theology of Bernard of Clairvaux.[46] Bach used the term *Gnadengegenwart* in a marginal note in his copy of the Calov Bible, which demonstrates that he was aware of both the term and the theological concept.[47]

Johann Sebastian Bach was familiar with writings by Johann Arndt, Johann Gerhard, and other Lutheran orthodox theologians from the seventeenth and eighteenth centuries. Furthermore, the doctrine of the threefold coming of Christ was still very much present in the theological discourse of his time.[48] An example that demonstrates the concept's presence in devotional literature of the early eighteenth century is a small book by Hamburg theologian Johann Joachim Neudorf (169?–1752). In his book for schoolchildren published in 1727, Neudorf explains the meaning of Advent, Christmas, and New Year's Day in a sequence of questions and answers that structurally resembles contemporary catechisms and schoolbooks.[49] Additionally, Neudorf included poems and hymns to help explain the theological concepts to the young boys. While Bach would probably not have been familiar with Neudorf's text, most of this supplemental material has direct connections to Bach's own devotional environment. Neudorf included texts by Benjamin Schmolck (1672–1737) and Erdmann Neumeister (1671–1756). In addition, he used prayers from the *Leipziger Kirchenstaat*, a devotional and prayer book published in 1710 for visitors in Leipzig that was still an important source for the liturgical practices in Leipzig in Bach's time. Like his predecessors, Neudorf differentiates between three modes of Christ's coming:

46. The idea of Christ's indwelling, or *inhabitatio*, can be found in numerous theological treatises and devotional books in the seventeenth and eighteenth centuries. An instructive example is Georg Serpilius, *Gloria, Pax Et Alleluja. Das ist: Gott geheiligte Sing- Und Früh-Stunden: Welche auß dem Geistreichen Psalm / Lob-Gesang und Lieblichen Advents-Liede: Gott sey danck durch alle Welt . . . Nach der Dreyfachen Zukunfft Christi angestellet* (Regensburg: Seidel und Hanckwitz, 1697). Serpilius's book is a collection of hymn sermons based on the Advent hymn *Gott sei Dank durch alle Welt*, which is interpreted according to the doctrine of the threefold coming of Christ.

47. Cf. Steiger, *Gnadengegenwart*, 243; see also Walter Wallmann's review of Steiger's study in *Pietismus und Neuzeit* 29 (2003): 327–32.

48. Eric Chafe has recently shown that the doctrine of Christ's *inhabitatio* has also influenced Bach's Weimar cantata *Erschallet, ihr Lieder, erklinget, ihr Saiten!* BWV 172; see *Tears into Wine: J. S. Bach's Cantata 21 in Its Musical and Theological Contexts* (New York: Oxford University Press, 2015), 529–67.

49. Johann Joachim Neudorf, *Christlicher Unterricht, für die Jugend, wie die H. Advents-Zeit, das H. Christ-Fest und das Neue Jahr GOttgefällig zu feyren sey*, preface by Erdmann Neumeistern (Hamburg: Kißner, [1727]).

1. Into the flesh (or for our salvation); this one has passed.
2. Into our hearts (for our sanctification); this one is the present [mode] (or happens daily)
3. For the [Final] Judgment; this one lies in the future.[50]

We can immediately recognize the structure developed by Bernard and used by Luther and others. Like Bernard and Gerhard, Neudorf emphasizes that the second, spiritual coming is central and that the two other advents of Christ depend upon it. Also important is that this second coming is mediated through words and sacraments, in other words, the church: "Without the second advent neither the first nor the third [advent] would save anyone. Therefore, one has to thankfully begin this new ecclesiastical year during this advent and remember that God comes to us through the word and the holy sacraments."[51] Not only is the presence of Christ a dogmatic statement, but Neudorf adds that the dwelling of Christ in the human heart provides consolation in times of distress and guides the believer from fear to happiness and joy:

> What is the purpose of this coming? The blessed indwelling of Christ and, through this, also of the Father and the Holy Spirit in us, as the highest happiness is in such a unification of the Trinitarian God with the faithful man. . . . How can we draw consolation from this indwelling when we suffer? Where God dwells, there he consoles the spirit of those who suffer. . . . This indwelling will not end with death but is eternal, and only in eternity will the glory of this unification [between Christ and man] be revealed.[52]

The same themes also appear in the libretto for the *Christmas Oratorio*. We have already explored the central importance of the second coming of Christ as the bridegroom for the interpretation of the Christmas narrative. We also find references to suffering and consolation in the text for the oratorio. For instance, the text of recitative 38 states,

---

50. "1. Ins Fleisch, (oder zu unserer Erlösung,) die ist vergangen. 2. In unsere Hertzen, (zu unserer Heiligung,) die ist gegenwärtig, (oder geschicht täglich.) 3. Zum Gericht, die ist zukünftig" (Neudorf, *Christlicher Unterricht*, 5).

51. "Ohne die andere Zukunft würde uns weder die erste, noch die dritte, heilsam seyn. Dahero man eben bey dieser Advents-Zeit das neue Kirchen-Jahr mit danckbarer Erkenntlichkeit solcher hohen Wohlthat billig anfangen soll, daß GOtt noch durchs Wort, und die heiligen Sacramente, zu uns kommt" (ibid., 7).

52. "Welches ist der Nutz dieser Zukunft? Die seelige Einwohnung Christi, und, um dessen willen, auch des Vaters und Heiligen Geistes, in uns: Als in welcher Vereinigung des Dreyeinigen GOttes mit den gläubigen Menschen dieser ihre höchste Glückseligkeit besteht. . . . Wie können wir uns dieser Einwohnung im Leiden getrösten? Wo GOtt wohnet, da tröstet er den Geist der Leidenden . . . Diese Einwohnung wird auch durch den zeitlichen Tod nicht getrennet, sondern bleibet ewig, und in der Ewigkeit soll erst die Herrlichkeit dieser Vereinigung offenbahr werden" (ibid., 21–24).

"Auch im Sterben sollst du mir das Allerliebste sein; in Not Gefahr und Ungemach" (Even in dying shall you be to me the most beloved of all; in need, danger, and affliction). While for a modern listener the reference to death and suffering seems to be out of place in a Christmas piece, it fits well into the theological framework provided by Neudorf and others.

The libretto for the *Christmas Oratorio* can even be read as the story of Christ's coming into the believer's heart. In part 1, the faithful soul asks Zion to prepare herself for the arrival of the bridegroom. In part 3, the text for the alto aria "Schliesse, mein Herze" urges the heart to embrace and welcome Christ. And finally, in the terzetto in part 5, the alto confidently testifies to the presence of Christ, "Er ist schon würklich hier" (He really is already here), while tenor and soprano still ponder when the time of his arrival will come. It is noteworthy that Bach sets these three pieces for alto, the voice that, as Ernst Koch has shown, was often used by Bach and other composers to symbolize the soul of the faithful believer.[53] In other words, the alto movements in particular reflect the idea of mystical unity and the second coming of Christ in the *Christmas Oratorio*.

Finally, the threefold coming of Christ provides the larger framework for the libretto of Bach's *Christmas Oratorio*. The first coming is narrated in the biblical sections, which tell the story of Jesus's birth in Bethlehem. In addition, several movements relate the second coming of Christ into the human heart, often by using the bride-and-bridegroom imagery from the Song of Songs. References to the third coming appear for the first time in the hymn setting in part 2, *Brich an, du schönes Morgenlicht*: "Dazu den Satan zwingen / und letztlich Frieden bringen" ([Shall] vanquish Satan, too, / and finally bring peace). A similar soteriological perspective is present in the hymn stanza "Ich will dich mit Fleiß bewahren" from the third part of the oratorio:

Dir will ich abfahren,	To you will I retreat;
Mit dir will ich endlich schweben	With you will I at last hover,
Voller Freud	Full of joy,
Ohne Zeit	Time no longer,
Dort im andern Leben.	There in the afterlife.

The third coming is confirmed in the closing movement of the oratorio, a festive hymn setting with interpolated trumpet fanfares:

Nun seid ihr wohl gerochen	Now you all are well avenged
An eurer Feinde Schar,	Of your band of enemies,

---

53. Ernst Koch, "Die Stimme des Heiligen Geistes: Theologische Hintergründe der solistischen Altpartien in der Kirchenmusik Johann Sebastian Bachs," BJ 81 (1995): 61–81.

Denn Christus hat zerbrochen,	For Christ has broken apart
Was euch zuwider war.	What was against you.
Tod, Teufel, Sünd und Hölle	Death, devil, sin, and hell
Sind ganz und gar geschwächt;	Are completely diminished;
Bei Gott hat seine Stelle	The human family
Das menschliche Geschlecht.	Has its place by God.

Thus, the text of the *Christmas Oratorio* follows the doctrine of the threefold coming of Christ in a loose way. The beginning of the oratorio focuses on the historical event and its implication for *unio mystica*. Christ appears as the beloved bridegroom, and the text expresses the believer's longing for both his historical and his spiritual presence. Just as Bernard highlighted and later theologians reiterated, the focus here is also on the current presence of Christ in the believer's heart. However, toward the end of the oratorio, the focus shifts more and more to the return of Christ at the end of times, when he will defeat "death, devil, sin, and hell."

In the Beginning Was: Bernard

Lutheran theology in the seventeenth and early eighteenth centuries was deeply influenced by older traditions that were rooted in the mystical theology of Bernard of Clairvaux, Johannes Tauler, and others. Martin Luther's appreciation for mysticism shaped his theology, and the application of mystical thought only increased during the seventeenth century with theologians such as Johann Arndt and Johann Gerhard. While Arndt's writings influenced the development of the Pietist movement in the second half of the seventeenth century, they were also frequently read by orthodox Lutherans. Indeed, Arndt himself ensured that his theological beliefs were in line with Lutheran orthodoxy. This orthodox Lutheran alignment is particularly clear in the way that Arndt links the idea of Christ's mystical presence to the Lutheran paradigm of *sola scriptura*.

Just as the second coming of Christ had been central to Bernard's concept of salvation history, it is also the central and recurring theme in the libretto for Bach's *Christmas Oratorio*. Bach's composition reflects the libretto in numerous ways. The solo movements for alto trace the stages of the second coming from expectation to fulfillment. The two chorale tropes in part 4 of the oratorio highlight the emotionality that accompanies the presence of Christ in that they employ harmonious voice leading between the soprano and bass, the two voices that commonly feature in Bach's love duets.

Bach might not have been aware to what degree the basic ideas of his oratorio were indebted to the medieval theologian; even Bach's anonymous librettist might not have noticed the parallels between his libretto and the ideas developed by Bernard of Clairvaux. However, the frequent references to Bernard in theological treatises from the sixteenth and seventeenth centuries that dealt with the threefold coming of Christ (Lohner, Dieterich) show that Lutheran theologians were well aware of the origin of these ideas. Furthermore, Johann Arndt in his devotional books does not hide the fact that he was deeply indebted to the theology of Bernard of Clairvaux. If Bach read Arndt's *Von wahrem Christenthumb*, he might have noticed some of these similarities between Bernardian theology and the text of the *Christmas Oratorio*.

Bach and his librettist created the *Christmas Oratorio* as a piece for the Lutheran liturgy in Leipzig. The six parts were to be performed during the Christmas season 1734–35. The theology of the oratorio is Lutheran theology as it would have been sanctioned by the Lutheran orthodox theologians at Thomas Church and the faculty of theology at Leipzig University. The central idea of the libretto is already expressed in the Lutheran hymn stanza that closes part 1, "Ach mein herzliebes Jesulein." The following movements expand upon this idea of Christ's presence in the human heart. These subsequent sections borrow language and images from the Song of Songs, from Luther's writings, and not least from a theologian esteemed by Luther and Arndt—the medieval mystic and theologian Bernard of Clairvaux. To paraphrase Leppin's assessment: in the beginning was: mysticism; in the beginning was: Bernard.

The Church under Persecution

Bach's Cantatas for the Fourth
Sunday after Epiphany

Derek Stauff

At key points in the liturgical year, early modern Lutheran worshipers heard confessional polemics and warnings about persecution, past and present. Lutherans of Bach's age worried about persecution from rival confessions. Although Luther's Reformation had met with early successes, by 1600 Catholic Reform had begun to reverse many Protestant gains in central Europe. Persecution against Protestants, as Thomas A. Brady Jr. has noted, "became far more systematic and purposeful among the Catholics," in part because Catholics had a uniform program of reform and the advantages of better political and ecclesiastical organization.[1] Even during Bach's lifetime, Lutherans still feared that their Catholic rivals would subvert the legal and political agreements that normally kept religious strife in check. European Protestants of the late seventeenth and early eighteenth centuries, according to Joachim Whaley, sensed renewed persecution directed against them.[2]

These fears could be reawakened on Sundays and during feast-day worship through gospel and epistle readings that allowed preachers to bring up the topic in their sermons; congregants would sing hymns long associated with religious persecution; and composers and their librettists raised the issue in their music. Cantatas for some of these occasions, such as Reformation celebrations, are already well known.[3] Confessional

1. Thomas A. Brady Jr., "Limits of Religious Violence in Early Modern Europe," in *Religion und Gewalt: Konflikte, Rituale, Deutungen (1500–1800)*, ed. Kaspar von Greyerz, Kim Siebenhüner, et al. (Göttingen: Vandenhoeck und Ruprecht, 2006), 137–38. On the avoidance of the term "Counter-Reformation" in this volume, see the preface.

2. Joachim Whaley, "The Return of Confessional Politics?," in *Germany and the Holy Roman Empire*, 2 vols. (Oxford: Oxford University Press, 2012), 2:151.

3. On Bach's role in various Reformation festivals, see NBA I/31, KB (*Kantaten zum Reformationsfest und zur Orgelweihe*, ed. Frieder Rempp); Alfred Dürr, *The Cantatas of J. S. Bach with Their Librettos in German-English Parallel Text*, rev. and trans. Richard D. P. Jones (Oxford: Oxford University Press, 2005), 707–14; Robin A. Leaver, "The Libretto of Bach's 'Cantata No. 79': A Conjecture," BACH 6,

polemics in cantatas for other points in the calendar, however, are easier to miss. Their significance depends on listeners having a strong background in Lutheran theology and history. Often the language of persecution is couched in metaphors. In addition, modern commentators, consciously or not, have usually stressed the most broadly inclusive and nonsectarian interpretations of Bach's cantatas, ignoring the ways his texts and music tried to separate Lutherans from rival confessions and creeds.[4] In their early modern religious context, though, cantatas for these overlooked Sundays kindled their listeners' fears of confessional unrest and persecution.[5] Most often, congregants were told that their opponents had long sought to wipe out the Lutheran church, and they were admonished to remain steadfast against impending persecution. As such, these cantatas show how eighteenth-century music could solidify loyalty to Lutheranism at the expense of competing confessions.

Cantatas for the fourth Sunday after Epiphany by J. S. Bach and his contemporaries offer a good case study. This Sunday became a place where composers and their librettists reminded listeners of the kinds of persecution that the Lutheran church had already suffered and would, in their view, continue to suffer. In fact, many of the words and images found in cantatas for this Sunday make sense only when understood against early modern Lutheran writings on persecution.

We currently know of just three cantatas that Bach performed on the fourth Sunday after Epiphany. All performances date from his Leipzig period (see table 1). The number is so few because the historical evidence is sparse and because the fourth Sunday after Epiphany did not occur every year. Sometimes it coincided with and was superseded by the Feast of the Purification of Mary.[6] If Easter fell early, the fourth

---

no. 1 (1975): 3–11; Leaver, "Bachs Motetten und das Reformationsfest," in *Bach als Ausleger der Bibel: Theologische und musikwissenschaftliche Studien zum Werk Johann Sebastian Bach*, ed. Martin Petzoldt (Göttingen: Vandenhoeck und Ruprecht, 1985), 33–47.

4. For the Sunday under consideration here, two recent commentators, Martin Petzoldt and John Eliot Gardiner, can serve as examples. Both offer credible exegesis of Bach's cantatas and the gospel passages to which they relate, both base their examination on theological writings of Bach's age, and yet both arrive at relatively abstract, spiritualized, or universalized points. These points certainly mirror strains of early modern Lutheran theology but are still incomplete. See Martin Petzoldt, *Bach-Kommentar* (Stuttgart: Internationale Bachakademie, 2007–), 2:503–25, esp. 507; John Eliot Gardiner, *Bach: Music in the Castle of Heaven* (New York: Knopf, 2013), 309–10.

5. Michael Marissen has recently pointed to Quasimodogeniti and Exaudi as Sundays when librettists raise the topic of actual and metaphorical Jews persecuting Christians; see *Bach & God* (New York: Oxford University Press, 2016), chap. 4.

6. When this happened in Leipzig in 1727, Bach performed cantatas wholly related to the Purification of Mary (BWV 82 and possibly BWV 83). Elsewhere in Lutheran Germany the practice differed during this same year. Frankfurt celebrated the fourth Sunday after Epiphany, performing Telemann's

Table 1. Cantatas Performed by Bach on the Fourth Sunday after Epiphany

Year	Cantata	Comments
1724	*Jesus schläft, was soll ich hoffen?* (BWV 81)	First performance[1]
1726	Johann Ludwig Bach, *Gott ist unser Zuversicht* (JLB 1)	Composed ca. 1714–15[2]
1735	*Wär Gott nicht mit uns diese Zeit* (BWV 14)	First performance

Source: This repertoire can be gleaned from Andreas Glöckner, ed., *Kalendarium zur Lebensgeschichte Johann Sebastian Bachs*, expanded new edition, Edition Bach-Archiv Leipzig (Stuttgart: Carus; Leipzig: Evangelische Verlagsanstalt, 2008).

1. Ulrich Leisinger has pointed to evidence that Bach performed this cantata again, though the date has not been determined. NBA I/6, KB 121.
2. Konrad Küster, "Die Frankfurter und Leipziger Überlieferung der Kantaten Johann Ludwig Bachs," *Bach-Jahrbuch* 75 (1989): 65.

Sunday after Epiphany would be omitted entirely. This happened in 1725, Bach's second year in Leipzig. As a result, his second cantata cycle initially lacked a cantata for this Sunday. Not until 1735 did Bach fill in this gap, writing the chorale cantata *Wär Gott nicht mit uns diese Zeit* (BWV 14). Bach's repertoire for this Sunday also included the cantata *Gott ist unser Zuversicht* by his Meiningen cousin Johann Ludwig Bach.

The Church Allegorized
Cantatas for the fourth Sunday after Epiphany become polemical, first, by bringing to mind the Christian church under duress. Listeners in Bach's age were used to hearing allegorical representations of the church in cantatas and oratorios, sometimes made explicit by librettos where the speakers are labeled.[7] Even when the church was not explicitly named, listeners could be cued in other ways, most notably by referencing passages from the Bible commonly understood typologically to be about the church.[8]

cantata *Herr, die Wasserströme erheben sich* (TWV 1:737), but in Hamburg, Telemann himself performed a cantata for the Purification of Mary, *Der Gerechten Seelen* (TWV 1:248).

7. A famous example, albeit confessionally unmarked, opens Bach's *St. Matthew Passion*: Daughter Zion, represented by the first chorus, calls out to her daughters, that is, believers, who are urged to join in lament over Christ's suffering and death. As Michael Marissen has pointed out, the libretto presents all of these characters—the Daughter Zion, her daughters, and the believers—as metaphors for the church; see *Bach's Oratorios: The Parallel German–English Texts, with Annotations* (New York: Oxford University Press, 2008), 29n1.

8. See Daniel J. Treier, "Typology," in *Dictionary for Theological Interpretation of the Bible*, ed. Kevin J. Vanhoozer (Grand Rapids: Baker, 2005), 823–27; J. Blenkinsopp, "Type and Antitype," in *The New Catholic Encyclopedia*, 2nd ed. (Detroit: Thomson/Gale, 2003), 14:254–55; for the current discussion, the terms "allegorical" and "typological" are used interchangeably.

I label such passages as ecclesial. A long-standing tradition encouraged Lutherans to view places in both the New Testament and Hebrew scriptures this way.[9] These interpretations were not limited to elite theologians: a broad range of Lutheran-approved writings—everything from commentaries and sermons to hymnals—apply them.[10] Christians throughout the centuries might have been drawn to these passages in part because the language is more vivid than the doctrinal statements on the church found in the New Testament. Such passages also allowed Lutherans to raise more easily the topic of religious persecution.

Bach's Cantata 14, *Wär Gott nicht mit uns diese Zeit*, is based on two biblical passages, both of which received ecclesial interpretations by early modern Lutherans. First, the cantata borrows the tune and text of Luther's chorale paraphrase of Psalm 124. (Table 2 shows the psalm in Luther's Bible translation and in his chorale paraphrase.) Like many of Bach's chorale cantatas, the opening and closing cantata movements literally quote Luther's first and last chorale stanzas along with the melody. The inner movements then paraphrase ideas from the middle stanzas without using the chorale tune.

Lutheran polemics had long put both Psalm 124 and Luther's chorale paraphrase to work because they offer God thanks for victory over enemies. For example, the Dresden court preacher Christoph Laurentius delivered a sermon on the psalm in 1632 when Saxony celebrated the first anniversary of the Battle of Breitenfeld, a major Protestant victory of the Thirty Years' War.[11] For Lutheran polemicists, it also helped that some commentators took an ecclesial view of the psalm. The first two points in Johann Arndt's summary of the psalm are:

1. About the miraculous protection and rescue of the church of God, about their enemies, and [about] all those who trust God.
2. From whence the fierce wrath and persecution against Christendom arises and against whom?[12]

9. For a discussion of several ecclesial texts commonly set to music in the seventeenth century, see Derek Stauff, "Lutheran Music and Politics during the Thirty Years' War" (PhD diss., Indiana University, 2014), chap. 2.

10. Hymnals, for instance, encourage ecclesial interpretations by placing certain hymns, particularly psalm paraphrases, under headings such as "On the Christian Church."

11. Laurentius, ΔΟΞΟΛΟΓΙΑ [*Doxologia*] *Davidica, Oder / Eine Christliche Dancksagungs-Predigt aus dem CXXIV. Psalm* (Dresden: Bergen und Krüger, 1632).

12. "1. Von dem wunderbarlichen Schutz und Errettung der Kirchen Gottes / von ihren Feinden / und aller derer / so GOtt vertrauen. 2. Woher der grimmige Zorn und Verfolgung wider die Christenheit entstehet / und wider wen?" (Johann Arndt, *Außlegung deß gantzen Psalters Davids*, vol. 2 [Lüneburg: Stern, 1699], C6r).

Table 2. Psalm 124 in Luther's Translation and Paraphrase

Ps. 124 (Luther 1545)		Luther's Paraphrase (1524)[1]	
1 Wo der HERR nicht bey vns were / So sage Jsrael.	If the Lord had not been with us, thus Israel may say.	1 Wer GOtt nicht mit vns diese zeit / So soll Israel sagen.	Were God not with us this time, / So shall Israel say,
2 Wo der HERR nicht bey vns were / Wenn die Menschen sich wider vns setzen.	If the Lord had not been with us, when men rose up against us.	Wer Gott nicht mit vns diese zeit / Wir hetten müssn verzagen. / Die so ein armes heufflein sind / Veracht von so viel Menschenkind / Die an vns setzen alle.	Were God not with us this time, / We would have been dismayed, / We wretched little band, / Despised by so many children of men, / Who all set upon us.
3 So verschlingen sie vns lebendig / Wenn jr zorn vber vns ergrimmet.	Then they would have swallowed us alive, when their wrath was kindled against us.	2 Auff vns ist so zornig jhr Sinn / Wo Gott hett das zugeben. / Verschlungen hetten sie vns hin / Mit gantzem Leib vnd Leben. / Wir wern als die ein Flut erseufft	Against us their intent is so wrathful / Had God but permitted it. / They would have devoured us / With all our life and limb. / We would have been as those drowned in a flood
4 So erseuffte vns Wasser / Strömen giengen vber vnser Seele.	Then the waters would have drowned us, the stream gone over our soul.	Vnd vber die groß Wasser leufft	And the great waters streamed over us,
5 Es giengen Wasser allzu hoch Vber vnser Seele.	The waters would have gone all too high over our soul.	Vnd mit gewalt verschwemmet.	And washed away with force.
6 Gelobet sey der HERR / Das er vns nicht gibt zum Raube in jre Zeene.	Blessed be the Lord, who has not given us as prey to their teeth.	3 Gott Lob vnd Danck der nicht zugab / Daß jhr Schlund vns möcht fangen.	Praise and thanks to God, who did not allow / Their jaws to trap us.

Table 2. Continued

	Ps. 124 (Luther 1545)	Luther's Paraphrase (1524)[1]	
Our soul has escaped as a bird from the snare of the fowler; the snare is torn and we are free.	7 Vnser Seele ist entrunnen Wie ein Vogel dem stricke des Voglers Der strick ist zurissen vnd wir sind los.	Wie ein Vogel des stricks kömpt ab Ist vnser Seel entgangen. Strick ist entzwey vnd wir sind frey	As a bird gets away from the snare, Our soul has escaped: The snare is asunder and we are free;
Our help remains in the name of the Lord, who made heaven and earth.	8 Vnser Hülffe stehet im Namen des HERRN Der Himel vnd Erden gemacht hat.	Des Herren Namen steh vns bey Des Gotts Himmels vnd Erden.	The Lord's Name stands by us, The God of heaven and earth.

1. *Gesangbuch Christlicher Psalmen und Kirchenlieder / Herrn D. Martini Lutheri / und anderer gottseligen Lehrer und frommen Christen . . . Jtzo auffs newe Revidirt / nach der Jahrzeit und Herrn Lutheri Catechismo sein ordentlich zugerichtet* (Dresden: Andreas Krüger, 1625). [VD17 12:112706H]; translations of stanzas 1 and 3 modified from Dürr, *The Cantatas of J. S. Bach*, 217.

The commentator Hieronymus Mencel described the psalm similarly: "Allegorically, we understand it as the true church of God, which is like a sheep among ravenous wolves (Matthew 10), which has against it the gates of hell, that is, Satan with all his might, along with heretics and tyrants."[13] Christoph Laurentius, too, describes the psalm as an "apt description and portrayal of the enemies of the true Christian church."[14]

These ecclesial implications carried over to Luther's chorale: some hymnbooks, like the 1713 Weimar hymnal, placed it under the category "On the Christian Church," surrounded by other well-known polemical hymns like *Erhalt uns Herr* and *Ein feste Burg*.[15] Luther's chorale was also sometimes linked to the fourth Sunday after Epiphany as a *de tempore* hymn.[16] (Because the hymn is also a psalm paraphrase, a number of hymnals, including Vopelius's 1682 Leipzig hymnal, obscure the hymn's intended use and significance by placing it under psalm-hymns.)[17] But taken together with interpretations of Psalm 124, ecclesial readings of *Wär Gott nicht mit uns diese Zeit* were common enough in the seventeenth and eighteenth centuries.

Second, Bach's librettist drew on Matthew 8:23–27, the gospel account of Jesus's calming of the sea, the reading for the fourth Sunday after Epiphany:

> [23] And he [Christ] entered into the ship, and his disciples followed him. [24] And, behold, there arose a great tempest in the sea, so that the ship was covered with the

---

13. "*Allegoricè* verstehen wirs von der rechten Kirche Gottes / die ist / wie ein schaff mitten vnter reissenden Wölffen / Matth. 10. welche die Pforten der Hellen / das ist / der Sathan mit aller seiner macht / mit ketzern vnd tyrannen wieder sich hat" (Hieronymus Mencel, *Psalterium Davids: Auslegung aller Psalmen* [Leipzig: Grosse, 1594], 702r–v).

14. "Eine artige vnd eigendliche Beschreibung vnd Abcontrafeyung der Feinde der wahren Christlichen Kirche" (Laurentius, *ΔΟΞΟΛΟΓΙΑ Davidica*, sig. D1r).

15. *Schuldiges Lob Gottes, Oder: Geistreiches Gesang-Buch* (Weimar: Mumbach, 1713), 419–20. The hymn also appears under the same heading in the following hymnals: *Gesangbuch Christlicher Psalmen und Kirchenlieder* (Dresden: Bergen und Krüger, 1625), 388–89; *Dreßdenisch Gesangbuch Christlicher Psalmen und Kirchenlieder* (Dresden: Bergen, 1656), 734–35; *Das Privilegirte Ordentliche und Vermehrte Dreßdnische Gesang-Buch* (Dresden: Eckels, 1727), 519; *Nürnbergisches Gesang-Buch* (Nürnberg: Spörlin, 1690), 878; *Neu-vermehrtes Rochlitzer Gesang-Buch* (Rochlitz: Stephan; Leipzig: Köhl, [1759]), 402. In a few other hymnals the chorale falls under similar but more generic headings: under "Von Creutz / Verfolgung" in *Geist- und Lehr-reiches Kirchen- und Hauß-Buch* (Dresden: Matthesius, 1694), no. 293; under "Religions-Gefahr" in Christian Gotthelf Blumberg, *Deliciæ Cygneæ: Das ist, Geistliche Schwanen-Lust, Oder Zwickauisches Gesang-Buch* (Zwickau: Büschel, 1703), no. 308.

16. See the Dresden hymnals of 1625, 1632, 1656, and 1727.

17. Gottfried Vopelius, *Neu Leipziger Gesangbuch* (Leipzig: Klinger, 1682); see also *Wittenbergisches Gesang-Buch* (Wittenberg: Henckel, 1673); and *Geistreiches Gesang-Buch, An D. Cornelii Beckers Psalmen und Lutherschen Kirchen-Liedern* (Dresden: Hamann, 1676).

waves: and he slept. [25] And the disciples came to him, and awoke him, and said: Lord, save us: we perish. [26] And he said to them, O ye of little faith, why are ye fearful? And he arose and rebuked the winds and the sea; then it was completely calm. [27] But the men marveled and said, What manner of man is this, that the wind and sea are obedient to him?[18]

This passage, like Psalm 124, was often given ecclesial and allegorical interpretations on two accounts: first, commentators saw the ship in which Jesus and the disciples sailed as a type prefiguring the church, and, second, the raging sea represented persecution.[19]

Luther's sermon on Matthew 8 from his 1525 *Fastenpostille* assumes an ecclesial interpretation. The spiritual meaning of the passage is that "Christ here prefigures the Christian life, especially the ministry. The ship signifies Christendom, the sea the world, the wind the devil. His disciples are the preachers and pious Christians."[20] Luther clearly links the raging sea to persecution. The sea, he claims, only became stormy when Christ's ship drew near.[21] This is an analogy for Christ and the Christian's own ministry, since faithful preaching causes persecution: "This is now the comfort of Christians, and especially of the preachers, that they should be certain and consider well that where they introduce and preach Christ, they must suffer persecution. That is how it is. And it is a very good sign that the preaching is truly Christian where they are persecuted, especially by the great saintly, learned, and wise people. And on the

---

18. "[23] VND er trat in das Schiff / vnd seine Jünger folgeten jm / [24] Vnd sihe / da erhub sich ein gros vngestüm im Meer / also / das auch das Schifflin mit Wellen bedeckt ward / Vnd er schlieff. [25] Vnd die Jünger tratten zu jm / vnd weckten jn auff / vnd sprachen / HErr / hilff vns / wir verderben. [26] Da sagt er zu jnen / Jr Kleingleubigen / Warumb seid jr so furchtsam? Vnd stund auff vnd be-drawete den Wind vnd das Meer / Da ward es gantz stille. [27] Die Menschen aber verwunderten sich / vnd sprachen / Was ist das fur ein Man / das jm Wind vnd Meer gehorsam ist?" (Martin Luther, *Biblia: Das ist: Die gantze Heilige Schrifft: Deudsch* [Wittenberg: Lufft, 1545]; English adapted from the KJV).

19. For iconography related to the subject, see Derek Stauff, "Schütz's *Saul, Saul, was verfolgst du mich?* and the Politics of the Thirty Years War," *Journal of the American Musicological Society* 69 (2016): 359–61.

20. "Es hat Christus hyrynn furgebildet das Christlich leben, sonderlich das predig ampt. Das schiff bedeutt die Christenheyt, das meer die wellt, der wind den teuffel. Seine junger sind die prediger und frumme Christen" (Martin Luther, *Fastenpostille* [1525]; WA 17/2: 107; see also LW 76: 286).

21. Abraham Calov's commentary quotes this very passage from Luther's sermon; see *Die Deutsche Biebel D. MARTIN LUTHERI. . . . Mit beyfügung der Auslegung / die in Lutheri Schrifften zu finden . . .* (Wittenberg: Schrödter und Brünning, 1681–82), vol. 5, col. 94; otherwise, Calov does not examine the typological significance of Matthew 8. The Calov Bible commentary, bibliographically in six volumes but bound as three, owned by Bach is now in the library of Concordia Seminary, St. Louis; see Robin A. Leaver, *Bachs theologische Bibliothek / Bach's Theological Library* (Stuttgart: Hänssler, 1983), 46–51, no. 1.

contrary, [the preaching] is not honest where it is praised and honored."[22] Luther's followers in the seventeenth century continued to draw similar meaning from Matthew 8. A sermon from 1633 by Christoph Megander mentions it as a place where the Bible foreshadows future persecution of the church: "We also prove *ex Scripturae typis*, from the models of Holy Divine Scripture, with what kind of troubled condition the church is prefigured. For this reason, the same is compared to a little ship with Christ's disciples inside, which floats in the greatest danger from pirates, storm winds, waves, shoals, sandbars, and the like on the violent, raging sea of this world."[23] Another sermon on Matthew 8, from 1683, specifically for the fourth Sunday after Epiphany, treats the ship typologically, as its title page reads: "*NAVICULA CHRISTI FLUCTANS ECCLESIAE TYPUS*, Christ's little ship, floating in danger on the sea as a type of the church, according to the regular gospel reading from Matthew 8:23–27."[24] The sermon's author, Johann Kemmel, a religious refugee from Hungary, dwells heavily on the metaphor of the church as ship, stressing the ship's poverty and weakness in the face of persecution. Most often he, like other writers, spoke of persecution in metaphors or in general terms, pointing to biblical or older historical examples.[25] But on occasion he mentions events within recent memory such as the Thirty Years' War and unrest in his native Hungary.[26]

22. "Das ist nu der Christen trost, sonderlich der prediger, Das sie gewiss seyn sollen und sich des erwegen, wo sie Christum furen und predigen, das sie verfolgunge müssen leyden. Da wird nicht anders aus. Und eyn recht gut zeichen ist, das die predigt recht Christlich ist, wo sie verfolget wird, sonderlich von den grossen heyligen, gelerten und klugen leutten, Widderumb nicht rechtschaffen ist, wo sie gelobt und geehret wird" (WA 17/2: 108; see also LW 76: 286).

23. "So beweisen wir auch solches *ex Scripturae typis*, aus denen Vorbilden heiliger Göttlicher Schrifft / mit welchen vns der Kirchen betrübter Zustand *adumbriret* vnd vorgebildet wird. Denn zu dem ende / vnd vmb dieser Vrsachen wird dieselbige verglichen einem Schifflein / welchs mit Christi Jüngern in höchster Gefahr / von Meerräubern / Sturmwinden / Wellen / Steinklüfften / Sandbäncken vnd dergleichen auff dem vngestümen / wüsten Meer dieser Welt daher schwimmet / Matth. 8 v. 24" (Christoph Megander, *Christi Hexameron, Christi Jesu / seiner Kirchen und Bekenner Heilige Creutz-Wochen: Von dem uber alle maß hochbetrübten Zustande derer hin und wieder im H. Röm. Reich / von freyer Religions-Ubung / außgesetzten und vertriebenen Christen* [Zwickau: Göpner, 1633], 118).

24. Johann Kemmel, *Navicula Christi Fluctuans Ecclesiae Typus, Das auf dem Meer in Gefahr schwebende Schifflein Christi / Als der Kirchen Vorbild / Nach dem ordentlichen Evangelio / aus dem* Matthaeo *am 8. v. 23–27* (Nürnberg: Spörlin, [1684]).

25. Ibid., 20.

26. Ibid., 34.

Heinrich Müller's sermon on Matthew 8 also adopts the ecclesial view: "This little ship is a lovely image of the Christian church."[27] The sea represents the godless world: "Not at all unfittingly, the world is compared to the tumultuous sea. For what the waves in the sea are, so are the godless in the world. The waves hurtle and rush horridly against the little ship, and thus the godless rage and roar against the pious children of God."[28] Müller even links the passage to contemporary persecution, though disguised by metaphors: "Even to this day, the little ship of Christ—understood [as] the Christian church—floats on the tumultuous sea of the world. There one finds many dangers. Often the danger is so great that it [the ship] begins to sink. As a result, work is required so that it might come through."[29] Two years later, August Pfeiffer's published sermon for the fourth Sunday after Epiphany repeated many of the same points.[30]

The same typology and imagery recur in eighteenth-century cantatas for the fourth Sunday after Epiphany. Erdmann Neumeister's cantata from his 1705 cycle contains explicit reference to the "church-ship" under persecution:

Das Meer der Tyranney	The sea of tyranny
Mag wüten / toben / wallen /	May storm, rage, seethe
Und auff das Kirchen-Schiff mit	And crash against the church-ship
wilden Wellen fallen	with wild waves.[31]

Another cantata libretto for the same Sunday, *Herr, die Wasserströme erheben sich* by Johann Friedrich Helbig, eventually set by Telemann (TWV 1:737), introduces similar

---

27. "Diß Schifflein ist ein schönes Vorbild der Christlichen Kirchen" (Heinrich Müller, *Evangelisches Praeservativ wider den Schaden Josephs* [Rostock: Andreae, 1681], 284). Bach owned a copy of Müller's sermons; see Leaver, *Bachs theologische Bibliothek*, 108, no. 19. John Eliot Gardiner has recently applied Müller's sermon to Bach's cantatas for the fourth Sunday after Epiphany; see *Bach: Music in the Castle of Heaven*, 309–10.

28. "Nicht gar ungleich wird die Welt einem ungestümen Meer verglichen. Dann was die Wellen im Meer / das sind die Gottlosen in der Welt. Die Wellen sausen und brausen greulich auff das Schifflein zu / so wüten und toben die Gottlosen wider die frommen Kinder GOttes" (Müller, *Evangelisches Praeservativ*, 282).

29. "Noch heut zu Tage schwimmet das Schifflein Christi auff diesem ungestümen Welt-Meer / verstehe die Christliche Kirche. Da findet sich manche Gefahr. Offt ist die Gefahr so groß / daß es beginnet zu sincken / dahero gehöret Arbeit dazu / daß es hindurch gebracht werde" (ibid., 282–83).

30. August Pfeiffer, *Evangelische Erqvick-Stunden* (1664) (Leipzig: Fritsche, 1706), esp. 1:140, 145; see Leaver, *Bachs theologische Bibliothek*, 157–59, no. 42.

31. Erdmann Neumeister, *Geistliche Cantaten, Uber alle Sonn- Fest- und Apostel-Tage* (Halle: Renger, 1705), 26.

ideas but without explicitly mentioning the church. Instead, it is alluded to as "your little ship, Lord, the poor bark" (i.e., a small boat):

Erhalte selbst bey Sturm und Krachen,	Preserve through storm and calamity
Dein Schifflein, HErr, den armen Nachen,	Your little ship, Lord, the poor bark,
Biß es erfreut in Hafen läufft.	Till it sails joyfully into port.
Wenn es um nahe Syrten schweifft,	If it swerves near sandbanks,
Der Feind auf allen Seiten streifft,	The enemy strikes on all sides,
Die Wolcken blitzen, Winde blasen,	The lightning flashes, winds blow,
Und die erzürnte Wellen rasen;	And the furious waves dash;
Reich deine Hand, die es ergreifft,	Stretch out your hand, which it [the ship] grasps,
Und in Gefahr kan sicher machen.	And can make safe in danger.
Erhalte selbst bey Sturm und Krachen,	Preserve through storm and calamity
Dein Schiflein, Herr, den armen Nachen,	Your little ship, Lord, the poor bark,
Biß es erfreut in Hafen läufft.	Till it sails joyfully into port.[32]

Just like earlier Lutheran writers, Neumeister and Helbig interpret the waves casting the ship to and fro as the raging of the church's enemies.

Although all these authors considered the ship and sea to represent Christendom and trouble, respectively, not all authors drew the same conclusions from Matthew 8. Lutherans remained sure that the winds and waves stood for various troubles, but some tended to spiritualize them, making them less about attacks by rival confessions and more about the devil, sin, sickness, and death. Heinrich Müller, especially, represents this trend, and we find no explicit confessional polemic in his sermon on Matthew 8. Preachers like Müller raise the issue of persecution solely in metaphorical terms, leaving the listener to connect them to current confessional disputes. They, like Müller, emphasize the ship's personal over its collective significance. The waves represent persecution against an individual rather than the Lutheran confession as a whole. All writers, furthermore, aimed not merely to polemicize and strike fear but to teach their readers and strengthen their faith. As a rule, Lutheran writings on persecution

---

32. The libretto comes from Helbig's *Auffmunterung zur Andacht: Oder Musicalische Texte, über Die gewöhnlichen Sonn- und Fest-Tags Evangelien* ([Eisenach]: Johann Adolph Boetius, 1720). This text is for the second of two arias that Telemann later excerpted in his *Auszug derjenigen musicalischen und auf die gewöhnlichen Evangelien gerichteten Arien* (Hamburg: Kißner, 1727). The modern edition, which includes facsimiles of the libretto from which this text excerpt comes, is Telemann, *Geistliche Arien (Druckjahrgang 1727)*, ed. Wolfgang Hirschmann and Jana Kühnrich, Musikalische Werke 57 (Kassel: Bärenreiter, 2012), LIV.

sought both to warn believers of impending troubles and to admonish them to remain steadfast to Lutheran doctrine by placing their trust in God.

Bach's Cantatas for the Fourth Sunday after Epiphany

In most cantatas for the fourth Sunday after Epiphany, including Bach's, the ecclesial interpretation remains implicit yet necessary to account for the language of persecution that saturates these works. Especially in BWV 14, the libretto cannot be understood fully without acknowledging ecclesial readings in both Matthew 8 and Psalm 124. This becomes most apparent in the cantata's middle movements, which bring up topics that would not normally come to mind in a literal reading of Matthew 8. For example, the second movement, a soprano aria, uses words like "enemy" and "tyranny," both closely linked to persecution:

Unsre Stärke heißt zu schwach,	Our strength is too weak
Unserm Feind zu widerstehen.	To withstand our enemy:
Stünd uns nicht der Höchste bei,	If the Highest did not stand by us,
Würd uns ihre Tyrannei	Their tyranny would
Bald bis an das Leben gehen.	Soon threaten our life.[33]

Topics like resisting enemies and potentially succumbing to their tyranny belong to ecclesial interpretations of the gospel passage and to Psalm 124. Moreover, this is the only place in Bach's cantatas where the word "tyranny" appears.[34] As previous commentary on Matthew 8 and Psalm 124 shows, the word was commonly linked with religious persecution.

Bach's music stresses the word "tyranny" and the dangers of persecution in several unusual ways. In particular, he adds greater musical weight to this aria's middle section, the spot where the librettist introduces these ideas, and Bach paints the words in this section with greater vividness than elsewhere. His anonymous librettist clearly designed the aria to fit the simple tripartite da capo form, and while Bach's division of the text conforms to the standard, the musical form matches the so-called modified da capo or, to adopt David Schulenberg's terminology, the through-composed da capo form (see Table 3).[35] Simply put, the aria's opening A section modulates to the dominant, and Bach must fully rewrite its return. The result is a sonata-like recapitulation entirely in the tonic. Furthermore, unlike the standard eighteenth-century da capo aria, where the

33. All texts and translations of Bach's cantata libretti are cited from Dürr, *The Cantatas of J. S. Bach*.

34. The word also appears in stanza 6 of the hymn/aria *Jesus, unser Trost und Leben* (BWV 475), from the *Schemelli-Gesangbuch*. Here the reference is to death's tyranny undone by Jesus's death.

35. David Schulenberg, "Modifying the Da Capo? Through-Composed Arias in Vocal Works by Bach and Other Composers," *Eighteenth-Century Music* 8, no. 1 (2011): 21–51.

Table 3. The Structure of BWV 14/2 (*Unser Stärcke heißt zu schwach*)

Section	A			B			A'		
Measures	1	21	44	47	71	78	94	98	117
(text)	Rit.	Solo (a)	Rit.	Solo (b)	Rit.	Solo (b)	Rit.	Solo (a)	Rit.
Key	I	I → V	V	V → ii	ii → IV	IV → iii	I	I	I
Ritornello segments	aabc		c'		a' a'		a		aabc

A section receives the most attention at the expense of the B section, here Bach adds an unusual degree of musical weight to the middle. The B section is equal in length to the opening: A (forty-seven measures), B (forty-seven measures), and A' (forty-four measures). Furthermore, whereas in most da capo arias the soloist twice repeats the first half of the text, with a ritornello separating these repetitions, here Bach reverses this scheme: the A section has only one single solo section (mm. 21–44) and no intervening ritornello, while the B section has two different solo sections (mm. 47 and 78), separated by a ritornello at measure 71. This also happens to be the aria's longest internal ritornello, the others at measures 44 and 94 simply having one phrase.

Instrumentation also gives the middle section extra emphasis. While most composers reduce the instrumentation throughout the middle, this B section has some of the aria's most interesting interaction between vocal and instrumental forces. The brass instrument participates in the first part (mm. 49–54 and 72–78), whereas such instruments usually rest at this moment.[36] Then the vocalist and first violin work in imitation from measure 62 to measure 69.

Bach also skillfully paints the words of the B section, including the word "Tyrannei": the first or last syllable of this word is usually dissonant against either the underlying harmony or in relation to the previous bars. (See in example 1 the diminished seventh against the bass at m. 54; the leap of a diminished fourth in the voice at m. 55; the leap of an augmented fourth into a major seventh against the bass at m. 61, etc.) Underlying this section is the aria's most unstable harmony, continually moving forward without a firm sense of key, in contrast to the ritornello. The soprano must also negotiate complex melismas on the word "Leben." All these difficulties are potentially symbolic: the singer must endure the snares and pitfalls of Bach's harmony and vocal writing, just as the believer must remain steadfast against persecution. As a result, Bach's music

36. The brass instrument in this aria might be a horn or a trumpet. In the autograph part, this aria alone is written for an instrument transposing from C to B-flat but without indication to change instruments from the horn in the movement before. Bach's autograph, however, labels the part *Tromba*. The NBA editor, Peter Wollny, interprets the latter as reflecting only Bach's intent while composing, which he then discarded while writing out the parts; see preface to NBA I/6, KB 149–50.

Example 1. J. S. Bach, "Unsre Stärke heißt zu schwach," BWV 14/2, mm. 51–62.

Example 1. Continued.

particularly stresses the moment when the aria brings up the language of persecution in the strongest of terms (example 1).

The theme of raging enemies continues in the following movements, including the tenor recitative:

Ja, hätt es Gott nur zugegeben,	Yea, had God but allowed it,
Wir wären längst nicht mehr am Leben,	We would long have been alive no more,
Sie rissen uns aus Rachgier hin,	They would tear us away out of thirst for revenge,
So zornig ist auf uns ihr Sinn.	So angry with us is their disposition.
Es hätt uns ihre Wut	Their rage,
Wie eine wilde Flut	Like a wild torrent
Und als beschäumte Wasser überschwemmet,	And like foaming water, would have swamped us,
Und niemand hätte die Gewalt gehemmet.	And no one would have impeded their force.

Here the water imagery, which also appears in other movements, can be credited both to the gospel reading and verses 4 and 5 of Psalm 124. This helps explain why Luther's paraphrase became a *de tempore* hymn for this Sunday and why Bach's librettist drew on the chorale. Most importantly, this imagery is obviously connected with persecution. While the recitative might remind listeners that God preserved them individually from both literal and spiritual death, these words should also be understood ecclesially and collectively: had God not spared his "church-ship," the Lutheran confession, it would have perished long ago in the wild torrent of listeners' confessional and political enemies. All this shows that to make sense of the language in Bach's libretto, we need to recognize the ecclesial significance of gospel and psalm, and we need to see how this encouraged listeners to hear persecution at the hands of their confessional enemies.

Ecclesial readings of Matthew 8 can also help interpret the other cantatas that Bach performed on the fourth Sunday after Epiphany. In both BWV 81 and J. L. Bach's cantata, the librettists have introduced typical storm-and-sea imagery drawn from the gospel reading but clearly informed by the tradition of interpreting these images as metaphors for persecution. Most vivid is the third movement of *Jesus schläft, was soll ich hoffen?* (BWV 81) in which Bach depicts the raging sea through rapid sixteenth- and thirty-second-note string figuration (example 2).

The tableau painted here was not just meant to satisfy eighteenth-century listeners' thirst for the sublime, though a storm at sea certainly ranks among the most popular sublime topics. Here Bach's musical imagery is linked to the onslaughts of persecution.[37]

37. In the third line, "Felsen" in Bach's score and parts, as well as in the printed libretto, appears as "Wellen," which may be a mistake; see NBA I/6, KB 120.

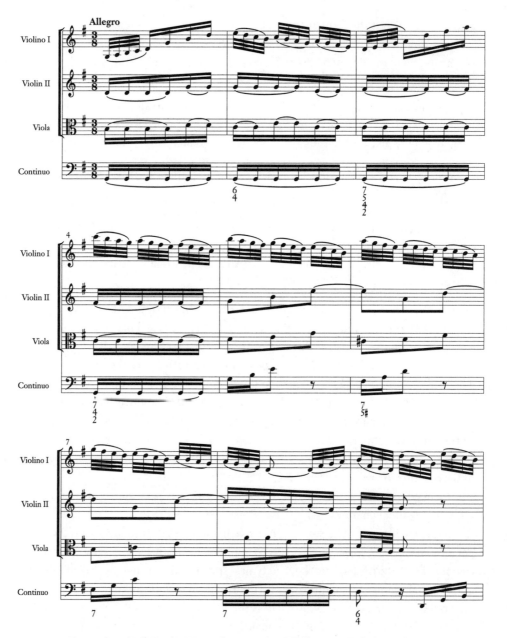

Example 2. J. S. Bach, "Die schäumenden Wellen von Belials Bächen,"
BWV 81/3, mm. 1–16.

Example 2. Continued.

Die schäumenden Wellen von Belials Bächen	The foaming waves of Belial's waters
Verdoppeln die Wut.	Redouble their rage.
Ein Christ soll zwar wie Felsen stehn,	A Christian should indeed stand like a rock
Wenn Trübsalswinde um ihn gehn,	When affliction's winds go round him,
Doch suchet die stürmende Flut	Yet the storming torrent seeks
Die Kräfte des Glaubens zu schwächen.	To weaken the strength of faith.

The waves come from the "devil's streams" ("Belials Bächen"), and the believer must stand up to the floods that try to "weaken the strength of faith." These same themes are repeated in the cantata's closing chorale, the second verse from the hymn *Jesu meine Freude*:

Unter deinen Schirmen	Under Your shadow
Bin ich für den Stürmen	I am free from the storms
Aller Feinde frei.	Of all enemies.
Laß den Satan wittern,	Let Satan nose about,
Laß den Feind erbittern,	Let the enemy be exasperated:
Mir steht Jesus bei.	Jesus stands by me.
Ob es itzt gleich kracht und blitzt,	Though it now crashes and flashes,
Ob gleich Sünd und Hölle schrecken,	Though sin and hell terrify me,
Jesus will mich decken.	Jesus will cover me.

Johann Ludwig Bach's cantata *Gott ist unser Zuversicht* (JLB 1) contains similar imagery linking the storm at sea to persecution. The libretto goes back to an anonymous 1704 cantata cycle from Meiningen that had earlier been set by Johann Ludwig's predecessor, Georg Caspar Schürmann.[38] Like BWV 81, J. L. Bach's cantata contains an aria in which rapid string figuration illustrates the raging of nature:

Ob die Wellen rasen,	Whether the waves rush,
Ob die Winde blasen,	Whether the wind blows,
Ob die Felsen splittern	Whether the rocks splinter
Erd' und Himmel zittern:	Earth and heaven tremble:
Wenn des Höchsten Obhut wachet,	If the highest's care keeps watch,
Ungestüm kein Grauen machet.	Tumult causes no dread.

In this short aria, Johann Ludwig illustrates the contrast between wild, uncontrolled nature and God's protection (example 3): at measure 13 the tempo changes to adagio, the rapid string figuration and the bass line drop out, and the string accompaniment begins to pulse eighth-note chords on every beat.

In J. L. Bach's cantata, though, the link between storms and persecution by various enemies is never explicitly drawn. Only briefly in the seventh movement, another storm-like soprano aria, does the listener get a hint of this:

38. *Sonn- und Fest-Andachten Uber die ordentlichen Evangelia Aus gewissen Biblischen Texten* (Meiningen: Hassert, 1704); exemplar in the Meiningen Museum. The librettist is anonymous, though Küster (1987) proposed Duke Ernst Ludwig I of Saxe-Meiningen, known to have written two cantata cycles. Schürmann composed at least six cantatas on texts from this cycle. These survive in the Bockemeyer collection in Berlin (D-B, Mus. ms. 30272).

Example 3. Johann Ludwig Bach, "Gott ist unser Zuversicht," third movement.

Example 3. Continued.

Example 3. Continued.

Example 3. Continued.

Dünkt dir deine Schuld gleich groß,	Though you think your guilt be great,
Will dich alles Unglück kränken,	And all misfortune try to hurt you,
Stürmt gleich Welt und Teufel los	If both the world and devil break loose
Dein Vertrauen zu ertränken:	To drown your confidence:
Laß' das Schiflein krachen,	Let the ship break,
Dein Erretter wird wachen	Your savior will awake,
Winde, Meer und Wellen	To still at last
Endlich stille machen.	Wind, sea, and waves.

Otherwise the imagery of crashing waves and rushing wind stands alone. In contrast to BWV 14, these two cantatas tend to stress the personal, spiritual significance of persecution. While they equate the storms and raging sea with enemies, the collective and confessional view of the ship is not to be found. We therefore cannot know for certain if Bach's listeners heard references in these two cantatas to broader attacks on Lutheranism. We can be sure, though, that at least some listeners still knew the long Lutheran exegetical tradition that encouraged believers to hear just this.

The fourth Sunday after Epiphany was not the only time of the year when Lutherans could rekindle their confessional fears and remember various persecutions that they had suffered in the past or that they feared in the future.[39] For instance, the first Sunday after the New Year became an occasion to bring up religious exile, since its gospel reading was Mary and Joseph's flight into Egypt. Here, just like the fourth Sunday after Epiphany, librettists could potentially raise political and confessional issues in ways that we might overlook. Through biblical references interpreted as ecclesial in Lutheran exegesis or through the metaphorical language of persecution, cantata librettists strengthened the congregation's loyalty to Lutheranism by raising the alarm over confessional foes while at the same time offering promises of safety within Christ's little ship.

And yet a caveat: by Bach's time, the fears and grievances expressed in the liturgy did not normally lead congregants toward violence against their opponents. One explanation for this is the political and legal structures of the Holy Roman Empire as they had developed over the previous two centuries. These structures, as Brady has explained, worked "to set limits to confessional strife by sublimating impulses to violence into conventionalized symbolic forms of insult with little or no material damage or recurring disruption of public life."[40] Under Brady's category of "conventionalized symbolic forms of insult" we might place the sermons, scripture reading, hymns, and

39. This includes the two Sundays explored by Marissen, cited in note 5 above.

40. Brady, "Limits of Religious Violence," 139–40.

cantatas for the fourth Sunday after Epiphany. The law prevented Lutherans from directly taking action against their opponents, but they still might do so figuratively.

We also should not overlook important counterweights in the liturgy and in Lutheran theology that encouraged congregants to live in peace with their opponents. Although sermons might warn against enemies, they do not admonish congregants toward violence but toward prayer and trust in God. The liturgy, too, makes similar points. Consider, most notably, the epistle reading for the fourth Sunday after Epiphany, Romans 13:8–10, which Bach's listeners would certainly have heard along with each of his cantata performances: "[8] Be indebted to no one for anything, but love one another: for he that loves another has fulfilled the law. [9] For it has been said: you shall not commit adultery, you shall not kill, you shall not steal, you shall not bear false witness, you shall not covet; and if there be any other commandment, it is summed up in this saying: you shall love your neighbor as yourself. [10] Love does nothing wicked to his neighbor: therefore love is the fulfilling of the law."[41] And on the previous Sunday, congregants would have heard a passage from Romans 12:17–21 in which Paul exhorted his readers to live peaceably as far as possible and not to take vengeance upon anyone. As easy as it is today to note how early modern Lutheranism sought to distinguish itself from and warn against the errors of rival confessions, we also need to recognize theological strains within Lutheranism that also acted as a check, diffusing religious and social tensions.[42]

---

41. "[8] Seid niemand nichts schüldig / denn das jr euch vnternander liebet / Denn wer den andern liebet / der hat das Gesetz erfüllet. [9] Denn das da gesagt ist / Du solt nicht ehebrechen / Du solt nicht tödten / Du solt nicht stelen / Du solt nicht falsch gezeugnis geben / Dich sol nichts gelüsten. Vnd so ein anders Gebot mehr ist / das wird in diesem wort verfasset / Du solt deinen Nehesten lieben / als dich selbs. [10] Die Liebe thut dem Nehesten nichts böses. So ist nu die Liebe des Gesetzes erfüllung" (Luther, *Biblia*).

42. Older theories of confessionalization have tended to focus on how religion and the state in early modern Europe divided people, but for a recent counterargument, see the introduction and essays in *A Companion to Multiconfessionalism in the Early Modern World*, ed. Thomas Max Safley (Leiden: Brill, 2011).

Music Historicism

Sara Levy and the Jewish Enlightenment

Rebecca Cypess

In 1798 the Jewish writer Wolf Davidson published his treatise *Ueber die bürgerliche Verbesserung der Juden*, intended to justify the emancipation of Jews in Prussia and their full integration into the predominantly Christian society around them. Borrowing his title from a 1781 publication by Christian Wilhelm von Dohm, Davidson joined an ongoing discussion among both Jewish and Christian thinkers of the Enlightenment concerning the merits of Jewish emancipation and the participation of Jews in civic and cultural life. By way of justifying Jewish emancipation, Davidson cited a long list of Jews, from philosophers and educators to practitioners of the mechanical arts, who were already making significant contributions to Prussian society. Among these were musicians—some of them professionals, but more in the emerging category of *Dilettanten*.[1] Within that group, he wrote, "well known as prodigious keyboardists here in Berlin are Madame Lewy, Madame Wolff, and Madame Boser, née Flies."[2]

These women have emerged in recent histories of the Bach family as important figures in the Bach tradition of the late eighteenth and early nineteenth centuries. Zipora Wulff, née Itzig (later Cäcilie von Eskeles), and Karoline Luise Eleonore von Bose, née Flies, were well known in their day as talented keyboardists.[3] But it was Zipora's

The research that led to this project was supported by a William H. Scheide Research Grant from the American Bach Society. I am grateful to Douglas Johnson, Yael Sela, Robin A. Leaver, Daniel R. Melamed, and the anonymous reviewer for this journal for their insightful comments and suggestions.

1. On the rise of musical amateurs in late eighteenth-century Berlin, see Celia Applegate, "Musical Amateurism and the Exercise of Taste," in *Bach in Berlin: Nation and Culture in Mendelssohn's Revival of the "St. Matthew Passion"* (Ithaca, NY: Cornell University Press, 2005).

2. "Hier in Berlin sind als vortreffliche Klavierspielerinn, Madame Lewy, Madame Wolff und Madame Boser, geborne Flies bekannt" (Wolf Davidson, *Ueber die bürgerliche Verbesserung der Juden* [Berlin: Ernst Felisch, 1798], 109).

3. Biographical information on all three women is in Thekla Keuck, *Hofjuden und Kulturbürger: Die Geschichte der Familie Itzig in Berlin* (Göttingen: Vandenhoeck und Ruprecht, 2011).

sister Sara Levy, née Itzig, who had the most lasting effect on Bach performance, reception, and scholarship. A student of Wilhelm Friedemann Bach and a patron of both Friedemann and Carl Philipp Emanuel Bach, Sara Levy played, collected, and preserved a large quantity of their music, as well as music by Johann Sebastian Bach and others of his generation—especially composers who lived and worked in Berlin.[4] Levy eventually donated the majority of her holdings to the Sing-Akademie zu Berlin, and they were subsumed within the larger collection then being assembled by Carl Friedrich Zelter.[5] With the repatriation of the Sing-Akademie collection to Berlin at the end of the Cold War, the archival work of such scholars as Christoph Wolff and Peter Wollny has assured Levy's place (if one still largely unknown outside specialist circles) as a crucial link in the Bach tradition in the generation before the revival of Bach's music on the public stage, which began with the performance of the *St. Matthew Passion* directed by Levy's great-nephew, Felix Mendelssohn Bartholdy.[6]

4. On Levy's biography, collection, and impact on the musical culture around her, see especially Peter Wollny, *"Ein förmlicher Sebastian und Philipp Emanuel Bach-Kultus": Sara Levy und ihr musikalisches Wirken, mit einer Dokumentensammlung zur musikalischen Familiengeschichte der Vorfahren von Felix Mendelssohn Bartholdy* (Wiesbaden: Breitkopf & Härtel, 2010); Wollny, "Sara Levy and the Making of Musical Taste in Berlin," *Musical Quarterly* 77, no. 4 (1993): 651–88; Wollny, "'Ein förmlicher Sebastian und Philipp Emanuel Bach-Kultus': Sara Levy, geb. Itzig, und ihr literarisch-musikalischer Salon," in *Musik und Ästhetik im Berlin Moses Mendelssohns*, ed. Anselm Gerhard (Tübingen: Niemeyer, 1999), 217–55; Wollny, "Anmerkungen zur Bach-Pflege im Umfeld Sara Levys," in *"Zu groß, zu unerreichbar": Bach-Rezeption im Zeitalter Mendelssohns und Schumanns*, ed. Anselm Hartinger, Christoph Wolff, and Peter Wollny (Wiesbaden: Breitkopf & Härtel, 2007), 39–50; and Christoph Wolff, "A Bach Cult in Late-Eighteenth-Century Berlin: Sara Levy's Musical Salon," *Bulletin of the American Academy of Arts and Sciences* 58, no. 3 (Spring 2005): 26–31.

5. On Zelter's collecting habits, see Matthias Kornemann, "Zelter's Archive: Portrait of a Collector," in *The Archive of the Sing-Akademie zu Berlin: Catalogue / Das Archiv der Sing-Akademie zu Berlin: Katalog*, ed. Axel Fischer and Matthias Kornemann (Berlin: De Gruyter, 2010), 19–25. On Levy's donation of her collection to the Sing-Akademie, see p. 21.

6. On the repatriation of the collection, see Christoph Wolff, "Recovered in Kiev: Bach et al. A Preliminary Report on the Music Collection of the Berlin Sing-Akademie," *Notes* 58, no. 2 (2001): 259–71; and Ulrich Leisinger, "The Bach Collection," in Fischer and Kornemann, *The Archive*, 37–42. The complete literature on Mendelssohn's performance of the *St. Matthew Passion* is too extensive to list here; see, for example, Applegate, *Bach in Berlin*; Gottfried Eberle, *200 Jahre Sing-Akademie zu Berlin: "Ein Kunstverein für die heilige Musik"* (Berlin: Nicolaische Verlagsbuchhandlung, 1991), 87–99; R. Larry Todd, *Mendelssohn: A Life in Music* (New York: Oxford University Press, 2003), 122–29, 180–98. See also Yael Sela, "Longing for the Sublime: Music and Jewish Self-Consciousness at Bach's *St. Matthew Passion* in Biedermeier Berlin," in *Sara Levy's World: Gender, Judaism, and the Bach Tradition in Enlightenment Berlin*, ed. Rebecca Cypess and Nancy Sinkoff (Rochester: University of Rochester Press, 2018), 147–77.

The complex relationship of the Bach family and Bach scholarship with Judaism underlies the story of Sara Levy and her circle.[7] In 2005 Wolff suggested that Levy had until then been "underemphasized, underresearched, or neglected if not suppressed by earlier historical German scholarship for reasons of an apparent anti-Semitic bias."[8] Since then, Levy's role within music history has received more attention, yet she is generally discussed from the perspective of her contribution to the Bach legacy, rather than as an autonomous figure in her own right. This problematic manner of thinking was initiated by Davidson, among others, who suggested that emancipation and tolerance were justified by—and, by implication, contingent upon—the "usefulness" of Jews to society. (If Levy and her circle had not made "contributions" to Prussian society, would the emancipation of the Jews not have been justified?)[9] Levy as a complete historical figure—a woman who sought to bridge the worlds of enlightened Judaism and German culture—has thus far remained elusive. I argue that she cannot be understood in this manner without a more thorough explication of the aesthetic, intellectual, and cultural trends that informed both her activities as a musician and her status as a modernizing yet committed Jewish woman. A multidisciplinary approach allows us to ask not only what she contributed to musical history, and the Bach tradition in particular, but what engagement with music meant to *her*.

In this essay I propose to address one aspect of this question: What was the significance of her music historicism as expressed in her collection of musical scores? To be sure, such historicism was not unique during the Enlightenment, but it takes on new meaning in light of her adherence to Judaism—remarkably strong compared with many other men and women in her family and social circle, many of whom chose radical assimilation or conversion—as well as her commitment to Jewish philanthropy and her engagement with the Jewish Enlightenment (Haskalah).[10] Indeed, recent archival work by Natalie Naimark-Goldberg has underscored the significance of Levy's patronage of Haskalah intellectual causes and Jewish communal institutions, which suggest a

---

7. These issues are explored in Michael Marissen, *Bach & God* (New York: Oxford University Press, 2016), and in Marissen, *Lutheranism, Anti-Judaism, and Bach's "St. John Passion" with an Annotated Literal Translation of the Libretto* (New York: Oxford University Press, 1998).

8. Wolff, "A Bach Cult," 26.

9. On the problems of the "contribution discourse" in Jewish history, see Moshe Rosman, *How Jewish Is Jewish History?* (Oxford: Littman Library of Jewish Civilization, 2007), 111–30.

10. On the tendency toward conversion among Levy's generation of enlightened German Jews, see Amos Elon, *The Pity of It All: A Portrait of the German-Jewish Epoch, 1743–1933* (New York: Picador, 2002), 81–86. Elon's observation, that "before conversion most converts were non-practicing Jews; after conversion they were non-practicing Christians" (82), highlights the distinctiveness of Levy's situation.

purposeful Jewish self-identification.[11] As a result of her awareness of Haskalah ideas on music—a point to which I will return below—Levy is likely to have known of the persistent and sometimes contentious debates over the history of Jews in music and over the potential of contemporary Jews to be "musical." I argue that her collection of scores may be fruitfully understood as a contribution to the history of music making among Jews. In collecting, playing, and transmitting this music, Levy reframed it as a component of Jewish history, thus fulfilling the call by leaders of the Haskalah for members of the Jewish community to engage with all of the arts and sciences. Levy's collection forged a common musical history accessible to both Christians and Jews.

Christian Views of Hebrew Music and the *neue Juden* of the Eighteenth Century

Numerous thinkers of the Enlightenment wrote about the history of music among the ancient Israelites. Basing their observations on the poetry of the Hebrew Bible, including passages such as the Song at the Sea (Exodus 15), the Song of Deborah (Judges 5), the Song of Solomon, and the book of Psalms as a whole, historians and literary theorists of the latter half of the eighteenth century described the sung poetry of the ancient Hebrews as a pinnacle of artistic creation. Johann Gottfried Herder's *Vom Geist der Ebräischen Poesie* (1782–83) cast the poetic song of the ancient Israelites as an ideal mode of "natural" expression: "Since Hebrew musick was probably free from the restraints of artificial rules, it could on that account approximate more nearly to the movements of the heart."[12] For Herder, the spirit of the Hebrew Bible was one of idyllic simplicity, primitive yet more expressive than the poetry of his own day. Moreover, music and poetry were perfectly united in the biblical art, and neither dominated the other: "So soon as musick was invented, poetry acquired a new power, a more graceful movement, and greater harmony of sound."[13]

Although the study of Hebrew letters had long been part of humanist education, the eighteenth century saw a rising interest in the incorporation of Hebraist learning among Christian scholars, and Herder's text is an example of the elevation of

11. Natalie Naimark-Goldberg, "Remaining within the Fold: The Cultural and Social World of Sara Levy," in Cypess and Sinkoff, *Sara Levy's World*, 52–74.

12. "Da die ebräische Musik wahrscheinlich noch ohne ermattende Kunst war, so konnte sie sich desto mehr dem Schwunge des Herzens nähern" (Johann Gottfried Herder, *Vom Geist der Ebräischen Poesie: Eine Anleitung für Liebhaber derselben und der ältesten Geschichte des menschlichen Geistes*, ed. Johann Georg Müller [Tübingen: Cotta, 1805], 30, translated in Herder, *The Spirit of Hebrew Poetry*, 2 vols., trans. J. Marsh [Burlington: Edward Smith, 1833], 2:25–26).

13. "Sobald Musik erfunden war, bekam die Poesie neuen Schwung, Gang und Wohllaut" (Herder, *Vom Geist der ebräischen Poesie*, 28, translated in Herder, *The Spirit of Hebrew Poetry*, 2:23).

the biblical art of poetry within the new field of aesthetics. For many writers of the period, analysis of the ancient Hebrew text had practical ramifications for contemporary artistic creation. Herder celebrated poets who captured the "spirit of Hebrew poetry" by imitating its classical forms and styles. Although, he explained, the German language was not naturally conducive to the pure expression and simple constructions of Hebrew, he praised Friedrich Gottlieb Klopstock, among others, as a latter-day King David, since Klopstock had captured some of that eloquence in his German odes and in his epic *Der Messias*.[14] Herder and other admirers of biblical poetry no doubt understood the ancient Hebrews as proto-Christians, and for that reason, admiration of the ancient art in no way undermined their own adherence to Christianity. Yet for Herder, the artistic value of the Hebrew Bible had implications for Jews in the eighteenth century as well; as he wrote, "Can one call a nation barbaric that has even a few such national songs?"[15]

Johann Nikolaus Forkel, too, admired the loftiness of the sung poetry of the ancient Hebrews. Yet Forkel's account is a darker one, reflecting the biases that had dominated Lutheran Germany until the age of Enlightenment and that continued as a common theme even after ideals of tolerance and coexistence had begun to spread. Forkel's *Allgemeine Geschichte der Musik* (1788) includes an impressively detailed history of ancient Hebrew music that draws on a wide range of previous scholarship, some written by Jews and some by Christians, including Athanasius Kircher, Charles Burney, and many others. At least one of the texts by Jewish writers had not been translated, so Forkel may have read it in the original Hebrew.[16] His discussion treated the poetic structures of biblical song, with special emphasis on the book of Psalms. Indeed, discussion of the Psalms formed the greatest part of Forkel's history of ancient Israelite music, for he viewed this work, composed and assembled during the reign of King David, as the pinnacle of the art of Hebrew poetry. Furthermore, evidence from the Psalms allowed

14. Herder, *The Spirit of Hebrew Poetry*, 2:246. On Justin Heinrich Knecht's setting of Klopstock's *Wechselgesang der Mirjam und Debora*, held in the collection of the Itzig daughters, and its relationship to the aesthetics of the Hebrew Bible, see Rebecca Cypess, "Ancient Poetry, Modern Music, and the *Wechselgesang der Mirjam und Debora*: The Meanings of Song in the Itzig Circle," BACH 47, no. 1 (2016): 21–65.

15. "Könnte man ein Volk barbarisch nennen, das nur einige solche Nationalgesänge hatte?" (Herder, *Vom Geist der Ebräischen Poesie*, 314, translated in Herder, *The Spirit of Hebrew Poetry*, 2:240).

16. Forkel's discussion of ancient Hebrew music appears in Johann Nikolaus Forkel, *Allgemeine Geschichte der Musik* (Leipzig: Schwickert, 1788), 1:99–184; of that chapter, the bibliography occupies 174–84. The author whose work had not yet been translated was Shabbethai ben Joseph "Bass" (1641–1718), a singer who had started his career at the Great Synagogue in Prague, later moving throughout Europe; he printed Hebrew books and wrote a supercommentary (a commentary on a commentary) on the Pentateuch.

Forkel to discuss the identity of the instruments used in the ancient world, especially during the reigns of David and of Solomon, who built the first Temple in Jerusalem, where music was an important part of liturgy and ritual. He wove interpretations by Christian theologians together with sources by Jewish writers from the Talmudic age to the seventeenth century.

Forkel introduced and concluded his discussion of Hebrew poetry and music with observations on the music of Jews during his own day and sprinkled references to *neue Juden* throughout the text. At the beginning of his chapter, he noted how different the ancient music must have been from anything heard in his own lifetime. Citing Herder's work, Forkel wrote that "the nature of music is, like the nature of speech, as easily changeable as a breeze. . . . [I]t floats in on a whim and on a whim it flies away."[17] He contrasted the changeable nature of music with the more static nature of the other arts. For example, whereas speech may be preserved through writing, "only music must live, that is, it must sound or it is no music."[18]

Forkel's reasons for starting with these statements were, on one level, entirely methodological: he needed to establish that the music of the ancient Hebrews was lost and that attempts to recover it were therefore speculative and uncertain. Yet, on another level, this portion of his history was not merely academic but rather polemical: through it, he sought to discredit the music of the Jews in the eighteenth century and, in doing so, delegitimize Judaism itself. This point is made clear at the end of the chapter, where he connected the loftiness of ancient Hebrew music and poetry to the high spiritual and ethical status of the ancient Jews. Conversely, he provided evidence of the *unmusicality* of contemporary Jews, and he cited this as proof of their immorality and their errant ways. Since the Jews had been dispersed among other nations, they had been unable to preserve their own musical-poetic tradition. Their resulting unmusicality was both a function and a reflection of their spiritual baseness. Mixing his words with those of Claude François Xavier Millot, whose *Élémens d'histoire generale* accused ancient Jews of the most heinous crimes, including human sacrifice, as well as purposeful ignorance of all the arts and sciences,[19] Forkel confirmed that the loss of the Hebrew musical tradition by Jews across the millennia was the fault of the Jews themselves:

> In the end, even the music of the prophets of every nation progresses only hand in hand with the other arts and sciences, as with the culture of customs. Above all, good and pure feelings of the heart are the most fertile soil for it [i.e., music]. But how were the sciences, arts (excluding poetry), traditions, and feelings of the Hebrews obtained? General opinion sees them as ignorant. All strangers, their languages, arts, sciences,

17. "Das Wesen der Tonkunst ist, wie das Wesen der Sprache, ein fein modificirter Hauch, der . . . auf den Lüsten schwebt, und auch mit den Lüsten vorüber fliegt" (ibid., 1:99).

18. "Allein die Musik muß leben, das heißt: sie muß klingen, oder sie ist keine Musik" (ibid.).

19. See Claude François Xavier Millot, *Élémens d'histoire générale* (Paris: Durand, 1778), 1:152–60.

and so forth, were for them [the Jews] objects of contempt or detestation. . . . Our holy books give us many examples of their inhuman barbarism; no less of their affinity for superstition and for unfaithfulness to God, who overwhelms them constantly with benefactions. In short, even with the direct guidance of Heaven the culture of this people remained in every respect so far behind that it has hardly earned the right to be counted among the number of cultivated nations.[20]

In Forkel's view, while the ancient Hebrews were of a high ethical standing, their place in modern times had been supplanted by Christians, who followed the true calling of God. The ignorance of the Jews in music and in every other art and science was a result of their own contempt for other nations—a circumstance that they brought upon themselves. It was unlikely that their traditions could ever be rehabilitated, for they were "without sciences, without customs, without fine feelings of the heart, without good instruments, without a singable language, without an art of musical notation."[21]

Forkel's history of Hebrew music was not the first in the Western tradition to assert that contemporary Jews were inherently unmusical. As Ruth HaCohen has shown, European music history is littered with examples of a "music libel against the Jews," which held that while Christianity produced music that was beautiful and spiritually edifying, Jews were capable of nothing but noise.[22] Indeed, while Forkel acknowledged that there were some *Virtuosen* in the tradition of synagogue music, these were "rare." In general, "in the synagogue itself, modern Jewish music is nothing but either a musical prayer, which is more or less growled or muttered in a few tones, or (when a chorus joins in) a frightful shouting."[23]

20. "Endlich ist auch die Musik von Seher bey allen Nationen nur mit andern Künsten und Wissenschaften, so wie mit der Kultur der Sitten, Hand in Hand vorwärts gegangen. Vorzüglich sind gute und reine Empfindungen des Herzens der fruchtbarste Boden für sie. Aber wie waren die Wissenschaften, Künste, (Poesie abgerechnet) Sitten und Empfindungen der Hebräer beschaffen? Ein fast allgemeines Urtheil erklärt sie für unwissend. Alle Fremde, ihre Sprache, Künste, Wissenschaften, u.s.f. waren für sie Gegenstände der Verachtung oder der Verabscheuung. . . . Von ihrer unmenschlichen Grausamkeit werden uns in den heil. Büchern eine Menge Beyspiele erzählt; nicht weniger von ihrer Neigung zum Aberglauben und zur Untreue gegen Gott, der sie ununterbrochen mit Wohlthaten überhäufte. Kurz, selbst mit dem unmittelbaren Unterrichte des Himmels blieb die Kultur dieses Volks in jeder Rücksicht doch so weit zurück, daß es kaum unter die Zahl der kultivirten Nationen gerechnet zu werden verdiente" (Forkel, *Allgemeine Geschichte*, 1:172). My thanks to Douglas Johnson for his assistance with this translation.

21. "ohne Wissenschaften, ohne Sitten, ohne feine Gefühle des Herzens, ohne gute Instrumente, ohne eine singbare Sprache, ohne eine musikalische Schreibekunst" (ibid.).

22. Ruth HaCohen, *The Music Libel against the Jews* (New Haven, CT: Yale University Press, 2011).

23. "In den Synagogen selbst ist die heutige jüdische Musik nichts, als entweder ein musikalisches Beten, welches in einerley Ton gleichsam gebrummt oder gemurmelt wird, oder (wenn der Chor einfällt) ein fürchterliches Geschrey" (Forkel, *Allgemeine Geschichte*, 1:162).

Jewish Thinkers on Ancient and Modern Music

The educated Jews of Prussia were doubtless aware of these characterizations of synagogue music. They were also aware that they lacked a coherent national or religious
music that could be compared with the Christian church traditions. In German and
in Hebrew, Jewish writers lamented the loss of their ancient music. Moses Mendelssohn's German translation of the Psalms, published in 1783, attempted to minimize the
gap between the Jewish and Christian traditions of sung poetry. The work, intended
for both Jewish and non-Jewish readers, presented the Psalms in a new guise—in
Michah Gottlieb's words, "as a great work of lyric religious poetry that could inspire
both Jews and Christians rather than as a repository of Christian or Jewish messianic
predictions."[24] Indeed, in the text of his dedication to the poet Karl Wilhelm Ramler,
Mendelssohn placed the project of his Psalm translations within the context of his
iconic friendship with the Christian writer Gotthold Ephraim Lessing, a friendship
that epitomized and exemplified the promise of enlightened tolerance.[25] Mendelssohn's translation departed from both Jewish and Lutheran traditions, but it did so by
reaching into their common history. In its multiconfessional aims, it sought to reclaim
the Psalms as an aesthetic space available to both religions and one that could bridge
the gap between them.

In his Hebrew writings, Mendelssohn was explicit about the loss of a Jewish musical heritage. In his commentary on the Pentateuch, published as *Sefer netivot ha-
shalom* (Book of the paths of peace) but commonly known as the *Bi'ur* (Explanation)
(1780–82),[26] Mendelssohn admitted that "we have lost this ancient musical science,

24. Michah Gottlieb, prefatory note to the Psalm translations, in Moses Mendelssohn, *Writings on
Judaism, Christianity, and the Bible*, ed. Michah Gottlieb, trans. Curtis Bowman, Elias Sacks, and Allan
Arkush (Waltham, MD: Brandeis University Press, 2011), 182.

25. Mendelssohn's German translations of the Psalms are in Mendelssohn, *Die Psalmen*, in *Gesam-
melte Schriften: Jubiläumsausgabe* (hereafter *JubA*), ed. Fritz Bamberger et al., 24 vols. (Stuttgart–Bad
Canstatt: Frommann, 1971), vol. 10.1. For more information on the Psalm translations, see David Sorkin, "Psalms," in *Moses Mendelssohn and the Religious Enlightenment* (London: Halban, 2012),
chap. 5. On Mendelssohn's friendship with Lessing, see Alexander Altmann, *Moses Mendelssohn: A
Biographical Study* (Tuscaloosa: University of Alabama Press, 1973), 36–50, 66–71, and 553–82. On
the persistence of anti-Judaism even in the thought of Lessing, see Martha Helfer, "Lessing and the
Limits of Enlightenment," in *The Word Unheard: Legacies of Anti-Semitism in German Literature and
Culture* (Evanston, IL: Northwestern University Press, 2011), chap. 1.

26. On the significance of Mendelssohn's Pentateuch translation as the first German-language trans-
lation of the Hebrew Bible, see Abigail E. Gillman, "Between Religion and Culture: Mendelssohn,
Buber, Rosenzweig and the Enterprise of Biblical Translation," in *Biblical Translation in Context*, ed.
Frederick W. Knobloch (Bethesda: University Press of Maryland, 2002), 93–105; and Sorkin, *Moses
Mendelssohn*, chap. 6.

and no remnant of the musical art used by our ancestors remains."[27] His introduction to Exodus 15, the Song at the Sea, includes a lengthy explanation of the poetics of the Hebrew Bible, but it, too, acknowledges that, with the passage of time and the geographical dispersion of the Jewish people, the oral traditions of the text—including its music—were lost. Still, he claimed, "There nevertheless remains in our sacred poetry much sweetness that is sensed by every wise reader, even if he does not grasp its cause. This sweetness is not merely auditory sweetness, which is intimately connected to the language in which a poem is composed. . . . Rather, it is the sweetness of the content, which is connected to the meaning and intention of the statement."[28] In fact, the aesthetic power of biblical poetry even in the absence of music provided Mendelssohn with a justification for translation of the text out of its original Hebrew. Just as the text alone, without its musical recitation, retained that original "sweetness of content," a translation into German would do the same. Although the poetry's "flavor is weakened and its fragrance made bitter by the translation, there nevertheless remains the sweetness of the content that we have mentioned."[29]

Mendelssohn's earlier writings on aesthetics indicate that, like other (non-Jewish) writers of the Enlightenment, he understood music, together with the other fine arts, as capable of shaping the ethical understanding and behavior of the listener: "Through different senses, poetry, rhetoric, beauties in shapes and sounds pervade our soul and dominate all its inclinations."[30] Mendelssohn himself was strongly engaged with mainstream German musical traditions, as shown both in his aesthetic writings and in his collaboration and famous studies with Johann Philipp Kirnberger.[31] Yet he cautioned

---

27. "אבדנו חכמת המוזיקא הקדומה, ולא נשאר לנו שריד מכל מלאכת הנגון, אשר השתמשו בה קדמונינו."
(Mendelssohn, *Sefer netivot ha-shalom* [*Bi'ur*], in *JubA* 16:126, translated in Mendelssohn, *Writings*, 214).

28. "מכל מקום נשאר עריבות רב בשירי הקודש, נרגש לכל קורא משכיל אף אם לא ידע סבתו, והעריבות ההוא אינו עריבת אוזן בלבד, הדבק ונצמד בלשון אשר בו הוסד...כי אם עריבת ענין, דבק במובן וכוונת המאמר."
(Mendelssohn, *Sefer netivot ha-shalom* [*Bi'ur*], in *JubA* 16:126, translated in Mendelssohn, *Writings*, 214–15).

29. "אף אם יפג טעמם הרב וימר ריחם ע"י ההעתקה, מכל מקום ישאר להם העריבות הענייני שזכרנו."
(Mendelssohn, *Sefer netivot ha-shalom* [*Bi'ur*], in *JubA* 16:127, translated in Mendelssohn, *Writings*, 215).

30. "Die Dichtkunst, die Beredsamkeit, die Schönheiten in Figuren und in Tönen dringen durch verschiedene Sinne zu unserer Seele, und beherrschen alle ihre Neigungen" (Moses Mendelssohn, "Ueber die Hauptgrundsätze der schönen Künste und Wissenschaften," in *JubA* 1:428, translated in Mendelssohn, "On the Main Principles of the Fine Arts and Sciences," in *Philosophical Writings*, trans. and ed. Daniel O. Dahlstrom [Cambridge: Cambridge University Press, 1997], 169–70).

31. See the account in Laurenz Lütteken, "Zwischen Ohr und Verstand: Moses Mendelssohn, Johann Philipp Kirnberger und die Begründung des 'reinen Satzes' in der Musik," in Gerhard, *Musik*

that Jews should not think the music they heard around them was anything like the music of the ancient Hebrew poets and instrumentalists:

> *On account of our great suffering and dislocation*, all of this wondrous science . . . has been lost from us, including the art and form of these instruments, the system of voices, the modes of playing, and the pleasantness of the music. Nothing remains for us except the names of the instruments and songs, which in most cases are mentioned in the book of Psalms by the sweet singer of Israel. Yet we know that this science was widely disseminated within the nation, and that the great men, sages, and prophets of the nation were experts in poetry, excellent performers of music, and exceedingly learned in this science. . . . [D]o not liken the musical art [*muzika*] that we possess today to the glorious science that these perfect individuals used, since it appears that there is absolutely no resemblance between the two.[32]

It is significant that Mendelssohn attributed the loss of the science of music among the Jews to their "suffering and dislocation." This narrative pervaded the discourse of Haskalah writers and their Christian allies in the causes of Enlightenment and emancipation, and it stood in sharp contrast to the narrative of moral degeneracy adopted by Forkel and others. For Mendelssohn, the musical disarray and the loss of the musical history of the Jewish community were the result of the oppressive regimes that had kept them shrouded in darkness. Logically, then, a regeneration of music among the Jews required both a lifting of oppression by means of emancipation and an intellectual awakening among the Jews themselves.

The place of music in the budding Jewish Enlightenment was advocated by the Venetian rabbis who contributed a letter of endorsement to the treatise *Divrei shalom ve-emet* (Words of peace and truth, 1782), compiled by Mendelssohn's friend and collaborator Naphtali Herz (Hartwig) Wessely. These rabbis strongly favored the involvement of Jews in all fields of inquiry, including *muzika* (music), a category that

---

und Ästhetik, 135–64. Kirnberger responded to the cross-confessional aims of Mendelssohn's Psalm translations by setting some of them to music. Two recorded examples are "An den Flüssen Babylons," Vocal Concert Dresden, directed by Peter Kopp, *Bachs Schüler: Motetten*, Carus 83.263, 2008; and "Erbarm dich, unser Gott," Rheinische Kantorei, directed by Hermann Max, *Johann Hermann Schein: Fontana d'Israel, "Israelis Brünnlein 1623,"* Capriccio 10 290/91, 1990.

32. "והנגונים נשכחו ממנו באורך הגלות, ומרוב העוני והטלטול אבדה ממנו כל החכמה הנפלאה ההיא, מלאכת הכלי' ותבניתם, מערכת הקולות ואופני הנגון ונעימות הזמירה אשר השתבחו בה גדולי עמנו , ולא נשאר לנו כ"א שמות הכלים והשירי' לבד, הנזכרים על הרוב בספר תהלות נעים זמירות ישראל. ואולם ידענו שהיתה החכמה ההיא מפורסמת באומה, וגדולי העם וחכמיו ונביאיו היו יודעי שיר מטיבי נגן ובקיאי' מאוד בחכמה ההיא....ואל תדמה בנפשך מלאכת המוזיק' המצוי' בידינו היום אל החכמה המפוארה אשר השתמשו בה השלמי' ההם, כי הנראה שאין דמיון ביניהם כלל."

(Mendelssohn, *Sefer netivot ha-shalom* [*Bi'ur*], *JubA* 16:126, translated in Mendelssohn, *Writings*, 213, emphasis added).

encompassed both the sung poetry (*shira*) of the Hebrew Bible and the art of instrumental performance. Both, these rabbis argued, could be fruitfully revived, along with
all other fields of inquiry, among an enlightened, emancipated Jewish population in
the diaspora. They cited a long list of stories and characters from the Hebrew Bible
that attest to the importance of music for Jewish worship and tradition, on the basis
of which they asked, "Why should a person who wishes to learn [music] be chastised,
after he has filled his stomach with meat and wine, which are the written Torah and
the oral Torah? And if he has inclination to learn it, why should he not occupy himself with it? For also today there is a need for this science."[33] Again, Jewish history
provided the precedent and the impetus for modern engagement with music. Despite
his incorporation of this letter in his treatise, however, as Yael Sela-Teichler has noted,
Wessely himself omitted any mention of music in his own words on the subject of
secular education, thus betraying some ambivalence about the study of "the arts for
the sake of aesthetic pleasure," as advocated by Mendelssohn.[34] Although Wessely's
treatise emphasized the need to revive the science of music in the context of Jewish
worship, his nephew Bernhard Wessely epitomized, at least temporarily, professional
Jewish engagement with music outside the synagogue. Before Bernhard's conversion
to Christianity, his cantata commemorating the death of Moses Mendelssohn in 1786
was celebrated by enlightened Jews and Christians alike.[35]

If Naphtali Herz Wessely equivocated about the need to incorporate music into contemporary Jewish learning, Mendelssohn's lament for the lost art of *muzika* underlies a
remarkable Hebrew-language publication that appeared in five volumes between 1785
and 1791 and that engaged directly with Forkel's history of ancient Hebrew music in
the *Allgemeine Geschichte der Musik*. Intended for a Jewish readership, this collection,
entitled *Sefer zemirot Yisra'el* (Book of the songs of Israel), included the text of the
original Hebrew Psalms alongside Mendelssohn's German translation. However, like
Mendelssohn's translation of the Pentateuch, the *Zemirot Yisra'el* printed the German
text in Hebrew characters, thus endowing the work with a sense of traditionalism
despite its radical departure from Jewish tradition, which had long resisted translation
to the vernacular until Mendelssohn's lifetime.[36]

---

33. "למה יגונה מי שהוא חפץ ללמוד אותה, אחר שימלא כרסו בשר ויין, זו תורה שבכתב, ותורה שבעל פה,
ויהיה לו הכנה ללמדה, למה לא יתעסק בה? וכי גם בזמן הזה איכא מצטרכת החכמה הזאת?"
(Naphtali Herz Wessely, ed., *Divrei shalom ve-emet* [Berlin: Ḥevrat Ḥinuch Ne'arim, 1782], 3:29).

34. Yael Sela Teichler, "Music, Acculturation, and Haskalah between Berlin and Königsberg in the
1780s," *Jewish Quarterly Review* 103 (2013): 376.

35. Ibid., 352–84; and David Conway, *Jewry in Music: Entry to the Profession from the Enlightenment to
Richard Wagner* (Cambridge: Cambridge University Press, 2012), 148–49.

36. On a similar choice in the print layout of the *Bi'ur*, see Gillman, "Between Religion and Culture,"
100–104.

The introduction to the *Sefer zemirot Yisra'el*, which appeared in the volume of 1791, was written by one of Mendelssohn's disciples and followers in the Haskalah movement, Joel Brill (Löwe). Brill's contribution dealt first with biblical poetics (*melitza*), emphasizing the manifestation of poetic principles in the book of Psalms.[37] He described linguistic devices and constructions that had also been observed by Christian Hebraists such as Herder, as well as in the German-language writings of Mendelssohn.[38] And, like Herder, Mendelssohn, Robert Lowth, and numerous other writers of the period, Brill identified the pinnacle of the biblical art in its union of poetry and music. In Brill's words, "When these two sciences are joined together—poetics and music—each one strengthens the other. . . . and from this is born the most pleasant category of poetics, that is *shir*, or what is known in the vernacular as lyric poetry [*lirische poesie*]."[39]

In the second section, however, Brill presented a history of ancient Hebrew music proper, considered as a separate subject from poetry. Given the importance of Forkel's *Allgemeine Geschichte* for the music-historical narrative of the Aufklärung, it comes as no surprise that Forkel's is one of two German sources that Brill cited at the outset of this essay. The other was August Friedrich Pfeiffer's *Ueber die Musik der alten Hebräer* (1779), which likely served as the basis of Brill's illustrations of the instruments used by

---

37. Mendelssohn is listed on the title page as an author of the *Sefer zemirot Yisra'el*, along with Brill. See *Sefer zemirot Yisra'el: Hu sefer Tehilim 'im targum Ashkenazi me-ha-rav Rabenu Moshe Ben Menaḥem* [Book of the songs of Israel: That is, book of Psalms with a German translation by the rabbi, our teacher Moses son of Menaḥem] (Berlin: Shoḥarei ha-tov vehatushiyah, 1791). On the changing meanings of the term *melitza*, see Moshe Pelli, *Haskalah and Beyond: The Reception of the Hebrew Enlightenment and the Emergence of Haskalah Judaism* (Lanham, MD: University Press of America, 2010), 135–60. On Brill's other activities within the Haskalah movement, see Shmuel Feiner, *The Jewish Enlightenment*, trans. Chaya Naor (Philadelphia: University of Pennsylvania Press, 2002), 236–37, 266–67; and Pelli, *Haskalah and Beyond*, 50–55.

38. Mendelssohn's review of the *Praelectiones Academicae de Sacra Poesi Hebraeorum* (1753) by Robert Lowth synthesized many of the issues in biblical poetics, and it allowed Mendelssohn to articulate his deviation from Lowth and other Christian writers based on Mendelssohn's own Jewish identity and adherence to Jewish tradition. See Moses Mendelssohn, review of *Robert Lowths akademische Vorlesungen von der heiligen Dichtkunst der Hebräer; nebst einer kurtzen Widerlegung des harianischen Systems von der Prosodie der Hebräer*, in *Bibliothek der schönen Wissenschaften und der freyen Künste* 1, no. 1 (1757): 122–55, and no. 2 (1757): 269–97. See also Cypess, "Ancient Poetry."

39. "כאשר יצטרפו שתי אלה החכמות יחד, המליצה והנגון, יחזקו זו את זו....ומזה יולד החלק היותר נעים שבמליצה, זהו השיר, המכונה בל"ז (לירישי פאעזיא)."
(Brill, introduction to *Sefer zemirot Yisra'el*, 8v–9r). On the history and significance of the *Sefer zemirot Yisra'el*, see Natalie Naimark-Goldberg, "Entrepreneurs in the Library of the Haskalah: Editors and the Production of Maskilic Books" (Hebrew), in *The Library of the Haskalah: The Creation of a Modern Republic of Letters in Jewish Society in the German-Speaking Sphere*, ed. Shmuel Feiner, Zohar Shavit, Natalie Naimark-Goldberg, and Tal Kogman (Tel Aviv: Am Oved Publishers, Ltd., 2014), 112–16.

the ancient Israelites;[40] indeed, a discussion of the identity of the biblical instruments dominates this portion of the *Sefer Zemirot Yisra'el*. Brill began his history of music with Jubal (Genesis 4) and proceeded through the destruction of the Temple. Like Herder and other Christian writers, he identified the art of King David, to whom most of the Psalms are ascribed, as the most accomplished musician in the Jewish tradition. Like Mendelssohn, Brill acknowledged that the greatest music of the Jews had been lost to time. Yet he argued that it would be worthwhile to attempt to reconstruct the history of the art as much as possible: "Still, it is proper to investigate even these few words that are before us, and to seek as far as we can in these matters, for even from this little bit will emerge a great reward in the understanding of some Scripture."[41]

Both Forkel and Brill drew on a wide array of sources in describing the characteristics of the ancient Hebrew instruments mentioned in the Bible. Both writers compared the ancient instruments to their modern-day counterparts, suggesting that they were seeking an ancient justification for contemporary musical practice. In some cases, the biblical text clearly describes the instruments as string, wind, or percussion instruments. In other cases, however—especially those associated with the Babylonian exile, which bear Aramaic names rather than Hebrew ones—such an identification is not clear from the text, and Forkel and Brill call on Jewish and Christian commentaries to explain the meaning of a term.

One point of disagreement helps to highlight the relevance of ancient music history for debates over Jewish participation in music of the late eighteenth century. Among the instruments that Forkel sought to define was the *magrepha*, which is mentioned not in the Bible but in the Mishna and, with greater explanation, in the Talmud, assembled during and after the period of the Second Temple (compiled ca. 200–500 C.E.). Citing Athanasius Kircher and Wolfgang Caspar Prinz, Forkel defined the *magrepha* as a pneumatic organ, similar to modern-day pipe organs. Forkel expressed frustration at the "opaque and nearly incomprehensible descriptions that the writers of the Talmud, ignorant in most musical things, gave us of this odd instrument."[42] He relied on the interpretations of the Christian writers Kircher and Prinz, who enabled him to claim

---

40. While Naimark-Goldberg is correct that the presentation of these illustrations is similar to that of Daniel Chodowiecki in Bernard Basedow's *Elementarwerk* (Dessau: Crusius, 1774), Brill's images are much closer in appearance to Pfeiffer's. See Naimark-Goldberg, "Entrepreneurs," 112–16.

41. "מכל מקום ראוי להתבונן גם במעט הדברים האלה אשר לפנינו, ולחקור כפי אשר תשיג ידנו בענינים האלה, כי גם מזה המעט יצא לנו תועלת רבה בהבנת כמה כתובים."
(Brill, introduction to *Sefer zemirot Yisra'el*, 14v).

42. "[Außer den] dunklen und fast unbegreiflichen Beschreibungen, die uns die in musikalischen Dingen meistens unwissenden Talmudisten von diesem sonderbaren Instrumente gegeben haben" (Forkel, *Allgemeine Geschichte*, 1:137).

that its power, like that of the organs of his own day, was surprisingly great: "Its sound was said to be so strong that one could hear it from ten thousand paces—others say ten miles—away, and when it was played in the Temple in Jerusalem, people throughout Jerusalem could not understand each other if they wanted to converse."[43]

Forkel's explanation of the *magrepha* enabled him both to disparage the knowledge of the Talmudists concerning music and to locate a precedent for the modern-day organ in ancient practice: "The arrangement of this *Pfeiffenwerk* was more or less similar to the arrangement of our modern-day organ."[44] On this issue Forkel did not consult Pfeiffer, who had put forth a different opinion. Although Pfeiffer had likewise noted Kircher's opinion that the *magrepha* was an *Orgelwerk*, Pfeiffer classified the *magrepha* as a percussion instrument. In Pfeiffer's view, it was the *ugav* that came closest to the modern-day organ.[45]

As for Brill, he did not locate a precedent for the modern-day organ in any ancient Jewish instrument. This is not to say that sources such as Kircher were overlooked; indeed, reformers of Jewish synagogue practice in the early nineteenth century cited Kircher's opinion about the *magrepha* as justification for their own inclusion of the organ in synagogue worship.[46] In fact, Brill did not discuss the *magrepha* at all. He offered several explanations for the *ugav*—all of them from Jewish sources dating from the Talmud through the seventeenth century. The first definition he offered was that of the *Shiltei ha-gibborim* (Shield of the heroes, 1612),[47] which equated the *ugav* with the modern-day viola da gamba.[48] Indeed, rather than focusing on the characteristics of the *ugav* per se, Brill listed the properties of the viola da gamba itself, likening it to the violin, explaining that its bow consisted of horsehair and its six strings of animal gut, and so forth. His explanation was short and moved on to other opinions from Jewish sources that classified the *ugav* as a wind instrument. But Brill's discussion of the *ugav* seems most intent on claiming a place for modern-day Jews in contemporary

43. "Der Schall desselben soll so stark gewesen seyn, daß man ihn zehntausend Schritte, andere sagen zehn Meilen weit habe hören können, und wenn es im Tempel zu Jerusalem gespielt wurde, konnten sich die Leute in ganz Jerusalem nicht verstehen, wenn sie miteinander reden wollten" (ibid.).

44. "Die Einrichtung dieses Pfeifenwerks ungefähr eine ähnliche Beschaffenheit gehabt hätte, wie die Einrichtung unsere jetzigen Orgeln" (ibid., 1:138).

45. August Friedrich Pfeiffer, *Ueber die Musik der alten Hebräer* (Erlangen: Walther, 1779), 48–49. Kircher's understanding of the *magrepha* is cited on page 52.

46. See Tina Frühauf, *The Organ and Its Music in German-Jewish Culture* (New York: Oxford University Press, 2009), 12–15.

47. On the *Shiltei ha-gibborim*, see Don Harrán, *Three Early Modern Hebrew Scholars on the Mysteries of Song* (Leiden: Brill, 2015), 177–253; and Daniel Sandler, "The Music Chapters of 'Shiltey Hagiborim' by Avraham Portaleone: Critical Edition" (PhD diss., Tel Aviv University, 1980).

48. Brill, *Sefer Zemirot Yisra'el*, introduction, 26v–27r.

music. In discussing all of these instruments and their eighteenth-century counterparts in Hebrew and in placing them along a continuum of development from the ancient sources, Brill sought to reclaim music as a component of the Jewish heritage.

Sara Levy's Historicism:
The Cultural Work of Collecting and Performing

If the topic of scholarship on ancient Hebrew music seems far from my starting point—the musical practices and collection of scores assembled by Sara Levy in the decades around 1800—the *Sefer zemirot Yisra'el* brings my discussion full circle. For among the many names printed in the subscription list of Brill's Hebrew edition of Mendelssohn's translations of the Psalms is that of Sara Levy. As Naimark-Goldberg has shown, the presence of Levy's name on this list should be understood within the context of her extensive philanthropy in the Jewish community of Berlin, especially her active support for and intellectual engagement with the Haskalah movement, which exceeded that of other women in her circle. Although it is unclear that Levy read Hebrew, she must have been aware of the contents of the *Sefer zemirot Yisra'el*, along with the other Hebrew-language books that she supported. Whether through the text itself, through popular journals, or through the discussions with Maskilim (adherents of the Haskalah movement) and other Jewish intellectuals with whom she socialized and whom she hosted in her home, she was surely aware of the aims and purposes of the quest for Jewish Enlightenment, as well as this music-historical project in particular.[49]

Among the aims of the Haskalah was the recovery and conceptualization of Jewish history. Indeed, Shmuel Feiner has located in the maskilic texts a concerted effort to legitimize academic history and introduce a historical consciousness into Jewish discourse, and Elias Sacks has argued that Mendelssohn's framing of contemporary Jewish practice relies upon both historical and aesthetic consciousness.[50] Whereas Jewish writers in the preceding thousand years or more had viewed the field of history predominantly as an instrument of theology designed to explain and justify Jewish exclusivity, the Maskilim sought to understand Jewish history, alongside the general history of humanity, for its own sake. The history of music presented in Brill's intro-

---

49. See Naimark-Goldberg, "Remaining within the Fold." On the reading habits of women in Levy's circle, see Natalie Naimark-Goldberg, *Jewish Women in Enlightenment Berlin* (Oxford: Littman Library of Jewish Civilization, 2013), 64–101. One example of a Maskil who socialized with Sara Levy was Solomon Maimon; see Sabattia Joseph Wolff, *Maimoniana: Oder Rhapsodien zur Charakteristik Salomon Maimon's aus seinem Privatleben gesammelt* (Berlin: G. Hayn, 1813), 108–13.

50. See Shmuel Feiner, *Haskalah and History: The Emergence of a Modern Jewish Historical Consciousness*, trans. Chaya Naor and Sondra Silverston (Oxford: Littman Library of Jewish Civilization, 2004), 1–70; and Elias Sacks, *Moses Mendelssohn's Living Script: Philosophy, Practice, History, Judaism* (Bloomington: Indiana University Press, 2017).

duction to the *Sefer zemirot Yisra'el* should be understood in this context: written in Hebrew, engaging both Jewish and Christian sources, but carefully distinguishing itself from the polemics and a posteriori justifications of the Christian discourse on music, Brill's introduction to the Psalms represents the first step in Jewish efforts to reclaim their own musical history.

The maskilic historical consciousness did not manifest itself only in written treatises and histories like Brill's. Moshe Pelli has noted that Jewish historical consciousness may be discerned in a wide array of literary genres adopted by the Maskilim.[51] Perhaps most famously, the fictionalized dialogue *Siḥa be'eretz ha-ḥayyim* (Conversation in the land of the living) by Aaron Wolfssohn projected a historical awareness by setting the medieval philosopher Maimonides into dialogue with Moses Mendelssohn, as they criticize the benighted rabbinic leadership of Mendelssohn's own day.[52] Through this text, Wolfssohn affirmed the place of Haskalah Judaism along the continuum of Jewish tradition but simultaneously set off the different historical periods of his protagonists from one another.

A work still farther from the genre of the historical treatise yet nevertheless displaying a strong historical consciousness is one that I have already discussed: Mendelssohn's German translations of the Psalms of 1783. In this work, as noted above, Mendelssohn reached into the history of both Christianity and Judaism for his source material, reframing it for the aesthetic, ethical, and spiritual needs of his own generation. In loosening the Psalms from a distinct religious context—whether Christian or Jewish—Mendelssohn presented a sacred text valued by both groups in a new and neutral guise. He described his emotional reactions to the Psalm translations as aesthetic works in a letter to his friend Sophie Becker in 1785. The Psalms had, he wrote, "sweetened many a bitter hour for me, and I pray and sing as often as I feel the need in me to pray and sing."[53] Moreover, the Psalms were not merely for prayer to God; instead, they were the spontaneous eruptions of a soul that needed to sing:

> The most common person, it seems to me, does not sing so that God hears him
> and finds pleasure in his melodies. We sing for our own sake, and this does as much

51. See Moshe Pelli, *In Search of Genre: Hebrew Enlightenment and Modernity* (Lanham, MD: University Press of America, 2005).

52. [Aaron Wolfssohn], "Siḥa be'eretz ha-ḥayyim," *Ha-mea'sef* 7 (1794–96): 93–97, 120–58, 203–28, 279–98. For more on this play, see Feiner, *The Jewish Enlightenment*, 330–31.

53. "mir haben die Psalmen manche bittre Stunde versüßt; und ich bete und singe sie, so oft ich ein Bedürfniß zu beten und zu singen bei mir verspüre" (Moses Mendelssohn to Sophie Becker, 27 December 1785, *JubA* 13:334, cited in and trans. Elias Sacks, "Poetry, Music, and the Limits of Harmony: Mendelssohn's Aesthetic Critique of Christianity," in Cypess and Sinkoff, *Sara Levy's World*, 122).

good for the wise man as it does for the fool. Have you ever read the Psalms with this purpose? It seems to me that many Psalms are of such a type that they must be sung with true edification by the most enlightened people [*sie von den aufgeklärtesten Menschen mit wahrer Erbauung gesungen werden müssen*]. I would once again recommend to you my translation of the Psalms, if this would not betray too much of the frailty of an author.[54]

It is significant that Mendelssohn did not merely advocate reading his Psalm translations silently. Instead, he explained that they need to be *sung aloud*. This idea is very much in keeping with Mendelssohn's claim that the Bible should be sung using the traditional Jewish cantillation system; as Sacks has noted, this act of singing aloud helps to impress the meanings of the words on both the singer and the listener.[55] Moreover, the experience of the Psalms as a performed work of art was not limited to either Jews or Christians; instead, the Psalms were available to all of "the most enlightened people." As noted above, Mendelssohn made this point clear when he dedicated his translation to Ramler and discussed his friendship with Lessing in the text of the dedication. Reaching into their common history, Mendelssohn offered his friends and readers a work of poetry that would both fulfill a spiritual need and create a bridge between them. It was through this experience of a historical artwork, read in a modern, cross-confessional translation and shared through sounding performance, that such a bridge could be forged.

If sounding performances of Mendelssohn's Psalm translations had the power to reclaim biblical poetry as a neutral aesthetic space available to both Christians and Jews, then Levy's acts of "musicking" may be understood as having a similar force.[56] Through her collection, with its strong historicist tone, Levy asserted her place in the tradition of German music—indeed, as a "grand-student" of Johann Sebastian Bach. In addition, as a performer, she had the capacity to reinterpret the music she played. Rather than seeing her merely as a receptacle—as a vehicle for the transmission of the music of the past—we may see her as an agent capable of spreading new understandings of older music. While the music that she played and collected was

---

54. "Der gemeinste Mensch, dünkt mich, singt nicht, daß Gott ihn höre und an seinen Melodien Gefallen finde. Wir singen unserthalben; und das thut der Weise so gut als der Thor. Haben Sie je die Psalmen in dieser Absicht gelesen? Mich dünkt, viele Psalme sind von der Art, daß sie von den aufgeklärtesten Menschen mit wahrer Erbauung gesungen warden müssen. Ich würde Ihnen abermals meine Uebersetzung der Psalmen vorschlagen, wenn es nicht zu viel Autorschwachheit verriethe" (ibid.).

55. Sacks, "Poetry, Music."

56. Christopher Small uses the term "musicking" to describe participation in aspects of music making that go beyond composition. See *Musicking: The Meanings of Performing and Listening* (Middletown, CT: Wesleyan University Press, 1998).

not composed by Jews, her acts of playing and collecting these works rendered them part of Jewish history.

How can we envision such a transformation taking place? Past writers have observed two apparently contradictory cultural tendencies in Levy's world. On the one hand, musicologists who have assessed Levy's collection have characterized it as reflecting a "conservative-enlightened musical taste."[57] Indeed, if one considers the music on its own terms, divorced from Levy's performances and their social context, this assessment seems accurate, and it is exemplified most obviously by her historicism. On the other hand, the social implications of the gatherings that she and other Jewish women held in their homes were decidedly progressive. These gatherings—generally, if anachronistically, referred to as "salons"—often involved a heterogeneous group, including Jews and Christians, men and women, philosophers and socialites, artists, scientists, and intellectuals.[58] Jews and non-Jews gathered to share cultural experiences, to discuss literature and the sciences, to read poetry, to hear music. That Jewish women were figureheads and hostesses at these gatherings attests to the significance of the salons in loosening earlier social hierarchies (though these women were generally excluded from salons hosted by their Christian counterparts). Ruth Dawson has emphasized women's "cultural roles," rather than merely their scholarly production (or paucity thereof), as vehicles for their participation in the Enlightenment, and the salon gatherings hosted by Levy and her peers exemplify these alternative modes of engagement with the social and intellectual trends of the era.[59] While recent reevalu-

---

57. See Wollny, "Sara Levy and the Making of Musical Taste," 659.

58. The problems with the historiography of the "salon" are laid out in Naimark-Goldberg, *Jewish Women*, 188–92; Ulrike Weckel, "A Lost Paradise of Female Culture? Some Critical Questions Regarding the Scholarship on Late Eighteenth- and Early Nineteenth-Century German Salons," *German History* 18 (2000): 310–36; Barbara Hahn, *The Jewess Pallas Athena: This Too a Theory of Modernity*, trans. James McFarland (Princeton, NJ: Princeton University Press, 2005); Liliane Weissberg, "Literary Culture and Jewish Space Around 1800: The Berlin Salons Revisited," in *Modern Jewish Literatures: Intersections and Boundaries*, ed. Sheila E. Jelen, Michael P. Kramer, and L. Scott Lerner (Philadelphia: University of Pennsylvania Press, 2010), 24–43. See also Petra Wilhelmy-Dollinger, *Die Berliner Salons: Mit historisch-literarischen Spaziergängen* (Berlin: De Gruyter, 2000); Deborah Hertz, *Jewish High Society in Old Regime Berlin* (New Haven, CT: Yale University Press, 1988); Deborah Hertz, *How Jews Became Germans: The History of Conversion and Assimilation in Berlin* (New Haven, CT: Yale University Press, 2007); David Lowenstein, *The Berlin Jewish Community: Enlightenment, Family, and Crisis, 1770–1830* (New York: Oxford University Press, 1994); and Cyril Reade, "Brendel Mendelssohn, Brendel Veit, Dorothea Veit, Dorothea von Schlegel: Identities in Transition," in *Mendelssohn to Mendelssohn: Visual Case Studies of Jewish Life in Berlin*, Studies in German Jewish History 8 (Oxford: Peter Lang, 2007), chap. 4.

59. Ruth Dawson, "Lights Out! Lights Out! Women and the Enlightenment," in *Gender in Transition: Discourse and Practice in German-Speaking Europe, 1750–1830*, ed. Ulrike Gleixner and Marion W. Gray (Ann Arbor: University of Michigan Press, 2009), 137–39.

ations of the Berlin salons caution against an overidealization of the social harmony that they seem to imply, there can be no doubt as to the intention of progressiveness in their agendas.

When considered within this social context or the equally heterogeneous performances that Levy gave at the Sing-Akademie, the apparently conservative music that she favored takes on a new aspect. In rendering this older music, Levy may indeed have executed most of the notes on the page, perhaps reviving the works as they were heard in the lifetime of Quantz or Sebastian Bach or in the heyday of musical life at the court of Frederick the Great. (In some cases, aspects of performance practice, especially with respect to instrumentation, seem to have changed in Levy's hands.) Yet the very act of performance within a new social context endowed this older music with different meaning, accomplishing what Ruth Solie and Suzanne Cusick, among others, have referred to as "cultural work"—work that may include the affirmation of or resistance to received understandings and associations.[60]

Writers focused on the act of performance have sought to challenge the hermeneutic tradition centered around the musical text or the "composer's voice."[61] Addressing the tension between the composer's intent and the performer's own persona, Cusick argues for an understanding that accounts for both, "redefin[ing] interpretation as a complex negotiation between performer and script, in which both have agency."[62] Attention to the moment of performance—and to shifting circumstances of performance over decades and centuries—highlights the changeable nature of musical meaning, even for works that have long been thought to form part of the canon. Indeed, in this respect, it is significant that Sara Levy's lifetime was a formative age for the musical canon; the performance practices in which she participated were among the factors that led to canon formation. Repeated performance within a group of connoisseurs of mixed religions may have contributed to the inscription of this music within the cultural consciousness of the enlightened Berlin community. The radical rereadings that Cusick advocates might be out of place in the historical situation of Sara Levy, but a nuanced understanding that accounts for both the conservative contents of her music

60. See Ruth Solie, "Whose Life? The Gendered Self in Schumann's *Frauenliebe* Songs," in *Music and Text: Critical Inquiries*, ed. Steven P. Scher (Cambridge: Cambridge University Press, 1992), 219–40; and Suzanne Cusick, "Gender and the Cultural Work of a Classical Music Performance," *Repercussions* 3, no. 1 (Spring 1994): 77–110.

61. See, for example, Carolyn Abbate, "Music—Drastic or Gnostic?," *Critical Inquiry* 30, no. 3 (Spring 2004): 505–36; and the colloquy "Studying the Lied: Hermeneutic Traditions and the Challenge of Performance," convened by Jennifer Ronyak, *Journal of the American Musicological Society* 67 (2014): 543–81. Their work presents a particular challenge to Edward T. Cone, *The Composer's Voice* (Berkeley: University of California Press, 1974).

62. Cusick, "Gender," 99.

collection and performing habits *and* the progressive nature of her social practices would be very much in keeping with her historical moment. While Levy's collection shows a strong historicist tendency, she had the power to shape the reception and understanding of the music that she played and collected among her social circle and her audience. Through her cultivation of a collection of scores and the resounding of the music in performance, Levy marked these works as objects of her admiration, and she also left her own mark on them as vehicles of expression and sociability available to Jews, as well as to Christians.

The contents of Levy's collection have been assessed in the past, but there is perhaps more to learn from the perspective I have proposed. Evidence from the scores in her collection suggests that she did not merely donate to the Sing-Akademie every item that she owned. Instead, she *created* a collection, just as Zelter did in assembling the larger collection of the Sing-Akademie—consciously and intentionally. The care that she took in assembling her collection is evident from the letter that Johanna Maria Bach, widow of Carl Philipp Emanuel Bach, sent to Levy in 1789, which implies that Levy wished to ensure that she owned a complete collection of Philipp Emanuel's music.[63] In making her donation to the Sing-Akademie, Levy held some scores back, and these later made their way into the hands of Abraham Mendelssohn, August Wilhelm Bach, Justus Amadeus Lecerf, and others.[64] She stamped hundreds of scores with the distinctive ex libris "SSLev^i" (Sara and Samuel Levy), but she did this sometimes long after a given score had first entered her collection. Such is the case, it seems, with the manuscript SA 1584, which bears an annotation in the hand of her sister Zipora Wulff in which Sara is called "Sara Itzig mariée pointe" (Sara Itzig, not married at all [i.e., with only a maiden name]) but which was later stamped with the ex libris showing Sara's married name.[65] How many scores survive that were once in her possession but that were never marked with her name? Peter Wollny has suggested that this is true for the manuscript SA 274, the *Konvolut* (a miscellany formed from various manuscripts) containing Friedemann Bach's song "Herz, mein Herz, sey ruhig" (Fk 97). Wollny has proposed that Friedemann wrote the song, described in the manuscript as a *cantinela* [*sic*, i.e., *cantilena*] *nuptiarum consolatoria* (wedding song of consolation) in honor of Sara's marriage.[66] To add her ex libris after the fact was to take ownership of the score,

---

63. The letter is transcribed in Wollny, *"Ein förmlicher Sebastian und Philipp Emanuel Bach-Kultus"* (2010), 49–51; see also Wollny, "Sara Levy," 657.

64. Wollny, *"Ein förmlicher Sebastian und Philipp Emanuel Bach-Kultus"* (2010), 37.

65. See Cypess, "Ancient Poetry."

66. Wollny, "Sara Levy," 659; and Wollny, *"Ein förmlicher Sebastian und Philipp Emanuel Bach-Kultus"* (2010), 74. David Schulenberg is more circumspect in connecting the song to Levy; see *The Music of Wilhelm Friedemann Bach* (Rochester, NY: University of Rochester Press, 2010), 263.

to declare it as part of her collection. To donate a score with her name on it to the Sing-Akademie was to connect herself with it for posterity.

It is true that Levy's collection favored instrumental music heavily over vocal music, but as I have shown elsewhere, vocal music was not absent from the collections and musical practices of Sara and her sisters. In at least one case—the *Wechselgesang der Mirjam und Debora* by Justin Heinrich Knecht—there is reason to think that the sisters took an interest in the piece because it was thought of as encapsulating "the true taste of the ancient Hebrew poetry" and the composition as constituting the ideal synthesis of ancient poetry and modern music.[67] And, as I suggested there, it seems possible that the handful of other vocal works in the collection of Sara and her sisters may likewise have held special meaning for the enlightened Jews of Berlin. Conspicuously absent are Sebastian Bach's sacred cantatas, which are firmly entrenched in a traditional Lutheran perspective and thus do not open themselves to the kinds of enlightened interpretation that would have been engendered by performance through Levy's hands. While Levy did not eschew sacred Christian music entirely, such works are the exception.[68]

While it is clear that Levy owned some scores of solo keyboard music, including sonatas, suites, and excerpts from *The Well-Tempered Clavier* (the work that would later become such an important vehicle for Lea Mendelssohn and her children), very few of these were included in her gift to the Sing-Akademie.[69] Indeed, it seems likely that she owned more scores for solo keyboard than those that survive with her ex libris. Her sister Zipora owned the solo keyboard works in the *Konvolut* GB-Lcm Ms. 2000; there, Sebastian Bach's French suites stand alongside fugues and fantasies by Friedemann and Philipp Emanuel in what reads as a keyboard instruction book for the generation of the Bach sons, albeit one assembled after the fact. Some, but not all, of these works survive in copies with Levy's ex libris, suggesting that others may no longer be extant or may never have been marked with her name. In addition, given the interest that she and her sisters apparently had in keyboard duos and double concertos, we may speculate that she owned and played Friedemann's concerto for two unaccompanied keyboards in F major (Fk 10), but that score also does not survive.[70]

67. See Cypess, "Ancient Poetry."

68. On Levy's approach to sacred music and its implications for Felix Mendelssohn Bartholdy's revival of the *St. Matthew Passion*, see Naimark-Goldberg, "Remaining within the Fold," 57–58, and Sela, "Longing for the Sublime."

69. On the place of *The Well-Tempered Clavier* in the Mendelssohn family, see R. Larry Todd, *Mendelssohn Essays* (New York: Routledge, 2008), 118.

70. The meanings of keyboard duos in the collection of Sara Levy are discussed in Rebecca Cypess, "Duets in the Collection of Sara Levy and the Ideal of 'Unity in Multiplicity,'" in Cypess and Sinkoff, *Sara Levy's World*, 181–204.

The collection that Levy gave to the Sing-Akademie eschews solo keyboard genres, focusing on chamber music—music to be made in company. Not all of these works were concertos of the sort that Levy played at the Sing-Akademie from 1807 onward.[71] RISM lists no fewer than seventy-seven quartets that would have been suitable for performance in her salon as well as the *Quartettabend* performances in which Levy participated at the home of Johann Carl Friedrich Rellstab, as his son Ludwig later reported.[72] Concertos, trio sonatas, sonatas for keyboard and obbligato instruments, including many involving flute (which her husband, Samuel Salomon Levy, apparently played)—these form the basis of Levy's collection.[73] Works by composers from the past—especially from Berlin—offered her an opportunity to insert herself into the history of the Prussian capital, recalling through sound a time when few Jews would have had access to the musical culture that she did. And in reviving the sounds of those pieces through her own performances, Levy had the capacity to remake them as part of her own musical inheritance and to make them accessible to her socially progressive listeners.

While it is true that Levy was not alone among collectors in displaying a historicist inclination, the interest in musical history reflected in her collection takes on a new layer of meaning in light of the historicist thinking that characterized the Jewish Enlightenment. As a woman, Levy may not have been engaged with Hebrew letters, but not all historical documents of the Enlightenment were made up of words.[74] Dawson's understanding of women's cultural roles as vehicles through which they left a mark on enlightened society is apt; thus, despite the paucity of surviving verbal documentation from Sara Levy's own hands, her collection of musical scores and the evidence of her performances demand engagement as evidence of intellectual history. As Mendelssohn's and Brill's aesthetic-historical project of the Psalm translations shows, historical consciousness may manifest itself outside the genre of historical or philosophical treatises. As Mendelssohn did when he translated the Psalms into German, Sara Levy reframed the music of the past. She loosened the bonds that linked the Prussian musical tradition to Christianity, forging a common musical heritage that would be accessible to both Christians and Jews.

---

71. Kornemann, "Zelter's Archive," 21.

72. See Ludwig Rellstab, *Aus meinem Leben* (Berlin: Guttentag, 1861), 117. Rellstab's concerts are also described in Karla Höcker, *Hauskonzerte in Berlin* (Berlin: Rembrandt, 1970), 13–18.

73. See Wollny, *"Ein förmlicher Sebastian und Philipp Emanuel Bach-Kultus"* (2010), 25–28.

74. For example, Annette Richards has shown that Carl Philipp Emanuel Bach's collection of portraits constitutes an example of music historicism in a genre other than verbal histories. See "Carl Philipp Emanuel Bach, Portraits, and the Physiognomy of Music History," *Journal of the American Musicological Society* 66 (2013): 337–96.

We should not assume that Levy and other modernizing Jews would have walked away from Christians who viewed them skeptically or disparagingly. Indeed, Levy's name appeared not only on the subscription list of Brill's *Sefer zemirot Yisra'el* but also on the subscription list for Forkel's published keyboard variations on "God Save the King."[75] Whether she was also aware of Carl Friedrich Zelter's anti-Jewish sentiments is unclear,[76] but it seems that anti-Judaism was simply a fact of life—and one that increased in the first decades of the nineteenth century. Indeed, it manifested itself in at least one infamous incident in Levy's salon.[77] Yet the normality of anti-Judaism in the late eighteenth century is made evident by Davidson's book, quoted at the outset of this essay. His special pleading for recognition of Jewish contributions to Prussian society must have been a response to the many people around him who refused to grant such recognition—who refused the enlightened call for tolerance across religions. I suggest that Sara Levy navigated this complex social and religious terrain by modestly but seriously staking out her claim in German musical history.

75. Johann Nikolaus Forkel, *Vier und zwanzig Veränderungen fürs Clavichord oder Fortepiano auf das englische Volkslied: God Save the King* (Göttingen: Vandenhoek und Ruprecht, 1791).

76. See Leon Botstein, "The Aesthetics of Assimilation and Affirmation: Reconstructing the Career of Felix Mendelssohn," in *Mendelssohn and His World*, ed. R. Larry Todd (Princeton, NJ: Princeton University Press, 2012), 21; also Jeffrey S. Sposato, *The Price of Assimilation: Felix Mendelssohn and the Nineteenth-Century Anti-Semitic Tradition* (Oxford: Oxford University Press, 2006), 52–53.

77. The incident in question, which took place in 1811, was an altercation between the writer Achim von Arnim and one of Levy's nephews, Moritz Itzig, which resulted in a challenge to a duel and subsequently a lawsuit. See, among other sources, Lowenstein, *The Berlin Jewish Community*, 110; and Hertz, *Jewish High Society*, 258–59.

CONTRIBUTORS

REBECCA CYPESS is an associate professor of music at the Mason Gross School of the Arts, Rutgers University, and a faculty affiliate of the Rutgers Jewish Studies Department. She is the author of *Curious and Modern Inventions: Instrumental Music as Discovery in Galileo's Italy* (University of Chicago Press, 2016) and numerous articles on the history and performance practices of music in the seventeenth and eighteenth centuries. She is coeditor, with historian Nancy Sinkoff, of *Sara Levy's World* (University of Rochester Press, 2018). A performer on early keyboard instruments, Cypess can be heard on the recording *In Sara Levy's Salon* (Acis Productions, 2017).

JOYCE L. IRWIN is a church historian affiliated with the Princeton Research Forum and previously with the University of Georgia and Colgate University. Her primary focus is on the theological basis of Lutheran church music in the early modern era. Her publications include *Neither Voice nor Heart Alone: German Lutheran Theology of Music in the Age of the Baroque* (Lang, 1993) and *Foretastes of Heaven in Lutheran Church Music Tradition: Johann Mattheson and Christoph Raupach on Music in Time and Eternity* (Rowman and Littlefield, 2015). She is also an active church musician and a colleague of the American Guild of Organists.

ROBIN A. LEAVER is emeritus professor of sacred music, Westminster Choir College, Princeton; honorary professor at Queen's University, Belfast, Northern Ireland; and recently visiting professor at the Institute of Sacred Music, Yale University. A past president of the American Bach Society, his most recent writings on Bach appear in *The Baroque Composers: Bach* (Ashgate, 2011), *Exploring Bach's B-Minor Mass* (Cambridge University Press, 2013), the *Bach-Jahrbuch* (2013), *Bach: The Journal of the Riemenschneider Bach Institute* (2011, 2015, 2017, and 2018), and *The Routledge Research Companion to Johann Sebastian Bach* (2017), of which he is also general editor.

MARK NOLL is Francis A. McAnaney Professor of History Emeritus, University of Notre Dame. His recent books include *In the Beginning Was the Word: The Bible in American Public Life, 1492-1783* (2016) and, as coeditor, *Protestantism after 500 Years* (2016), both from Oxford University Press. He has also coedited three books on the history of hymnody in North America, including *Sing Them Over Again to Me: Hymns and Hymnbooks in America* (University of Alabama Press, 2006); his article on connections between Martin Luther and J. S. Bach appeared in a special issue of *Christian History* magazine devoted to Bach (Summer 2007).

MARKUS RATHEY is a professor of music history at Yale University. His research focuses on music in the seventeenth and eighteenth centuries, Johann Sebastian Bach, and the Bach family. His books include a study of Johann Sebastian Bach's *Christmas Oratorio* (Oxford University Press, 2016) and an introduction to J. S. Bach's major vocal works (Yale University Press, 2016). He is president of the American Bach Society and associate editor of the *Yale Journal of Music and Religion*.

DEREK STAUFF is an assistant professor of music at Hillsdale College. His research focuses on Lutheran music, confession, and politics in central Germany in the early modern period. His most recent article, "Schütz's *Saul, Saul, was verfolgst du mich?* and the Politics of the Thirty Years' War," appeared in the *Journal of the American Musicological Society* (2016). In addition, he is also currently editing two separate editions of psalm concertos by Samuel Michael and Sebastian Knüpfer, respectively, organist and cantor in seventeenth-century Leipzig.

JANICE B. STOCKIGT is an associate professor and honorary principal fellow of the Melbourne Conservatorium of Music at the University of Melbourne. A major part of her research has been into the life and works of the Bohemian composer Jan Dismas Zelenka (1679–1745), which led to the award-winning monograph that has become the standard work on the composer (Oxford, 2000). Further research in the former collection of the Catholic court church of Dresden led to the discovery of previously unknown psalm settings by Antonio Vivaldi. Current research projects concern musicians of the Dresden court during the reigns of August II and August III, transmission of sacred music from Italy to Saxony via Bohemia, and Australia's earliest performance of the *St. Matthew Passion* (Melbourne, 1875). Recent publications include contributions to *Music at German Courts, 1715–1760*, edited by Samantha Owens, Barbara Reul, and Janice B. Stockigt (Boydell, 2011); *Exploring Bach's B-Minor Mass*, edited by Yo Tomita, Robin A. Leaver, and Jan Smaczny (Cambridge, 2013); and *Fasch-Studien* 13 (Ortus, 2016).

GENERAL INDEX

General Index

INDEX OF BACH'S WORKS

Bach Perspectives
is a publication of the
American Bach Society,
dedicated to promoting the study
and performance of the music of
Johann Sebastian Bach.
Membership information is available online at
www.americanbachsociety.org.

THE BACH PERSPECTIVES SERIES

The University of Illinois Press
is a founding member of the
Association of American University Presses.

Composed in 10/14 Janson Text
by Jim Proefrock
at the University of Illinois Press
Manufactured by Sheridan Books, Inc.

University of Illinois Press
1325 South Oak Street
Champaign, IL 61820-6903
www.press.uillinois.edu